The Greek Poetess
and
Other Writings

ARA BALIOZIAN

The Greek Poetess
and
Other Writings

SELECTED AND EDITED
BY C. K. GARABED

Armenian Literary Society
NEW YORK

For information, address: Armenian Literary Society, New York, c/o Arthur Hamparian, 77 Everett Road, Demarest, New Jersey 07627.

Printed in the United States of America

Library of Congress Cataloging-in-Publication Data

Baliozian, Ara.
  The Greek poetess, and other writings.

  Material which originally appeared in various publications.
    1. Armenians.   I Garabed, C.K.   II Title.
DS165.B27   1986   909'.0491992   86-7864

Acknowledgments

The material included here has appeared in the following publications, whose publishers and editors are thanked for permission to reprint:

Ararat Quarterly
The Armenian Mirror-Spectator
The Armenian Reporter
The Armenian Weekly
Asbarez
Echo
The Literary Tabloid
Meghou
Menk
Nor Gyank Weekly
World Literature Today

Furthermore, "The Greek Poetess" was broadcast on Radio Station CHYM-FM, Kitchener, Ontario; "Cross-Examinations" on CKWR-FM, Los Angeles; and "Conversations" on CFMU-FM, McMaster University, Hamilton, Ontario.

Contents

Editor's Note

As an ardent Berliozian, I should feel a strong attachment to Ara Baliozian for no other reason than his name. Such is not the case, of course, but we do share a common interest in Hector's music, although my interest extends also to Berlioz's literary gifts, which are known to relatively few people.

If I were to try to decide what it is about Baliozian's writing that makes it so special, I would have to begin by skirting the issue. So many people fancy themselves writers only because they have learned how to read and write in a particular language and have developed a certain facility with the use of words to express their ideas and feelings. In this country of universal education, everyone feels he is capable of writing a book. If more people could more easily learn to read and write music, we'd have a plethora of would-be composers.

What distinguishes a truly first-rate writer? Is it his choice of subjects? The development of a personal idiom? Or is it his style of phrasing or wordsmithing? It is none of these! Craftsmanship, though characteristic of the first-rate writer, is not the reason either. I'm reminded of "Method" actors who incessantly talk of their craft. Again skirting the issue, I am taken with the similarity between Baliozian and Joseph Conrad, in that English was their adopted language. But their stature as writers comes first and is not derived from the other fact.

Does Baliozian's concentration on matters Armenian detract from his universality? No more than Dvorak's on Slavonic themes.

Now to the heart of the matter. Three things come to mind: genius, magic, and inspiration. What is genius? No one knows and it certainly is not measurable. Some misuse the word to describe a specific level of intelligence as measured by IQ tests. It is neither so crass nor crude. It is a rare realm where the spirit dwells in sweet solitude. Mere mortals can only discern its existence in the way astronomers deduce the existence of unseen bodies. It has no correlation to intelligence, as even the man of genius can have his lapses, which are unaccountable. The word fills a need and so we use it.

Magic is the art of the spellbinder. Bach, Beethoven and Berlioz—the *original* 3Bs of music—practiced that art. Their music enthralls the listener and suspends him in space.

Inspiration is a useful term but not very definitive. The best works of art are said to be inspired. Whence the source of inspiration? The word *immediate* is recalled. It means "without medium." In other words, one is in touch with the source directly without any intermediate bridge. He who experiences immediately sees without eyes, hears without ears, and knows without learning. Platonic intuition!

These then are the thoughts that come to mind when I dwell on Baliozian's writing. No attempt has been intended to explain anything. Besides, to those who understand, no explanations are necessary.

C. K. Garabed

Teaneck, N.J.

Fiction

The Greek Poetess

IT WAS KAZANTZAKIS WHO REVIVED MY INTEREST IN THE GREEK LAN-
guage. I left Greece at an early age, and by the time I became
fascinated with the character of Zorba I had forgotten whatever
Greek I knew. I reestablished my contacts with the local Greek
community and had no difficulty whatever in finding several tu-
tors who, in exchange for English lessons, were willing to help me
with my Greek.

My first tutor turned out to be a homosexual, and when I failed
to respond to his advances he lost interest in the project.

My second tutor happened to have a jealous husband, and
when she failed to respond to *my* advances, *I* lost interest in the
project.

My third tutor, Vassili, lasted six months. And until he fell
foolishly in love and married a slatternly blonde, he would
faithfully come to my place every Friday night for a few drinks and
an exchange of lessons. "That's all Greek to me," he would say
whenever I failed to explain something properly to him. And
when he lost interest in the English lessons I taught him chess. A
mistake. He would become so engrossed in the game—reminding me of Karsh's portrait of Sibelius—that I would be compelled
to drag him away from the chessboard by physical force. To
improve my game and finish him off without wasting too much
valuable time, I would spend hours during the week poring over
the games of Fisher, Petrosian, and Luzhin.

Among the Greek books and magazines Vassili left behind, there
was a small volume of poems entitled *Privileged Moments* by
someone called Eleni Papachristou. They were not so much

poems as long, thin columns of word-caravans that crossed the desert of the page in curves, zigzags, and broken patterns of great variety. The book lacked pagination and the poems were untitled. The only thing I remember to have gotten out of them was a sense of isolation, a quest for communion, a futile effort to reach out from the printed page and touch the reader.

> I am the light-green sea wave
> that rises,
> breaks,
> then spreads on the white glowing sand.
> I am a polar bear on an iceberg,
> a tiger in the jungle,
> a soaring eagle in the sky,
> a leaping, prancing wild goat.
> I am the river thirsting for the waters of the sea,
> I am the earth,
> the sky,
> the sun,
> the stars:
> *You.*

I have always thought of poetry as a middle-class thing. It presupposes a private income, agreeable surroundings, leisure, pretty faces, elegant little miseries. Pretty faces, by their very inaccessibility, inspire me with thoughts of resentment, rage, rape, rather than stylish stanzas.

> I cover my flesh,
> but my soul
> like a stone
> is hard
> naked
> exposed.

Perhaps something is lost in my translation and in my not reproducing here the typographical extravaganzas.

> Words:
> I distrust them
> like scorpions and tarantulas.

This one even tries to look like an arachnid.

> A mirror
> hung from a star—that
> for the occasion
> has accepted the role of a nail—

       above the earth
       and reflecting it:
       the moon.

Through what must have been an obvious technical oversight, this one has a trapezoidal shape.

· 3 ·

I translated some of the poems into English as a form of exercise. And then, and only then, did it occur to me to write a fan letter to the poetess in the hope of thus acquiring a Greek pen pal. With the letter I enclosed samples of my translations and sent the whole thing to the publisher's address in Athens.

I forgot about it until I heard from her a couple of months later. It was a warm, friendly reply in which she praised my translations, apologized for being late in answering my letter (she had been out of the country), quoted fragments from her last unpublished poem, and wanted to know more about myself: my work, my friends, my habits, my dreams.

The correspondence lasted a little over a year, and in that space we had more disagreements than agreements. She believed, for example, in predestination, in supernatural phenomena, in ESP— but not in UFOs—and dismissed all the sciences as dangerous superstitions; dismissed also all the great writers, the giants, as she called them "because they are, like Cyclops, one-eyed. In their presence I tend to behave like Odysseus. I resent even friendly giants because by their very presence they eclipse my own personal vision of reality."

Being brought up in awe of authority, I must confess that her wholesale contempt for writers, ideas, and ideals was a constant source of delight to me. Delight, yes, and also a liberating force. For it seemed to me then that one needed much more than erudition and irreverence to express such opinions: one needed courage.

Listen to her opinion of Dostoevsky, whom I had idolized as a raw youth: "A narrow reactionary and a petty chauvinist who thought Christ was of Russian descent, and the tsar a member of the Holy Family."

On Tolstoy: "A man who labored under many delusions, one of which was that like God he could understand everything and everyone. He couldn't, and didn't! Actually his own muzhiks understood him far better than he understood himself, or his muzhiks for that matter."

On Napoleon: "A megalomaniac with the mentality of a Mafioso."

On Freud: "An excellent writer of detective stories, and some first rate literary criticism: see his stuff on Ibsen, Shakespeare, Dostoevsky, Mann, and *Oedipus Rex* . . . not to be confused with *Oedipus Complex*—the butler in his whodunits."

On Casanova: "A mental masturbator of elephantine dimensions. An intellectual exhibitionist whose only thrill was to offer his pudenda to the public gaze."

On Hemingway: "After he was awarded the Nobel Prize I read a book by him—something about bells, may have been bulls, probably balls . . . I dislike bulls, and have no affection for the rest. I prefer Twain's frogs, Melville's whales, Faulkner's bears, Steinbeck's mice, and Nabokov's butterflies."

On Nabokov: "Another one of your sick Russians whose sole preoccupations seem to be Pushkin, incest, mushrooms, chess, and *Schmetterlings*."

On Goethe: "A pompous ass who had the amazing ability of writing nice little poems—flowers on a dung heap."

On Dante: "An obscurantist and a cryptosadomasochist."

On Norman Mailer: "Who the hell is he?"

On Marx: "Which one, Groucho or Karl?—not that it makes any difference."

On her own writings: "A Negro chieftain was asked once to define what was good and what bad, and he said: 'When I steal my enemy's wives, it is good; but when he steals mine, it is bad.' Well, I say the same—or almost: My things are good whenever they make money, bad whenever they don't. Money for its own sake I detest, but money in so far as it manifests popular acceptance, I adore."

On ideals: "I knew sooner or later I would be confronted with that question: by the way, one reason I like you is that you are so predictable, and consequently so comfortably easy to deal with. I will not add hypocrisy to my other defects by saying that I am an idealist. As far as ideals go consider me a virgin. It is the powerful of this world, those who command divisions and shape the destiny of nations that should have ideals, and *they never do*. Which goes to show you that ideals are luxuries only slaves and superfluous people can afford."

Her favorite writers?

"I have none."

During a conversation, however, she spoke admiringly of Chekhov and La Rochefoucauld: "Chekhov was the only sane Russian," she said. "All the others suffered from some type of profound personality disturbance or neurosis. Chekhov was a civilized, decent modest man who did not hesitate to admit that he could not answer the important questions. How many writers have been willing to make that painful admission? . . . La Rochefoucauld had a few things to say and he said them without mumbo jumbo." Her own letters and conversations glittered with aphorisms.

• 4 •

She had the habit of enclosing a great variety of items in each letter: a yellow leaf, a blade of grass, a wild flower, a postage stamp, drawings, clippings from newspapers and periodicals with marginalia, cartoons, sketches for poems, old postcards . . . anything that could be fitted into an envelope.

In one long Proustian letter, full of childhood and adolescent reminiscences tinged with self-pity, that gradually became a boozy interior monologue, she spoke of her intimate, loveless life. At the age of twelve she had been seduced by a friend of the family.

"He used to spoil me with all kinds of little gifts and attentions, and one day, when there was no one in the house, his little kisses and caresses took an unexpected turn. When I wanted to free myself from his embrace he wouldn't let me, and as his behavior became more incomprehensible and frightening, his words acquired a tenderness and sweetness that were a revelation to me. I was confused. Well, perhaps a little curious too, eh? I was, I think, in some ways, a rather precocious child. And I now think the only reason I allowed it to happen was that it seemed to mean so much to him and nothing to me—on the physical level at any rate.

"In spite of what Freudians say, it was not a traumatic experience. So much so that I allowed it to happen again . . . Am I perhaps shocking your sensibilities? The liaison (which you would probably call *dangereux*) lasted two years. (I do hope you are still with me.) At the age of fourteen I went through a religious crisis. [They must have been caught in flagrante, I remember to have

thought at this point] after which, to this day, I have never felt the
need for masculine companionship. As a matter of fact I wanted to
be a nun, but my father wouldn't let me."

The subject matter of some of her poems, however, was far
from spiritual.

A glance
a word
and suddenly
the house is on fire
and the world is reduced to cinders:
Love.

Love:
Is it tears?
Cries?
Caresses?
Kisses?
Sighs?
A thousand deaths
and one resurrection?

As delicate
as a drop of water;
as cruel
as Chinese torture:
Love.

Where is love born?
In the eyes?
In the heart?
In the mind?
Between the legs?
Is love a torrential river
that flows downwards
from the heights of the spirit?
Or
like lava in a volcano
rises from the very roots
of one's being,
from the very beginning of time?
Is it a miracle
that reveals to us our infinity?
Or a curse
that threatens to reduce us
to nothingness?

That letter had a postscript: "Sometimes I wonder whether we
will ever meet. I hope not. It would be like meeting my own

conscience, my double. A crisis. I am sending you a photo, taken last year—the most recent I have. May I ask you to do likewise? I do want to know what you look like, so that when I write, I can write to *you* and not to some imaginary soul."

About her picture, I remember to have written: "You are much more beautiful than I had thought. Don't be surprised if my letters slowly degenerate into endless declarations of love."

To which she had replied: "Did you then think I was an old, fat, myopic, frustrated spinster?
Old: Is thirty-two old?
Fat: I was, as a matter of fact, fat. But during the last few months I managed to lose 42 kilos, so that I now look like Nefertiti.
Myopic: I plead guilty to that charge. I do wear glasses when I work.
Frustrated spinster: No comment!"

Several times she had invited me to go to Athens: "If you come, I promise to quit work for at least two weeks. We could go to one of our many beautiful islands: nothing but the sun, the sea, the white beach, a caique with an old mustachioed barefoot seawolf, a cool taverna . . . No rat race, no pollution, no mechanized traffic. We could have long talks. Writing is such a poor substitute for tête-à-têtes."

I had informed her that it was not one of my present ambitions to be a tourist. All I wanted from life was freedom. I was not speaking of metaphysical or physical or political freedom, I had added. I was speaking of financial freedom. If she wanted to see me, she must be the one to cross the ocean. She could afford it. Moreover, she enjoyed traveling. The year before she had gone to Spain. The following year she was planning to go to Japan. She had already covered North Africa, Israel, most of Europe. The matter rested there for a while until she surprised me with a telegram announcing her arrival.

• 5 •

At the airport I had trouble recognizing her. In the one photo she had sent me she looked cool, contemplative, serene—huge, chestnut-colored eyes, an enigmatic smile that had a disdainful quirk at one corner. But as I looked at her, what stood forth was her nervous restlessness. She had looked at me once, a quick inquisitive glance, a handshake, an exchange of smiles, and then, after some feverish rummaging in her duffel bag, she had extricated cigarettes and lighter, and smoking she had told me the story of her swollen ankle. She smoked greedily, like a man, blowing clouds of smoke from nostrils, mouth, ears, and fanning it away from her face with a hand. I may have stared at her without realizing it. Later, she was to ascribe her nervousness to that.

The accident had happened in the Athens airport. A heavy suitcase of monumental dimensions, a veritable cathedral, had landed on her, and she had let loose such a piercing scream that everyone in the place had been frozen with terror.

Fractures? I inquired.

A nurse had examined her, and to everyone's surprise (for by then she had gathered around her a small crowd of sympathizers, crypto- as well as not so damn crypto-sadomasochists, and just plain morbidly curious spectators of both sexes and all ages) the nurse had found nothing pulverized, shattered, or cracked. In the airplane a charming stewardess had given her a tiny hot-water bottle which had eased the pain somewhat—the martinis had also helped . . . There was inner tension in her voice, but also a cultivated casualness.

She wanted me to take her to a hotel. "We may have to discuss that over a drink," I said.
"Where?"
"My place."
"I don't wish to disagree, but—"
"Don't."
"But—"
"Enough buts."
"From one totalitarian regime into another. I already feel at home."
"That's the general idea."

• 6 •

"So this is where you live. And all the time I thought you lived in a mousehole. Now I see why you don't want to move. Books, piano, typewriter, records, Vermeer, Leonardo, Vermeer—he must be your favorite—Velasquez, Goya. On the conservative side, but good. I feel out of place. An intruder. You play chess? We must have a game soon." We never did. Too busy with other matters.

At first, she wouldn't allow me to make love to her, and when I insisted on an explanation, she said it had nothing to do with me personally and that I must please be patient.

"Maybe tomorrow," she said.

"Today. Now. Yesterday!"

"Such impatience. Aren't there any whorehouses in this godforsaken place?"

"I don't know."

"Haven't you made any inquiries?"

"I haven't."

"Why not?"

"Because I could never perform in such places."

"Why is that?"

"I don't really know."

"I do. You are an idealist, that's why."

"Oh?"

"Yes. An idealist. Ideals are good for the soul, and anything that is good for the soul is bound to hurt the rest. One should keep a certain balance in these things. You go to extremes. In spite of what you think and in spite of what I may have said on the subject, I do have a few ideals of my own too, by the way. But I refuse to sweat my soul to affirm them today, knowing that I might want to negate them tomorrow. Why, may I ask, *why* should I die for an idea, being always aware of the possibility that I might be wrong? Perhaps not necessarily wrong in the idea itself, but in thinking that to fight something to the death is a form of victory. I don't believe in so-called moral victories. In my eyes they are synonymous with defeat."

"That's all fine and dandy, but couldn't we discuss these matters some other time? Preferably by correspondence?'

"Let me finish! . . . What was I saying?"

"I forget."

"That's because you weren't paying any attention."

"Not true."

"You know, I have had this suspicion for a long time now, that all your difficulties stem from the fact that you were born in the wrong century. Probably you even think love and sex cannot be separated."

"How did you know?"

"Why do you think I understand you so well? We happen to be alike in many, many ways. Did I ever tell you that I've always wanted to have a brother but was an only and neglected child?'

"A horrible combination that: only *and* neglected."

"You think so too? Did I ever tell you that once I tried to kill myself?"

"You may have."

"No, I couldn't have."

"Of course not."

"It was a silly accident, actually. I had a few vodkas, perhaps one or two more than I should have had. Then I remember having taken some sleeping pills, perhaps also one or two more than I should have had—I was never good at arithmetic anyway. And when I came to I found myself in a hospital that used to be an asylum for the incurably insane. The cell wasn't padded but the windows were equipped with iron bars. It was there that I had one or two sessions with a Freudian analyst who was later to commit suicide—which goes to show you. Needless to say, never in my life did I seriously consider suicide as a way out."

"Good for you."

"I say, your contribution to this conversation is so slight that I might as well be delivering a soliloquy. Your mind must be on other matters."

"It is!"

"The least you could do is contradict me once in a while."

"I do not wish to waste valuable time on arguments."

"I see."

"Good."

"Well, I'll tell you what. It is not my intention to hurt your silly masculine vanity. Let's compromise. You promise me that you will behave and I will sleep with you in my pajamas."

"Agreed!"

"Promise first."

"I promise."

• 7 •

"But you promised! . . ." Some drops of blood from that night still adorn my bedsheets. Next morning, before we went out for a walk, she was to try soap and water, vinegar, vodka, lemon juice, and the devil knows what else, all of which behaved like mordants.

As for her love-making, I'll say this: the secret beauty of her *ars poetica* with all its literary and autobiographical allusions, verbal splendors, the multiple levels of perception which her Greek was meant to convey, may have been beyond my reach, but her performance in bed was complex and inventive without being snobbish or misleading or self-indulgent. Erudite and eclectic, yes, but also original—*Finnegans Wake* without mumbo jumbo.

• 8 •

During our walks I taught her how to distinguish several weeds, wildflowers, shrubs, and trees. Notwithstanding the fact that in the course of a year's correspondence she had enclosed in her letters enough botanical specimens to make possible an exhaustive study of the flora of Greece, she had no interest in their classification. Classes, divisions, ranks, categories, she said once, were invented by fools to deal with other fools; and that in nature everything was unique—even snow crystals, leaves of the same tree, grains of sand—and that there were no rules, only exceptions. I told her Thoreau agreed with her: "He says somewhere that if you want to be acquainted with trees and flowers, you must forget your botany."

"And you say this man was an American?'

"He was."

"I find that difficult to believe, I shall have to read his complete works. He sounds like a man after my heart. You see, I could never take Americans seriously. They are eternal adolescents fond of toys first, machines later. And machines are nothing but bigger toys, no?—more expensive, more dangerous. You mentioned a contemporary American writer once . . . I neglected to burden my memory with his name."

"Mailer? Norman Mailer?"

"That may well be the gentleman's name. I read some of his things . . ."

"What did you think?"

"He can be entertaining enough when he writes about boxers, bullfighters, soldiers, clowns—"

"Clowns?"

"I meant to say politicians. Forgive the Freudian slip. But the moment he steps into other fields, he reveals a deplorable lack of taste and judgment. And what arrogance! What imperialistic disregard for what has been said already by others, in other times and continents."

Speaking of wild flowers, she said: "They are nature's poems, infinitely more complex than your Eliot and Joyce. God may have had the mind of a mathematician and the wrist of an Italian Renaissance painter, but he must have had the heart of a poet.

What is even more astonishing is that he belonged to that group of decadent, *fin-de-siècle* poets who believed in art for art's sake. For, what could be the possible propaganda value of a lily, may I ask?"

We came across two highway fatalities: a garter snake and a muskrat. I enjoyed my role of cicerone. Showed her a hawk circling high up in the sky. On the wooden wall of a barn, a woodpecker rattling away like a pneumatic drill. We walked around a pond that was alive with a cloud of damsel-flies. On the opposite shore, on a pond, a fly-catcher with a grasshopper in its beak—"Either you have the wrong name or he has the wrong victim," she said. Every step we took started off half-a-dozen tiny olive-green explosions—leopard frogs that dived and plopped into the green waters, and when they came up for air, we could see their eyes like those of diminutive crocodiles. Then we stumbled on a tornado of blood-thirsty mosquitoes that chased us like a pack of ravenous wolves. We ran into the tall grass, jumped over fences, crawled under barbed wire, dodged ruminating cows, avoided ground-hog burrows . . . Love on the grass, *en plein air*, under the sky, in the nearby aspen grove, was out.

· 9 ·

"I remember you once wrote . . ." she began a conversation during another, less eventful walk.

"I hate to be quoted," I said.

"Did you write that? I don't remember."

"You mean to tell me you remember everything I wrote?"

"I refuse to flatter your silly masculine vanity. You once said: 'I love to love, and hate to hate'—"

"Doesn't everyone?'

"Let me finish. 'I love to love and hate to hate, but find myself hating most of the time.' "

"That's me all right."

"What are your feelings towards me?"

"That's a plantain, and that's called chicory—"

"Answer!"

"I should have said another thing: I hate to use the word *love*. And that's milkweed, so called because—here! let me show you. Observe."

"I will not. Answer my question first."

"I did."

"You did not."

"Shaw says—"

"Shaw was an ass! Don't quote Shaw to me. He didn't even make love to his wife."

"Why, a man could be chaste and wise at the same time."

"Ha! Is that what you want? Wisdom and chastity? *Shaw says!* Shaw, a millionaire masquerading as a socialist. He thought he had all the answers and next thing you know he was endorsing Stalin and Mussolini. He had no heart. No emotions. And you are no different. Shaw says indeed. Why don't you quote Kafka too? Now, there is your man. He spent most of his passion on postage stamps. He wrote two, sometimes three letters a day to his women, and the reason he refused to marry any of them was that he couldn't stand the idea of losing a pen pal. He may have been impotent too. Compared himself to a worm once—an obvious phallic reference. But *you* don't have that excuse . . . I know what it is: now that you have me here, with you, you take me for granted. Wait until I leave, then you will miss me."

She was right. The first night alone, wasn't bad. I could use the change of pace. The second, I was restless. The third, I felt a vacuum in my bed. The fourth, this vacuum transferred itself to the depths of my being and soon changed into a raging whirlpool of ache, despair, desire. I felt as though I had been amputated, dismembered.

• 10 •

She stayed twelve days.

"I shouldn't have come. It was a mistake. But I don't regret it. I'm glad I did," she said at the airport.

"I'm glad you did too," I said.

"I don't want *you* to be glad. I want you to be miserable, as I am."

"I am miserable too."

"You lie, as always. Tell me you will miss me."

"I will."

"Tell me you love me, or is that too much to ask?"

"I love you."

"Another lie. But I love you all the same. Hold me. I don't care what everyone makes of our tableau. Promise me you will do your best to come to Greece. Soon. Within a month. No, that's not soon enough. Today. Now. Yesterday! Remember? . . . I'll never forget that. All right, I am willing to compromise with you again. Make it two months. Don't worry about money. My poems will soon be translated into English by T. S. Eliot, and published in America, and I will achieve instant fame and fortune. All the television talk shows will beg me to appear on their programs, and naturally Hollywood will want to film the story of my life. Is there an actress who looks a bit like me? Ali MacGraw? Is she the *Love Story* kid? Pretty, but dumb—she'll have to do I guess."

When I pointed out that T. S. Eliot couldn't do the job, she said: "Why not? He did Saint-John Perse, didn't he? And Valery."

I told her why not.

"He's dead? That's not fair. He does all these second-raters, and when my turn comes, he croaks. Who is the next best poet in the English-speaking world. *I* know. W. H. Auden. What is your opinion of him? Do you think he can be trusted with the job?"

"Well, not quite."

"Why not? Didn't he do Cavafy or Saferis or something? If he liked them, he will love me. But if I want *him* to translate my stuff I'd better hurry because he won't be getting any younger. I saw a picture of him recently in a magazine. If one were to judge by appearances he must be at least say . . . two, three hundred years old. With my luck, he's sure to go to the devil too, before I get to him. O well! I can always get Kim."

"Kim? Kim who?"

"Kimon Friar. A good friend of mine. He translated Kazantzakis's *Odysseus*. And if that doesn't work out, I can always start taking karate lessons and become a spokeswoman for women's lib— that's where the money is—with a scandalously ambidextrous and omnivorous private life, and write a highly controversial book entitled *From Clytemnestra to Lady Chatterley* or *From Emma Bovary to Lolita Haze,* or some such nonsense, in which I will combine the total commitment of Sartre (minus the obfuscating jargon) with the brilliant precision of Nabokov (minus the aristocratic paternalism), the bombast of Kazantzakis with the philistinism of Thomas Mann; a Proustian delicacy of perception with a Joycean flair of word-play; and which eventually will be translated—although untranslatable—into forty-two languages, including Swahili and Eskimo, and be a universal best seller. I shall however refuse to rest on my laurels. I will write a merciless critique of this book under a pseudonym, of course—"

"Masculine?"

"Of course! And make another killing. After which—I'm not through yet—I will produce a revised edition, a kind of Toynbeean reconsideration . . . and so on. By the way, the idea of this book came to me, I should say *was conceived*—I may mention this in the preface—during our first night together, when you took me by force."

"I did not."

"Almost."

"You enjoyed it."

"Is that so?"

"You said you did—during *and* after."

"The animal in me may have. After all, I am human too. And if the book is a flop, no problem. I already have money for both of us, not to mention an army of old uncles and aunts, all of them filthy rich, who can't live forever. Promise you will come."

"I promise."

"I know all about your promises. You *must* come. Because if you don't, I'll come and drag you there by force. Which reminds me that I have an excellent friend, a belly-slitting lawyer, who I'm sure will be able to provide me with a good legal blackmail angle. For all I know I might even be in an interesting condition. If so, then you simply *have* to come to make an honest woman of me, no? As you can see, you have no choice. Whatever Lolita wants—"

"I thought you said you were on the Pill."

"I was—notwithstanding my doctor's warning that it might be dangerous to my health. He mentioned the possible side effects it might have on my liver, thyroid, adrenal glands, gall bladder . . ."

"Did he mention nausea?—"

"He may have."

"Vertigo? Double vision? Cancer?"

"That does it! I'll never take another one as long as I live."

"If you were on the Pill, then what's all this talk about blackmail and belly-slitting?"

"Nothing is one-hundred percent—didn't you know? The Pill is of course a little better than Vatican roulette, but it is not fail-safe. Only total abstinence is. And speaking of abstinence: You must also promise not to be unfaithful to me in the meantime; because if you even so much as touch another woman I will know it immediately. In addition to a network of spies I happen to be equipped with a set of highly developed extrasensory perceptions. I'll know in a jiffy and be here the next day, catch the bitch by the throat and strangle her, shoot her, cut her throat, bury her alive, dig her up, and stone her to death. As for you, a worse fate awaits you. I shall have to castrate you, then kill you, or kill you first, then castrate you—the order is not important."

• 11 •

In one of her first letters, she wrote: "You must have not only a black heart, but a black liver, and a black pancreas, black lungs, and black blood. If you don't come soon, I shall take a lover and live happily ever after, and you shall never hear from me again. Come! Besides chains (as Groucho says, or is it the other one?) what have you got to lose? How can you go on living in that crummy joint? In that hemispheric equivalent of Siberia. In that *enfer de merde* . . ."

She knew of course that I would never go: "If it weren't for your infernal pride, we could be so happy," she wrote once. But kept on urging me to join her.

She still does, after two years and several lovers of whose existence she has made only cryptic allusions. "Like Columbus before me, I discovered a new world when I crossed the Atlantic. And by that I don't mean Thoreau and wild flowers and weeds. And rats! Especially the kind that do not keep their promises.

"As for writing poetry, I agree with you: it is a form of bourgeois self-indulgence, like insanity and suicide. It seems to me it is far more important to enjoy the little details of life than to have a happy life, to care more about the next moment and hour, rather than the next month, or year, or life, or generation. Enough philosophy. Will I see you again? Last night I dreamed about you . . ."

• 12 •

I dream of her too, at least twice a month. Again I hold her in my arms and feel her soft body against mine. We don't say much. I don't even see her face, but I know it is she because of the many subtle ways of her body. She again abandons herself to the delirium of love. Her thighs envelope my hips, her knees touch my shoulder blades, and as I bring my mouth close to her ear (she had erotogenic ears) and brush some wisps of matted hair, I hear the plainsong of her soft moans and feel the successive floods of lava against my loins. To prolong the sweetness of the privileged moment, I keep my eyes shut, but it is too late. For by then, I have already become aware of my self-engendered soddenness, and that I am alone in my bed between the crumpled sheets damp with perspiration, alone in my hemispheric equivalent of Siberia.

Autobiographical
Narratives

In the New World

AFTER VISITING HIS SISTER in New York City and on his way to Montreal, where he has a brother, an old childhood friend from Athens, whom I have not seen for twenty-five years, drops in to see me. We have a couple of drinks and laughs. He has gained a few pounds, lost some hair, but retained his wit and humor. When I ask what made him decide to wander all over the world, he replies: "Death."

"Death?"

"I had a heart attack last year."

"Sorry to hear that."

"It opened my eyes, and I said to myself: Before you go to hell, you might as well go to America."

We laugh.

"So, tell me, how do you like our brave New World?"

"Big, different, strange . . ."

"All in all, not a bad place to visit, eh?"

"I'm glad *you* like it."

"I didn't say that."

"You said *not a bad place*."

"I said *to visit*."

"What made you decide to prolong your visit by a quarter of a century then?"

"Economic necessity. Sometimes one chooses because one has no choice. And when one has no choice, one doesn't always choose wisely."

"But you look pretty contented to me, well adjusted, happy . . ."

"Happy to see you, yes. As for the rest, call it gallows humor."

"Don't get me wrong. The place itself isn't what bothers me, but the natives—dollar-obsessed, indifferent to ideas, to people, to beauty. . . . At first I thought I had landed on a different planet—strange language, strange people, strange environ-

21

ment. . . . Men walking like robots; women walking like men; bread that looks white, soft, and inviting, but tastes like plastic; friends and relatives more interested in the TV set than in one another—"

"It's the same here."

"I was told Canada is different."

"The difference is so tiny that it might as well be invisible to the naked eye. Let me give you an example. Once a year, around Christmas, on my birthday, most of the dozen or so Armenian families within a radius of about six–seven miles pay us a visit. Mother does some baking, I get a few pounds of cashews, almonds, and mixed nuts. They come—Armenians of all ages. We exchange a few comments on the weather, the latest death, marriage, divorce, birth . . . about five–ten minutes of conversation in all, after which everyone sinks back into his solitude. The teen-agers cluster around the TV set, the old ones play *tavlu*, the younger ones poker, the women knit, and I go to my room and books."

"No."

"Yes."

"I find that hard to believe."

"Wait, there is more. On one occasion I made a declaration to the effect that since we get together only once a year, we should refrain from playing games and watching TV. 'What shall we do then?' someone said. 'Talk,' I said. No one said anything for a long time. Complete silence. 'Is this what you want?' someone shouted. 'Now then, get the *tavlu* and let's have a game!' And the silence was soon drowned by the clatter of dice, the canned laughter of sitcoms on TV—interrupted as always by oratorio-length commercials."

"Those commercials—they drive me *insane!*"

"You get used to them."

"Never!"

"The first twenty-five years are always the hardest."

More laughter.

"How can anyone stand them?" he says.

"Stand them? They *love* them. Their vanity is flattered. Even the most stupid among them feel smart and superior. That's democracy in action for you. The triumph of the lowest common denominator, or, to put it more technically, the indifference and vulgarity of the many, and the greed and self-interest of the few. Add to that the pressure to conform and you will have a fail-safe system impervious to ideas, outside influences, good taste, improvement. . . . Another important factor: everywhere else there are those who exploit and those who are exploited. Here, those who are exploited today hope to be exploiters tomorrow. Everybody is brought up to believe that with hard work and application he can be anything he wants—a leader of men, a millionaire, a star . . . and sometimes all three at once."

"This pressure to conform," my friend says; "I knew it existed, but not to this extent. They preach freedom but they are afraid to use it. You remember how it was with us in Greece. Greeks wouldn't allow us to speak Armenian. Made fun of us. Insulted us. What kind of gibberish is that? they would say. This is a civilized country. Speak Greek. You're in Greece now. You're eating Greek bread. You're living on Greek soil. They were rude, mean, merciless."

"Yes, I remember that very well."

"But that problem doesn't exist here. Besides, most Americans are themselves foreigners anyway. And yet, the majority of Armenians don't even know how to speak Armenian. Even those who know Armenian prefer to speak in English with one another—not only when they are out in the street, but also in the privacy of their own homes. They change their names . . ."

"This is true of all immigrants. They come here—rootless, poor, confused, disoriented—and spend the rest of their lives conforming. They look down at the 'old country' and they change not only their language and names, but also habits, mentality, outlook. Anagnostopoulos becomes Agnew, Hampartsoumian Hammer or Ham, Ardashes Koeroghlanian Archie Kerr."

We laugh.

"Let's sit crooked but talk straight," he says. "I prefer Kerr to Koeroghlanian."

"Me too. I am myself sometimes tempted to accept a friend's advice and change my own name to Ball—Ray Ball—make things easy for the natives, who prefer monosyllables: Bill, Jack, Smith, Jones, James, Dick, Joe. And then it occurs to me that I went through hell trying to adjust to the New World—took me twenty-five years and I'm still having problems. Let them be a little uncomfortable with my name. Why should I be so tender-hearted and compassionate? But let me tell you about this Koeroghlanian-Kerr character to illustrate a pet theory of mine that changing one's name is a symbolic act that ushers in an infinite number of other changes in one's psychological make up, conduct, identity, attitudes. I first met Ardashes about twenty-eight years ago in Venice. He was then a young, bright, happy, intelligent boy, very good at math. After graduation we didn't keep in touch and I had forgotten all about him, until about two–three years ago he telephoned to inform me that he was in the neighborhood and would like to drop in for a short visit. I told him he was welcome. He said he had his wife and children with him too. I told him they were all welcome, of course. They came. The children were mean, noisy, spoiled, and as they went about vandalizing everything in sight, he explained with an Anglo-Saxon cool voice that he no longer disciplined them because constantly telling children what to do and not do hampers their natural development."

"Not bad. In the name of Freud, they raise savages."

"I must have looked on with some degree of unbelief, perhaps even shock, because his *odar* wife hastened to explain that before becoming parents, they had taken a course in child psychology—as if to say, there is method in our madness. As soon as we were alone for a minute or two however, this friend of mine spoke in Armenian and said: 'You know,' he said, 'I have a very comfortable job as an executive in a financial corporation, a nice home in the suburbs with a swimming pool in the backyard; my wife is a wonderful girl and I am proud of my children, but I'm not happy here. I've never been happy.' How come? I said. 'Well,' he said, 'you see, I have no friends.' Too bad, I said. 'But now that we have established contact,' said he, 'let's keep in touch eh?' "

"And what did you say to that?"

"I said nothing. I believe in silence as a weapon of self-defense."

"Well, then, what happened?"

"Nothing. I haven't heard from him since."

"He got the message then."

"Or he joined a club. They have all kinds of clubs here—for alcoholics, fat women, single parents, rape victims, collectors of bottles, perverts of all kinds . . . you've got a problem, they've got a club, or a university course. I just read that they even have a university course somewhere in Boston to teach grandmothers how to suck eggs. . . . Nobody is allowed to have a problem. There are books on creative divorce—creative is an *in* word now— creative writing, creative living, creative financing, creative this, creative that . . . in other words: you want to be *creative?* Follow instructions."

"And no one sees a contradiction in that?".

"Of course not. And if you or I were to point that out to them, they would say, What the hell do you know? If you're so smart how come you're not rich? Or, if Armenians or Greeks are so

great, what have they done lately? They themselves may be a
tangle of complexes and insecurities, but when they deal with a
social inferior or a foreigner, they appear confident, secure, aggressive . . . because they live in the best of all possible worlds;
they know best; and anyone who disagrees with their way of life is
an ignoramus, a malcontent, an outcast, an eccentric who belongs to the lunatic fringe. Italians are dismissed as spaghetti, the
French as frogs. . . . Paris? a local farmer once said to me. What's
there to see besides pissoirs?"

"Which may explain Vietnam."

"Exactly. They dismissed not only the French experience there,
but they also ignored the North's fanaticism, the South's opportunism, and their own lack of values. Wars are fought with machines. Ideas, ideologies, values—these are all obsolete. Platonic
concepts. *Percentages*—that's what they go by. Moral or esthetic
values are taken into consideration simply because they cannot
be expressed in a language that may be understood by cal-
culators, computers, and electronic morons. Before making an
important decision, an American political leader reduces a complex issue to an either/or proposition, finds out what the majority
wants, then gives it to them. They follow the masses and call it
leadership."

"*Creative* leadership!"

"Right. But face to face with a real crisis, they are paralyzed. The
so-called hostage crisis, for instance—"

"For a whole year we heard nothing but the hostages in Iran.
While I was in New York it occurred to me that these hostages
were safer in Teheran. Had they been free men in New York, at
least one of them would have been killed in a traffic accident,
another two or three mugged, or perhaps even murdered. . . .
They wouldn't even let me go out for a walk. I *love* to walk—the
only way to get the feel of a city. No, they said, nobody goes out
for a walk here. You'll get mugged and robbed. You should see
the number of locks and bolts they have on their doors—a regular
fortress. Democracy in action looks more like a state of siege to
me. Everyone I talked to in New York has either been mugged or
knows someone very close who has been mugged. They live in
constant terror. At least the KGB in Moscow is more predictable. It
follows certain rules. Your average Soviet dissident knows what to
expect and when, where . . . Another thing: Until I saw New
York, I thought Greece was the land of pickpockets, burglars,
thieves, liars, and cheats. But I'm beginning to suspect that beside
Americans, we are just amateurs."

"Americans are ahead of the game because they are more versatile, better organized, technologically advanced, practical. Business functions like organized crime, and vice versa. And politics has adopted techniques from both."

"Tell me about Watergate. What was it all about?"

"The abuse of power, *they* said. The real crime, however, was stupidity—the fact that they got caught. Everyone knows here that politicians cheat and lie, and they have always done so . . . and why shouldn't they? It's part of the game. All is fair in love and war, they say. How much more so in business and politics! Who wants an honest moron as a leader?"

"They tried one and he made a mess of things."

"What you said about Greeks being amateurs however, is right. My professor of economics used to say that business is neither moral nor immoral, but amoral. He was wrong. Business—at least in its American context—is more versatile than that. It may adopt moral, immoral as well as amoral methods—so long as they work. Greeks are prejudiced against honesty and morality. The only time they feel comfortable is when they cheat and lie. After living under the Ottomans for six centuries, they have learned to dissemble and deceive. Americans have no such complexes. To them truth is as handy a tool as any lie. But again, to speak of truth in an American context would be misleading. These are obsolete, outmoded concepts that no longer apply. Americans have redefined everything. Words have no longer their original value and meaning. Sometimes they even mean the opposite of what they say. Take ambition, for instance. At one time it was regarded as a vice. It meant greed, ruthlessness, fanaticism, selfishness. When Hamlet makes a list of his defects to Ophelia, he includes ambition—'I am very proud, revengeful, *ambitious*,' he says. Americans, on the other hand, regard ambition as one of the cardinal virtues. A man without ambition is a weakling, a fool, a parasite, an aberration. And do you know why? Because an American businessman one day made the observation that America's business is business and that gentlemen make poor salesmen. 'What we need,' he said, 'are aggressive men, men with ambition!' On that day the word had to be redefined. Everything business touches is altered. That includes words. When a businessman speaks of free enterprise, for instance, he means license to rape the environment, pollute the air, exploit, mislead, convince the masses that when they buy a pack of cigarettes what they get isn't cancer but sex appeal."

"And your average American slob falls for that line?"

"Let's say after being exposed to the same commercial a thousand times, he begins to sing its tune—sometimes literally."

"Those damn tunes—they actually make me hate the stuff they push."

"A young student from Yerevan came to see me one day. He was visiting relatives in a neighboring town. We sat in the living room. Someone else was watching TV, and whenever a commercial came on, he would excuse himself and stomp out of the room muttering what sounded like Russian profanities."

"Beautiful!"

"That's exactly what I said. And yet, I never had the courage and initiative to do it myself. The pressure to conform. In a society of madmen, the sane try to cover up their sanity as if it were a crime, whereas the mad parade their lunacy with total impunity. Did you know that there are people here who regard Sinatra and Crosby as semi-classics, and Strauss waltzes as unbearably complex? Result? Rock and punk singers, yelling, screaming, and writhing like jungle savages are shown on educational TV—that is to say, they are subsidized by the government and supported by the people."

"That *is* insane! Why would the government want to subsidize criminal conduct?"

"Democracy in action, like Goya's reason, begets nightmares, contradictions, and absurdities. Let me give you more examples. Preachers and born-again Christians who are also ruthless politicians, shrewd businessmen, and millionaires. The brother of an American president accepts bribes from an African fascist leader and refuses to see anything wrong in that. The ex-hippie wife of our prime minister runs away from home, reveals herself to be a common groupie, writes her autobiography, and becomes a bestselling author. An American president tries to justify his criminal conduct in the eyes of the people by declaring that his mother was a saint. Another American president, a devout Catholic, has an affair with a Mafia moll—who, needless to add, writes her memoirs too, with the usual results. Upper middle-class matrons seated in comfortable living rooms, wearing fancy hairdoes and enormous diamond earrings, sip sherry and complain about inflation on the evening news, saying things like 'We can't make ends meet!' "

"This sort of thing should be exposed and ridiculed."

"It has been, many times. And that's another typical American absurdity. Every facet of American life has been thoroughly analyzed, exposed, and criticized by Americans themeselves. But since critics never run for office—and if they do, they invariably lose—nothing is done."

"Who runs for office—besides peanut farmers and second-rate actors?"

"Usually corporation lawyers and entrepreneurs—provided of course they are of Anglo-Saxon origin. In that sense the Byzantine Empire was far more liberal. A thousand years ago Armenians were allowed to occupy the imperial throne of Constantinople—the mightiest state of its time. The most important Armenian in Washington today is a young speech-writer for Reagan—a left-over from the Nixon administration."

"Now, that's what I call real progress."

"I once worked for a man here who would say things like 'So and so is a good man because he's Anglo-Saxon' or 'So and so is a man of integrity because he's an Anglo-Saxon.' And he would say this even to people of Hungarian, Jewish, and German origin, and no one saw anything wrong or questionable in that. At the time I dismissed him as an imbecile, which he certainly was—and forgot about him until the other day when I was reading the posthumously published diaries of Edmund Wilson, generally regarded as the foremost American literary critic of the 20th century. He too uses the term Anglo-Saxon synonymously with attractive, noble, great. And *these* are the people who call us racists whenever we try to explain to them what the Turks did to us in 1915. An old story, they say, let bygones be bygones."

"It's easy being magnanimous with someone else's injury—like being generous with someone else's money."

"Exactly!"

"For a whole year they talk of nothing but their precious 52 hostages, some of whom may have been spies; but they want us to forget the senseless massacre of at least a million completely innocent and harmless women, children, and old men."

"Even some Armenian-Americans think that way now. Let the Turks keep our territories, they say. Who needs them? We are better off here. They write editorials and letters to the editor to that effect. They deliver sermons against 'Armenian' terrorism."

"Am I right in assuming that you haven't been very happy here?"

"Define happiness."

"All right, let me rephrase my question: How in hell did you manage to take it for a quarter of a century?"

"Let's say I have no illusions about the rest of the world. At the moment I'm busy translating a book by Gostan Zarian, in which he writes about life in a suburb of Paris. 'How can anyone live here?' he wonders at one point. 'How can I live here?' I assure you, it sounds as bad as . . . this parody of Siberia. And speaking of Siberia, once in a while I think of following in Zarian's footsteps and going to Yerevan—Ararat, Aragats, Sevan, *ishkhanatsoug*, my own people, ancestral lands, dreams. . . . But, I suspect, there I would be shut in an insane asylum. Writers here are ignored; there, they are treated like civil servants and immature babes whose every step must be carefully watched lest they fall and rock the boat. But enough about myself and my problems. Tell me how are things with you?'

He speaks of his Greek wife (she can speak Armenian now), his work (he is a successful jeweler), his children (one of them is studying medicine in Paris), recent heart attack (made him see the world for the first time), mutual friends. . . .

Mutual friends:

"Remember Jirair Abdalian?"

"The pianist?"

"The same. Last year he fell in love with a visting coloratura soprano from Beirut. She gave a recital in Athens; he accompanied her on the piano; they had to practise together—"

"What did she sing?"

"Schubert, Brahms, Hugo Wolf, and Gomidas for an encore. Did a very good job too. I almost fell in love with her myself. But that *abdal* of ours went further. He ran away with her, abandoning wife, children, work."

"Must have been love at first sight, a tornado."

"Whatever it was, it didn't last. He's back with his wife now, trying to patch up things. As for Khosrovouhi Janashian, our classmate: someone—no one knows who and why—tried to stab her to death in her own apartment. She's all right now but under psychiatric care."

"I thought things like that didn't happen in Greece."

"They do, all the time. American influence—drugs, pollution, Coca Cola, rock and punk groups, the Mafia—we have them all. And speaking of the Mafia: remember your pal Movses, the one who went to school with you in Venice—had a breakdown there? . . Well, until very recently he ran one of the best nightclubs in town—politicians, diplomats, actors, visiting royalty, big shots, *la creme de la creme*—but then he got involved with shady characters and deals, and had to run away to South America somewhere."

"And our pal Antranik Zouloumian?"

"He got into trouble with his wife."

"Armenian or *odar?*"

"Armenian—someone from Salonica; you don't know her; an attractive wench. It seems she had a Greek lover there and he followed her down to Athens and they went on seeing each other. A long story. Four children. Big scandal. Anonymous letters, blackmail, detectives, murder threats, headlines—I wish I had more time. I need at least two hours to outline the drama. Dostoevsky stuff. If you ever run out of material, you should come to Athens. We'll give you enough plots for a dozen novels."

After he leaves, I count my blessings. I may be alone, on a strange planet, in the middle of nowhere, but at least I have my books, my peace, my bottle of booze.

Anonymous letters, blackmail, adultery, murder threats, detectives. What will man do in his unending struggle against boredom! Or is it search for happiness? Love. Man knows what he wants, but doesn't know how to get it. In his search for love, he generates hatred and intolerance. In his pursuit of happiness, he generates misery. A man will dream a dream and in his single-minded efforts to realize that dream, he will turn it into a nightmare. It happens all the time. In his efforts to build an empire that would last a thousand years, Hitler reduced his beloved fatherland into rubble; and in this he had the full cooperation, not to say adulation, of millions of fellow Germans. Still has. "Hitler is not dead," an old German (of whom we have several in our neighborhood) assured me over a bottle of schnapps recently.

"I've heard rumors to that effect too," I egged him on. "They say he is in South America somewhere."

"You bet! And he is coming back—this time, no monkey business."

"Why is it taking him so long?"

"He is working with his scientists."

"Working on what?"

"Machines."

"Doomsday machines?"

"Bombs, yes. Big ones. Powerful . . . "

The grouchy old brute has something to look forward to. He smiles. His eyes flash. He feels strong. He pours himself another drink.

He is a devout Christian. A practicing Catholic. We walk to

church together every Sunday morning—he to pray, and I to play the organ.

I look at him and think of the myth of the average man. The banality of evil. The serenity of old age. Average moralists preaching to equally imaginary average men about forgiveness, loving one's enemy, compassion.

We, all of us, harbor abysmal depths of rage, resentment, and revenge. And the older we grow, the more unsettled scores we accumulate. I once heard of a decrepit old man in his nineties, an Armenian, who after murdering his *odar* daughter-in-law, went to the nearest police station and said: "You can do what you like with me now. I don't care any more. I did what I had to do."

He had fulfilled his destiny.

I think of that old man often.

Though not yet ninety, I have myself accumulated enough injuries to justify a dozen homicides.

One must have a big belly, my mother is fond of saying— meaning one must swallow all kinds of insults without losing one's temper or charity. Perhaps. But when a mad dog bites you, it hurts.

There was a time when I replied to every single letter I received. No more. It's a waste of time. Not only because it is extremely difficult to please everyone, but also because it is impossible to please anyone to the extent he thinks he deserves to be pleased. Vanity, it has been said, is a monster with a voracious and insatiable appetite. Its favorite words are: "More, more, more!"

I am beginning to discover that no matter what you decide to do in this business, the outcome will always be the same: you'll make an enemy. First they ask for your understanding and cooperation; then your time (that is to say, a fraction of your life) and integrity (that is to say, your soul). Single-minded, rude, ruthless. Mephistopheles made a deal with Faust. He had something to offer. All you get these days is insults that masquerade as advice.

How does one deal with such people without going down into the gutter with them?

How does one deal with people who, though in a better position to help you, ask for *your* help? Pot-bellied princes begging for a crust of bread from a starving pauper.

How does one deal with scum whose sole principle seems to be: "What's yours is mine, and what's mine is mine too"?

Does one write a long, venomous letter?

Or does one ignore them?

I do both: I write long letters which I never mail. Why should I be the one to teach them ethics and etiquette? Provide them, as it were, with another weapon in their arsenal, help them to improve their tactics. I prefer to let them wallow in their own greed and filth. Sometimes the best way to teach a man a lesson is not to teach him at all. Let him find out for himself—the hard way.

Nothing exasperates me more than to read a letter from a shrewd, experienced operator who has been in the business for thirty-forty years—an established reputation, a famous name—who in exchange of a specific, present service offers future, vague favors. Promises. Verbal commitments. Bribes that, on close inspection, turn out to be counterfeit currency. What infuriates me more than anything else is their blind arrogance—their assumption that you are too stupid, greedy, and impatient to let such a golden opportunity slip by. Everywhere, they see reflections of themselves. *That* indeed is their crime as well as punishment.

I am beginning to suspect that in this world only God is in a position to make promises. The rest . . . the less said the better.

I once had a curious conversation with an old, experienced local writer, born, raised, and educated in the New World—a tough pro with very few illusions left about life and his fellow men. The subject was a poet whose integrity I tried to defend by asserting that (a) he was mentioned in several reference works, (b) he had taught at a prestigious university, (c) he had published a dozen volumes, (d) he now held a responsible position in the government. "Some of the worst crooks in the world are in *Who's Who*," he said. "I am personally acquainted with several poets who are alcoholic degenerates and child molesters; I have published over a dozen books myself and I assure you it doesn't mean a damn thing; and these days the only way to get a job and rise in the bureaucracy of our government is by being an incompetent fool and a swindler." I could only gasp in astonished disbelief. *I* should be talking like that, I thought. After all, it was *I* that was raised in an Ottoman environment, not he. . . .

A letter from a reader:

"Enclosed a copy of a letter I wrote to the editor of the *New York Times* on the subject of abortion, which I feel is one of the most important issues of our time. Would you care to comment on it in the Armenian press? About myself: I studied philosophy at the University of Denver, Colo. . . ."

"I studied philosophy for a while," an insurance salesman once told me. "Couldn't get interested. So I took up insurance."

"What didn't you like about philosophy?"

"The fact that it never made up its mind what to say . . . went around and around . . . know what I mean?"

After being exposed to slogans all their lives, it is only natural for them to want ontology and metaphysics by slogan.

How many times have I heard people say: "O yes! I've seen that product advertised on TV." Meaning: Must be good; you can rely on it.

In the old days they used to quote Aristotle and St. Thomas Aquinas. It's TV commercials now. Progress. As I switch channels on TV (which I do now automatically during commercials) I catch a glimpse of a dizzy blonde on a talk show saying: "Live and let live, that's my philosophy."

I have noticed that everyone has a philosophy here. They voice a prejudice and call it philosophy. They dislike someone and ascribe it to "philosophical differences." They pour ketchup on everything and call *that* too an act of philosophical speculation.

Philosophy: a Greek word meaning love of wisdom. That is to say, an effort to make sense of this world. If to repeat a worn-out cliché were philosophy, a parrot would be Socrates.

What would have happened to Socrates in New York City?

Somewhere in *The Traveller and His Road,* Gostan Zarian wonders what would have happened to Hamlet in Istanbul. "To begin with," he writes,

> with Oriental cunning and without the prompting of a revenant, he would have guessed immediately that his father had been poisoned. He would have pretended to be a close friend of the new king. He would have fondled his mother. Next, without wasting much time, he would have singled out palace officials sympathetic to his cause, and one night he would have ambushed the king and assassinated him. Ophelia would not have drowned in the Bosphorus. She would have been made a queen. His mother would have been immured in one of the island monasteries. Laertes would have been promoted to a minister of state. The populace would have mounted noisy demonstrations and the Ecumenical Patriarch would have promulgated a new religious policy.
>
> *To be or not to be?* A pointless question. *To be* at all cost. And to hell with philosophy, justice, morality. King Hamlet. A probable puppet in the hands of monks. Gentle, given to dreams, sweet—hence, the possible victim of a bold, rude, and uncouth Armenian commander from the interior provinces.

A fascinating game that.

What would have happened to Hamlet in Chicago? Very simple. He would have asked Rash (short for Horatio) to get in touch with one of the Mafia families and ask for a favor. Next day, his uncle would be ambushed and machine-gunned by Sicilian mobsters. After marrying and divorcing Hamlet, Ophelia would become an entertainer in Las Vegas, have an affair with Sinatra, appear on TV talk shows and say things like, "Live and let live, that's my philosophy." Asked about Hamlet, she would reply: "He is a wonderful, compassionate human being. We are very good friends."

In Montgomery, Alabama, Othello would be castrated by Klansmen; Desdemona would gradually degenerate into a nymphomaniac and an alcoholic and eventually inspire Tennessee Williams with one of his steamy, tawdry, morbid southern plays which would be a hit on Broadway.

Socrates in New York?

He would be dismissed as a harmless eccentric and a permanently unemployable welfare case; and after being mugged, robbed, and arrested a few times (on grounds of disturbing the peace and vagrancy) he would either freeze or starve to death in Central Park. Hemlock has been replaced with apathy—a far more lethal and slow poison. That's progress for you—the progress of a degenerative disease. And progress is our most important product.

Plato on the Dick Cavett Show:

"Dr. Plato, could you sum-up the message of your philosophy in a single sentence that would be accessible to our television audience?"

Cavett to Dante Alighieri:

"Signor Alighieri—may I call you Al? . . . thank you. Well, Al, last night I read your *Inferno,* and may I say it's one *hell* of a book—if you'll forgive the pun."

I remember the day I applied for a job with a paperback edition of Plato's *Dialogues* in my pocket. "You like reading! You like reading books. Plato, I see. Greek philosophy. You must be a philosopher. But this job isn't for a philosopher."

I tried to explain that, not being Mongoloid, I was already fully aware of that fact, and that I would not allow Plato, or any other philosopher for that matter, to come between me and my work. . . . I never got the job.

Next interview, when asked what my hobbies were, I said: "Collecting stamps, watching TV . . ." I got the job.

You want to survive? Pretend you are a robot with only enough intelligence to carry out a specific number of tasks.

You want to go ahead in this world? Guess what the other wants you to say and say it.

You want to be a leader of men? Find out where they want to go and lead them there.

About five years ago I wrote a series of radio plays one of which was particularly well produced and acted. After some inquiries I was able to obtain the name of the actor/producer, who turned out to be not an actor at all but a professor of English literature at a nearby university. One Sunday afternoon I called him on the telephone and congratulated him on his excellent performance. We had a long talk. We discovered we shared a common admiration for Chekhov and I promised to write a Chekhov soliloquy for him based on his correspondence. He performed that too on a number of occasions with a delicious Russian accent. Then, one day, he invited me to dinner and introduced me ("a playwright") to several of his friends and associates, including a long-haired gent in faded blue jeans and torn shirt whom he identified as Dr. Paul Something—"head of the sociology department at the Lousy University in Halifax."

"Lousy? did I hear you right?" I said.

"Dalhousie, yes."

"Of course."

Ten minutes later, someone made a derogatory remark about a prominent political figure, someone else added his two cents' worth, and Dr. Something seized this opportunity to deliver a lecture on Marxism as updated by Marcuse. We listened obediently. No one dared to contradict him. When I was invited to offer my own views on the subject—"from the point of view of a playwright"—I said that in politics, the cast of characters may change, but the plot of the play seldom does.

"Translation, please," someone said.

"What I'm trying to say," I explained, "is that ideas, ideologies, philosophies, and regimes may change, but rascals don't."

"That's metaphysics," Dr. Something snapped.

"No. I'm talking about Castro," I said. "I'm talking about Stalin and Mao."

"We maintain none of these characters was or is a Marxist."

"That's exactly what Marx once said about himself," I said.

"What did he say?"

"That he was not a Marxist."

"Maybe so. It seems to me however that what *you're* looking for is a utopian solution . . . final answers. . . . We live in an imperfect world. All we can do is try to eliminate present injustices."

"Injustices are only symptoms. Every system generates its own. Marxism only replaces one set of injustices with another."

"Again you are referring to imperfect models. We may do better than the Cubans."

"You may also do worse."

"Possibly, but I doubt it."

"Ah! doubt!—a beautiful word that, don't you think?"

"You must be a skeptic."

"When it comes to power, politics, politicians, civil servants, and bureaucrats, yes."

"What's left? Am I right in assuming that you are advocating passive acceptance?"

"Of course not. What I may be saying is that before we organize another bloody revolution, let us teach the masses to doubt, to question, and to mistrust their leaders and betters—including revolutionaries."

"That may bring about anarchy; and I doubt very much if anyone can ever convince a bunch of skeptics to rise against their oppressors."

"Let them not rise. Let them instead erode the power of their oppressors. Without the cooperation and consent of the oppressed, the oppressors are bound to go out of business."

"But skepticism as a philosophy has no appeal to the masses."

"You speak as though ideas, like consumer goods, must be packaged in such a way that they will *appeal* to the masses. Perhaps from now on thinkers and social scientists should consult publicity experts on Madison Avenue in order to see what their chances of success are. Or perhaps ask behavioral psychologists to try them on rats first."

"Why not? I'm all for a pragmatic approach. I'll go to the devil himself for a piece of useful advice."

"Pragmatic, utilitarian—those must be *your* favorite words."

"They are, yes. Frankly, I have little use for bleeding-heart liberals, idealists, and mystics, who feel more at home in abstractions than in real-life situations. Philosophy and metaphysics are, in my view, nothing but bourgeois pastimes. It's easy to contemplate noble thoughts and spin complex theories on a full belly. But when a man is cold and hungry, he'll gladly exchange all of Plato and St. Thomas Aquinas for a loaf of bread and a pair of boots."

"Am I right in assuming," I said, "that what you would like to see is capitalist production methods combined with Marxist distribution? In other words the marriage of America and Russia. More of the same."

"More and better, that's right. More goods, better services."

"And what happens to anyone who challenges the system?"

"You mean reactionaries and counter-revolutionaries?"

"I mean someone like Socrates."

"Socrates would be on our side."

"Do you think Socrates would give a hoot about your electric toothbrushes and unemployment insurance compensation?"

When, about ten years ago, I decided to dedicate my full time to such reactionary and antisocial activities as reading, meditating, and writing, I had an unforgettable and sinister encounter with a civil servant from the Unemployment Office—a tall, blue-eyed, cadaverous character with the shuffling gait and the long arms of an ape, who paid me an unannounced visit here, in my own home, demanding to know what the matter was and why I had failed to find another job. I replied that none of the jobs I had been offered so far had been, in my judgment . . .

"Your *judgment?*" the ape snapped—mean, stupid, arrogant. "How can you trust your own judgment?—you don't even have an income!"

This has happened to me many times. All kinds of people—total strangers as well as friends and relatives—come into my home, pretend to be concerned about me, to have my interest at heart, help me (though I haven't even dared to entertain the notion to ask for their assistance)—they question me, they find out things about me, then they proceed to abuse and insult me.

My mother is right when she says: "Honest and good people don't come to us. Only fools and crooks." And yet, she is as gullible as I am. Perhaps more so. She is taken in by anyone with good manners. That's her weak point—etiquette. Someone smiles and says good morning to her with a sweet, courteous voice, and she is overwhelmed. "He's such a nice person. So polite."

"Are we talking about the same person?'

"The man in the red house—walks with a cane—retired last year . . ."

"You mean the one with the Boris Karloff voice?"

"He said good morning to me today."

"The one with the Bela Lugosi smile?"

"He asked me how I was too."

"Big deal! Did you know that that man actually murdered his wife and fed her body to the alligators?"

"Why isn't he in jail then?"

"They couldn't find the body. He said to the police she fell and drowned. But it's common knowledge that he murdered her when they were vacationing in Florida."

"Do you believe that?"

"If I were to judge by his looks, yes. There is something sinister and evil about him."

"I think he's a very nice man."

"They also say he took a shot at his own son just because he went out with a girl he didn't approve."

"He did well. Children these days no longer listen to their parents."

"Even so, the punishment should fit the crime, *no?* If all parents shot and killed their children because they disobeyed, where would we all be?"

"He did not kill his son."

"He ran away. He might as well be dead to his father."

"These days they all run away; they prefer to live by themselves."

"Maybe so, but I want you to be careful. Stay away from that man. Don't talk to him. Say hello, if he says hello; a comment on the weather, if you must; but no more."

A French philosopher has written a book in which he proves beyond a shadow of a doubt that if people stopped committing crimes, the police would begin to terrorize the people in order to justify its own existence. To what extent could this also be said of politicians? To what extent do they use fear of the enemy's power to justify their own power? To what extent do they use fear of war to justify war?

And revolutionaries: to what extent do they exploit social injustices in order to seize power and perpetrate worse injustices? Perhaps this whole era—from prehistoric times to the present day—will be known to future historians as the Age of Misconceptions, Misunderstandings, and Deceptions.

The American Dream itself—that combination of a home in suburbia, an attractive wife, a car, two–three children, a cushy, executive job in a skyscraper, garage and supermarket doors that open up by themselves as if by magic—is probably one of the greatest frauds perpetrated on mankind. And yet, people cling to it like the drowning man is said to wrap himself around any-thing—including a snake.

A letter from my childhood friend in Athens: "All in all," he writes, "I'm glad to be home. Needless to say, I enjoyed our talk very much. I never told you this when I was there, but the truth is, after you left for Canada 25 years ago, I could not replace you with another friend . . . though I tried many times. And all these years I lived alone, unable to share my esthetic discoveries and joys. Do you remember the long hours we spent together discovering Beethoven's symphonies, discussing the 19th-century Russians, analyzing the French New Wave? You know me, I loathe all senti-mental talk and nostalgia; if anything, I am a cynic—one has to be—to survive. But I want you to know that I treasure these moments as if they were my most valued possessions. But I shouldn't complain. After all, I now have everything I wanted to have: a more or less comfortable life, a wonderful wife, three children, a car, a large bookcase with my favorite books in it, a beautiful stereo set, a vast record collection (which now includes Solti's complete *Ring*, Bach's *B-Minor Mass*, Cesar Franck's *Three Chorale Preludes*, and Bartok's *Quartets)*, and all the rest of the bourgeois paraphernalia. . . . Did I mention a boat and a nice little summerhouse on a nearby island?—which, by the way, we seldom use and which reminds me, how would you like to have it? Consider it yours. After your long, self-imposed Siberian exile, it should be a welcome change, no? I will provide you with all the liquor, coffee, and food you can consume. That's no problem. It's an ideal place for a writer. They say Kazantzakis did some of his best writing there. Just say yes and I'll handle the rest. I have worked out all the logistics. The expenses involved are, I assure you, insignificant. You don't have to worry about anything. You may stay for as long as you wish—a month, three months, a year, or, if you prefer, for the rest of your natural life. . . ."

"Dear friend:
   You must be a mind reader, because I have always dreamed of living on an island—alone with the sea, a Byzantine church on a hill, the ruins of a Doric temple on the beach, pine trees, solitude, meditation, a friend I can trust. . . . At the moment however, I am in the middle of several major projects which, I regret to say, I cannot interrupt. There are other reasons. One of them is that I have little faith in 'geographical' solutions. Twenty-five years ago I left Greece and instead of living in a Greek slum, I now live in a

Canadian slum. I sometimes suspect life is a maze because people look for an exit in the outside world, rather than within. . . ."

Another letter from an Armenian in Bulgaria who informs me he doesn't like Bulgaria any more and wants to emigrate to Los Angeles, via Beirut. To do that however, he needs $2,850, which he will repay shortly after he gets to Los Angeles. If I don't have that sum readily available, could I be kind enough to mention a few names and addresses of compassionate fellow Armenians who might consider helping a brother in need?

A third letter from a young Soviet-Armenian poet who wants me to send him a pair of blue jeans.

I have not yet decided how to reply to these letters. Perhaps I shouldn't reply at all. . . .

(1980)

The Horrible Silence

Every thinking Armenian is like a radio station in the middle
of a storm sending messages to distant places and receiving
no reply.

A horrible silence surrounds him.

With pleading eyes he peers at the demolished walls of
history. And like a wretched fisherman, in vain he casts his
torn net into the depths of the past.

Tradition is a beautiful graveyard.

Let us not deceive ourselves and let us not be deceived by
others. We walk with bare feet over fields that have already
been harvested.

GOSTAN ZARIAN

I T IS NOT EASY being an obscure writer. And being an obscure
Armenian writer is like compounding a felony. If you are not
dismissed by friends and relatives as a harmless eccentric—the
idiot of the family—you are regarded as a permanently unem-
ployed and unemployable misfit.

"Scribble, scribble, scribble," a lady friend of my mother's says
whenever she sees me writing. "Don't you ever get tired of scrib-
bling?" She is a devout, church-going, Bible-reading Christian—
mean, narrow, nasty. Her son works in a factory. He manufactures,
saves, invests, raises a family, pays taxes.

What do I do?

I trace words on a piece of paper. Someone else reads them—if
at all.

End result? Zero.

Cash value? Ditto.

I live in a small industrial town surrounded by farms, studded
with insurance head offices, trust companies, and banks. There
are as many banks here as there must have been churches in Ani.
Even little boys and girls are in the business of trafficking in
goods, making and saving money. They knock on doors at all

41

hours of the day, asking for empty pop bottles and baskets, selling chocolate-coated almonds, ballpoint pens, pickle jars, home-made cookies, pears, peaches, dew worms, or anything else they can get their hands on. In winter, they offer to shovel your snow for a quarter; in summer, to cut the lawn. "I made 40 bucks last week," I once heard a boy boast to his pal shortly after a snow-storm. "I already have 500 bucks in the bank."

"What are you gonna do with it?"

"Buy a car."

"What kind?"

"A Plymouth—my uncle got one."

An Irishman's definition of the English: "Asses who talk about horses." Replace horses with cars and you will observe that the more things change the more they stay the same.

It is not much different with the adults. Their time being more valuable, however, they deal in more expensive items—imported perfumes, encyclopedias, real estate, aluminum doors and win-dows. Sometimes they call you on the telephone to inform you that you have just won a prize, or that they are making a survey and would you please be kind enough to answer a few questions. But you can tell they are half-literate drop-outs in pursuit of the fast buck by the amount of trouble they go through trying to pronounce your name. Some of them don't even try and simply say: "Is this the man of the house?"

In his efforts to make his name more palatable to the natives, a friend of mine changed it to Art Hambersomian (from Artashes Hampartsoumian), and shortly thereafter to Hamian. For all I know he may be a Ham by now.

Like headless chickens, they run around shorn of name, tradi-tions, language, and religion, blabbering all the while about roots and identity.

There is something formidable about an Armenian from the Mid-dle East let loose in the New World. Levantine mercantilism seems to combine with American opportunism to produce an elemental force that in its obsessive pursuit of profit discards all sense of decorum and shred of decency.

You are introduced to a fellow Armenian at a picnic or at a wedding. A few weeks or months pass, and this individual, pre-tending to be your very close friend, comes into your home. After some harmless chitchat he informs you that he is now an insur-ance salesman and could he, if it is not inconvenient to you, pretend he is going to sell an insurance policy to you. He is new at this game, he explains, and he would like to acquire some practice. Needless to add, he adds, you must not feel in the least obliged to buy an insurance policy from him, unless of course—

In an effort to warn him that he will be wasting his as well as your time, you try to tell him that such an eventuality is most unlikely, not to say absurd, in view of the fact that having worked for eight years in the head office of an insurance company, you are already overinsured. Totally unimpressed and obviously impervious to such subtle hints, he replies that you couldn't possibly have the particular type of policy he will offer simply because no other company but *his* carries it, and that the instant he is through explaining all its financial benefits to you, you will definitely want to have one because it will solve all your past, present, and future problems in addition to reducing all your other policies to a state of abject redundancy.

Acquaintances from a nearby town drop in for a visit one Sunday afternoon. They bring along some fellow Armenians you have never seen before. One of these new faces delivers a speech saying this is a great country and that he has been all over the world but nowhere has he felt more welcome and free. He goes on and on counting his blessings, and before you know it he has whipped out an enormous catalogue from god knows where and is trying to persuade the rest of the company that if they order these items directly from him, they will get them at cost, whereas if they buy them from a regular outlet, they will have to pay two or three times as much.

A country, like a book, is a mirror; if an ass peers into it, you don't expect a philosopher to peer out. And what is heaven to a pig but an ocean of mud.

My life moves on a monotonous triangular pattern: the public library, where I read and research; my room, where I write; and the church, where I play Bach on the organ.

My daily walks to the library—a distance of about a mile—are uneventful affairs. Always the same faces—mostly retired old men and women. We exchange smiles, greetings, and comments on the weather.

"You're late," one of them tells me.

"Looks like rain," another says. "You'd better get your raincoat."

"How's everything?" I ask Jacob Dups.

He nods resignedly, as if to say: Thanks for asking, but don't ask.

Dups is in his late sixties—retired four years ago. Of German peasant stock. A man of few words. A hard worker. Grim, methodical, single-minded. He paints and repaints his house; he demolishes his porch and builds a new one; he raises fences. In winter he shovels the snow not only off his sidewalk but off his roof—risking his neck in the process. In summer he works incessantly in his garden, which he plants so thickly and efficiently that in a matter of weeks it acquires the appearance of a tropical rain forest.

"How's the wife?" I ask.

"Not so good," he replies.

His wife is a notorious hypochondriac.

"Been to the doctor?" I say.

"Yes."

"What did he say?"

"Needles."

"How many?"

"Two."

"A month?"

"Week."

"For how long?"

"Two."

"Weeks?"

"Months."

"She'll be all right, you'll see," I tell him. "Probably it's some virus that's been going around. I wasn't feeling so good myself last week. And how's the garden coming along?"

He loves his garden with a passion. Tears come to his eyes whenever hooligans vandalize it. "Why? Why?" he wants to know.

At the library, I am thought of as one of those harmless eccentrics whose hobby is accumulating scraps of esoteric information. Whenever at the Reference Department they are asked questions they cannot handle, they come to me for help. I have been asked questions about 1928 Broadway hit shows, Hindu mysticism, and African tribal customs. What's the name of the Brazilian tribe that worships ants and anacondas? What's the average lifespan of a Siamese cat? Could you suggest a middle name for a French poodle called Fifi La Petite? That type of thing.

I am not the only eccentric who visits the library every day. There are a number of other habitués; among them the one I call Ophelia—an elderly woman with the long, youthful hair of a teenage beauty—who carries on an endless and often acrimonious conversation with herself, occasionally bursting into very loud *Aha!s* and *Ha!s*, as if to say: Do you take me for a fool? No one knows her story. But I have a theory. Many years ago, when she was young and beautiful, she was seduced by a handsome devil who whispered all kinds of sweet things in her ear and she believed every word of it. She knew bliss. Seduced, abandoned, and probably pregnant, she suffered a mental collapse from which she never recovered.

Quasimodo, the other habitué, is the victim of an industrial accident. His story is widely known. Many years ago, a heavy object fell on his head, in the factory where he was employed, and left him permanently damaged. Ever since then he rides around on a bicycle gaudily decorated with brightly colored feathers, banners, ribbons, trophies, framed photographs, coffee pots, empty tin cans, and miscellaneous other utensils, in addition to a battery of bells which he rings with great gusto and persistence. His clothes are black with grease, muck, and filth; his boots of enormous size and weight; his gait that of Dr. Frankenstein's monster; the stench around him unbearable.

Another character, who may be normal, looks like an undertaker—tall, sinister, silent, sepulchral, always in a black raincoat; he doesn't walk, he slithers. He reads nothing but newspapers.

Still another, a very pale, emaciated woman, seems to be permanently engaged in transferring very slowly and methodically the contents of one plastic shopping bag into another. She doesn't read.

Every morning, around 9:30, the mailman arrives. On the average he delivers half-a-dozen English- and Armenian-language newspapers from Canada and the United States, two or three letters, and a book or a magazine from the Soviet Union.

"Why Armenian massacres?" I read in a letter today written by an assistant professor of sociology in Boston. "Was it the Armenians who committed the atrocities?" And: "What is the best book on Armenian political organizations? One of my students suggested that you may be in a position to help me."

Was it the Armenians who committed the atrocities?

Is he being Socratic, sarcastic, or just plain American naif? Hard to say.

Talaat, Enver, Jemal, and Kemal knew something we didn't know. The masses forget; and those who should remember end up confusing the victims with their murderers. History is a farce of mistaken identities. Who did what to whom?

"Imagine a fly trying to rape an elephant," an Armenian rug merchant once told me. "Our revolutionaries were that fly, the Ottoman Empire the elephant."

We were punished for our shameless daring. There is justice in this world after all. This rug merchant is rich. He has found his god, which is capital. He has all the answers. God helps those who help themselves. God abandoned the Armenians because they were on the wrong path. They were not satisfied with the privilege of amassing vast fortunes by exploiting the ignorant Turks. They wanted more. Their greed knew no bounds. They lusted after freedom of speech, ancestral lands, political self-determination, and other ideals and chimeras devoid of all cash value.

"An Armenian terrorist assassinated a Turkish official today in France," the voice on the radio states. "It appears that this incident is a result of events that occurred 65 years ago."

A long time indeed to hold a grudge, the voice seems to be implying.

We may be flies, but we have the memory of elephants.

"Your invariably friendly book reviews no doubt encourage many of our youthful and budding talents," I read in a letter today. "But they may also mislead your readers, in addition to lowering our already *mighty low* literary standards. If you continue praising the works of undeserving mediocrities, what are you going to say about the work of a real talent?"

In one of the newspapers I read a letter to the editor in which my work as book reviewer is vilified and I am described as a meddlesome fool who is incapable of understanding what he reads. The letter is written by an outraged author whose last book I reviewed with a touch of compassion.

It's always the same story. State a case as objectively as you can, add a dash of compassion to cushion the blow, and someone will always find enough reason to hang you.

After I published my first book on Armenian history and culture with a chapter devoted to the massacres, a Canadian critic with a Germanic surname asserted that I was a virulent racist—because of my dislike of the Turks.

It is only natural that nations guilty of genocide should resent all talk of genocide. An Englishman once said that it was bad manners to speak of ropes in the house of a man who had been hanged. In his efforts to explain the genocide of the Armenians, another Englishman (Toynbee) states that there is potential evil in all of us. Those who are not guilty today may be guilty tomorrow. Given the right combination of circumstances and motivations, a human being, any human being, group, or nation, will commit the most unspeakable crimes in the name of territorial integrity or some other ideal. Forgive and forget. That's the only humane and Christian thing to do. Forgive and forget. Revenge is mine, said the Lord.

You will note that even common criminals would be embarrassed to use this piece of cheap sophistry in a court of law. But law is one thing, history another. One must learn to departmentalize.

Departmentalize.

An employer of mine—the manager of a department store—was very fond of this concept. He believed that life was big enough to accommodate any number of contradictory principles and that one must learn to be flexible and adaptable. "Any day now I might ask you over to my place for dinner," he once said to me, "introduce you to the wife and the kids. We'll break bread together, have a couple of drinks, chat about this and that. I want us to be friends. But when on Monday morning we meet again in the store and I tell you to jump, the right thing for you to do is ask, *How high?* Know what I mean? Business is business. What do you think made this country of ours great? Democracy? Equal rights? Hell no! Free enterprise? Yes. The survival of the fittest? Of course. Even our preachers here are millionaires."

At this point I remember to have made a reference to the eye of the needle.

"The Eye of the Needle," he explained very patiently, "was the name of a gate in Jerusalem. It wasn't your average, regular-sized gate, but slightly lower. A camel could pass through it easily—all he had to do was lower his head a bit, that's all. You probably thought Jesus meant the actual, literal eye of the needle."

"That's what I was taught in the Old Country," I said.

"You were taught wrong! Ask any Biblical scholar."

Preferably an American scholar, eh? They know how to adjust God to capital. Or is it god to Capital?

In today's mail a letter from Dr. Paul Engelmann, Armenologist.

We met thirty years ago in Venice. He was then in his early twenties, I an impressionable boy of thirteen. He had come to study Armenian with the Mekhitarists of San Lazzaro. He had a passion for languages and he could already read (for pleasure) Homer in Ancient Greek, Kazantzakis in Modern Greek, Horace in Latin, Proust in French, Dante in Italian, Ortega in Spanish, Byron in English, Pushkin in Russian, and of course Thomas Mann in German. After staying in Venice for four years, he went to the Sorbonne in Paris and later to the State University of Yerevan, where, he once wrote, he was constantly mistaken for a German of Armenian descent. The author of a German-Armenian and Armenian-German dictionary, numerous essays on Armenian philology, and several articles on Armenian history and culture in German encyclopedias, he is now a professor at the University of Bonn and head of the department of Caucasian languages at the University of Bochum.

"I just finished reading Shahnour's *Retreat Without Song*," he writes. "An interesting work—for its iconoclastic approach rather than style. At the moment however, I am busy translating a volume of early Charents—*Dziadzan* (Rainbow), *Dagharan* (Songbook), *Gazelner*, etc. I am having some problems, however. As you probably know, German can coin new compound words as easily as Armenian—a facility which English as well as French and Italian lack completely. I am beginning to discover, however, that Armenian is much richer and more flexible than German. To give you an example: I am having a great deal of trouble trying to find a German equivalent of Charents's *anrtchatsar* (you became a dream)—one of those beautiful words that a translator ends up hating because they reduce him to a state of despair and paralysis. Enough of my problems. Tell me about yourself and your 'Siberian exile.' Do you still play Bach on the organ? And how's your novel *Semiramis* coming along? Will you send me a copy of the manuscript as soon as you complete it? I have some friendly contacts in the publishing community here and I might be able to do something about it—provided of course you trust me with the task of translating it into German first. After it comes out here, maybe publishers there might consider treating you with more respect."

Perhaps. But I doubt it. It is not enough to be good here. One must be *marketable*. "The material you have submitted is excellent," a New York literary agent once informed me. "My readers have nothing but praise for it. It is *literature*, they tell me. In my view, however, it would be more appropriate for university publishing houses or literary quarterlies, with which we do not deal."

They call themselves *literary* agents, but they no longer deal in literature but in marketable merchandise. After all, they have to live too. Business is business. What do you think made this country what it is? Ideas? Literature? Poetry?

Business is business.

Before World War I, our town (which is now the Octoberfest capital of the North-American continent) was called Berlin. Around 1916, however, it was hastily renamed Kitchener—after Lord Horatio Kitchener, a British field marshal with handlebar mustaches and the fixed stare of a boa. This, according to Fred Larsen, the local oral historian, aroused considerable bitterness in the German community. Things have never been the same since. If you think Armenian hatred of Turks is racist, you should have a talk about the English with a German over a bottle of schnapps.

Every year in October, our town is filled with German tourists. They gather around an enormous maypole erected especially for the occasion in the center of town, and listen to speeches and German folksongs played by a band of local boys in Tyrolean costumes. There are beauty and beer-drinking contests, parades, singing, and dancing (during which one partner slaps the posterior of the other). In all the supermarkets, several counters are heaped with such typical Octoberfest products as sauerkraut and thick, phallic pork sausages of a cadaverous hue. An enormous amount of beer flows. And inevitably some blood—as a result of traffic accidents by besotted drivers.

Rumor has it that these celebrations are just a cover for ex-Nazis, who congregate here from as far as Egypt and Argentina. German community leaders dismiss these allegations as cheap slander. Nevertheless, copiously illustrated investigative articles have already been published in a number of newspapers and magazines in Canada and the United States. Aroused to indignation, some of the townsmen, among them survivors of Buchenwald and Auschwitz, wrote outraged letters to the local paper, demanding that Octoberfest and related atrocities be banned. The mayor, however, put an end to that nonsense once and for all when he declared that Octoberfest was good for business.

Business is our business and anything that's good for business is good.

Writes the Viennese satirist Karl Kraus (who died in 1936): "The trading mentality is said to have evolved in the confines of the ghetto streets. In freedom they indulge in psychology. . . . What miracles a combination of trading mentality and psychology can produce we see every day."

To think that these words were written long before television commercials.

About a month ago I received a letter from a woman in Wisconsin, which said in part: "At the moment I am engaged in collecting and editing a volume of children's stories from around the world. Would you consider providing me with rough translations of some Armenian folktales? I will do the adaptation and a friend of mine will take care of the illustrations. You may not be aware of the fact that such adaptations happen to be in great demand these days. May I hope to hear from you soon?"

Today I read the following:

"Many, many thanks for the two charming Armenian folktales. I loved the finale with the apples. My editor agrees with me that the Armenian stories will add a new color and flavor to our international anthology. I have another proposition to make. Would you be interested in collaborating on a pornographic novel with me? I suspect we have an excellent chance of coming up with a best-seller, provided we take care of alternating the female and male points of view. By that I mean you could tell me what the masculine imagination finds appealing, and I would do the same with the feminine imagination. By emphasizing both the feminine and masculine angles for maximum impact, I have no doubt in my mind we stand a good chance of coming up with a highly popular product with possible spin-offs into the paperback market, and perhaps even a Hollywood adaptation. The royalties from these transactions would be, needless to add, far from negligible."

At the public library this morning I come across a new book titled *How to Sell Yourself*. "Before you sit at your typewriter," I read in another recently published how-to manual, "study the market carefully. That may indeed be the most important phase of your career as a writer."

In a land where everyone has a price and everything is for sale, prostitution has become an art and a science about which entire books are written, sold, and avidly read. They are no longer interested in becoming writers; they want to produce best-sellers. They don't want to sing; they want to appear at the Metropolitan Opera. They don't want to act; they want to go to Hollywood. And why? Because that's where the money is, of course.

One of the curses of being an obscure writer is that you invariably attract unpublished writers. These people know that they have little or no chance with established authors, so they seek out obscure ones. As a rule, they are extravagantly generous with praises. They devote an entire section of their letters to your virtues as a writer. The punchline, however, they reserve for the last paragraph, as an afterthought as it were.

"I have just completed a musical comedy based on a poem by Toumanian," I read in the finale of a letter today. "I plan to submit it to Charles Aznavour, who, I am sure will want to do it. Before I do so however I would like to have your opinion. Perhaps after reading it you might be inspired to write one of your perceptive reviews."

Twenty-five years ago, while crossing the Atlantic, I met a young student on his way home to Chicago after a visit to Israel. He is now a professor of Hebrew and one of my most prolific and regular correspondents. He writes letters that are more like entries in an intimate journal. He has been planning to write the Great American Novel for almost ten years now and keeps reminding me that I should not destroy his letters. Intelligent, well-informed, sensitive, he is also totally disoriented and disorganized. He writes of his problems with landlords, arguments with wife, extramarital affairs, snatches of conversations with colleagues, students, neighbors, children, rabbis, friends, enemies, winos and whores; new foods he tasted; experiments with drugs. I receive two, sometimes three letters a week from him: long, stream-of-consciousness letters, handwritten, which, more often than not, I don't even finish reading. They already fill four large cartons in the basement.

"Last night I ate in an Armenian restaurant," he writes in today's letter. "The food was okay, but the toilet filthy. What's the matter with you guys? You should write an exposé. . . . A cousin of mine—a wealthy, spoiled Jewish brat—is in the midst of divorce proceedings. Her husband is a self-made, aggressive, brilliant character. Filth, slander, and complications with no end in sight. Between moneyed folks divorce can be a nasty piece of business. I'd advise that if you get married, be sure to underestimate your wealth to your intended, and never take her into commercial confidentiality. . . . I have an Iranian friend whose mistress is an ex-nun. I find this Moslem-Catholic coalition disturbing. Why don't you write a letter to the Pope, and I'll handle Khomeini. Maybe together we might have those two excommunicated. . . . Did I tell you about the published poet I met last week? He read some of his stuff to me. It stank. But I liked him as a person.

Sometimes lousy poets make good people. . . . I used to write poetry in my younger days, but no more. The only people who read poetry these days are poets, and the only reason they read it is to know what the competition is up to. . . . How are things in that hick town of yours? I'll never know what made you decide to live there. Your efforts to clarify this point have been totally unconvincing. I think you should make an honest effort to get out of there."

If you want to be productive, I keep telling him, this is the ideal place. But in his view, a writer is first and foremost a witness to his time: he must see things, go places, have experiences, meet people. . . . I tell him masterpieces are forged in solitude and that what I have seen of the world has not made me curious about the rest.

I spent a weekend in New York City recently and was surprised to discover that the buildings were the only true inhabitants there.

Was it Piet Mondrian or Paul Valery who did not even want a window in his study, because he found the world outside distracting? Mondrian hated the color green; it reminded him of nature. And it was in Siberia, after all, that Dostoevsky discovered his mission as a writer. It occurs to me, however, that whereas Dostoevsky's Siberian exile lasted no more than six years, mine has already reached the quarter-century mark. In Siberia moreover Dostoevsky found a wife, friends, human beings with whom he could communicate, come to terms with, write a book about— one of his best: *The House of the Dead*. Solzhenitsyn himself met a number of fascinating characters there—men and women who were to inspire thousands of pages of impassioned prose. During the last quarter-century, have I met anyone about whom I could produce a single interesting paragraph?

Late one night, two–three years ago, I received a telephone call by a well-known (in her own estimation) actress (retired), whom I shocked when I said that I had never heard of her. She said she worked in Hollywood and New York and knew practically everyone who was someone in the business. She had heard one of my plays on the radio, she went on, and liked the way I handled the dialogue. She wanted to have a talk with me. She invited me over to her place. I went. I had never been in that particular neighborhood. I didn't even know such places existed four miles from the center of town. Imagine a forest that, as you drive on the highway, looks like any other thick wall of trees; and in its middle a lake; and around the lake houses that look more like small resort hotels with swimming pools, parks, orchards, flower gardens, pagodas. Her living-room alone was about the size of a small stadium. Mementoes everywhere—walls, desks, entranceway: books, posters, autographed pictures of Kaufman and Hart, Elmer Rice, Otto Preminger, Tennessee Williams, Katherine Cornell; an authentic Renoir drawing. At one point during our conversation—or rather her monologue, during which names dropped at the rate of about a dozen a minute—she excused herself, disappeared, and shortly thereafter returned in a bikini. She had remarkably youthful legs. Her face, however—wrinkled, old, and on the whole, totally unmarketable—made me think of a certain ill-fated pawnbroker in *Crime and Punishment*. She proposed that I go swimming with her. I said no thanks. She insisted. I was firm. She insisted some more. I was adamant. It occurred to me that, had I been confronted with the choice between succumbing to her charms and perishing, I would have chosen a third crime: Raskolnikov's.

Before I left, she made me promise to pay her another visit soon. I promised. Anything to get the hell out of there, I thought.

There you have the most unforgettable character I have met during the last twenty-five years. Was she really a retired actress or just an eccentric, rich, frustrated old lady fond of collecting show business memorabilia and gigolos? I am not sure. For all I know— and for all I care to know—she may have been Bormann in drag.

It's always the same story. People who are in a position to help end up asking for *your* help. And to make matters worse, they seem to be in a more desperate position than you.

Life here has been like a long stretch in solitary. I am surrounded by people who regard art and literature as occupations fit only for eccentrics and social outcasts. A sculptor committed suicide here last year at the age of twenty-six. He used a shotgun, like Hemingway. Some say he was experimenting with drugs, others that he had fallen in love with a woman who loved another. But I have a different theory. It was the drab vastness of the landscape and the hideous mediocrity of life.

A friend of mine who loved Bach and Brubeck gave up his piano and the weekly jam sessions, went back to school, and is now a teacher. Another friend forgot his dream of singing Radames and Cavaradossi at the Met and is now in the advertising racket. There was a time when he would appear regularly every Sunday afternoon and ask me to accompany him on the piano as he sang—

tried to, at any rate, and with such sincere longing and technical ineptitude—"Celeste Aida," "Una furtiva lagrima," "E lucevan le stelle." Unable to endure the torture any longer, my mother pleaded with me one day: "Why don't you teach him easier tunes, for heaven's sake? If he goes on like that he's liable to put a rip in his throat."

Still another friend with even more grandiose dreams—a publishing firm, a monthly literary periodical, an avant-garde theater, and a film-production unit—with no holds barred, no concessions to the bourgeoisie, tough, idealistic—took a course in industrial psychology and now works in the personnel department of an insurance company. "How's tricks?" he says, whenever we come face to face in the street. "We should get together one of these days. Have a couple of drinks. Tell me all about the latest Fellini. I haven't been to the movies for ages. Work, work, work. Still single, eh? Smart move. Raising a family is no picnic. Problems with no end."

He looks contented. In his element. *They* are the ones who don't mind complaining. He sees no conflict between his former dreams and present conformism. There is a time to cast stones around and a time to gather them together. A time to build castles in the air and a time to settle down and raise a family in suburbia. The world is a stage and life a succession of roles. But unlike a real actor, you have no choice in the matter. The role is chosen for you by society. In the land of the brave and the free, they are nothing but slaves to a thousand irrational fears, prejudices, and social pressures. And they resent it when you refuse to be intimidated, to conform, to ask *How high?* when they tell you to jump.

"Married?" I was asked once during a job interview.

"Single."

"Engaged?"

"No."

"We prefer our employees to be married."

I was naive enough to ask why.

"We feel . . . blah-blah-blah—responsible—blah-blah-blah—dependable."

Translation: Statistics as well as common sense suggest that a married man will take more abuse than a single man for the simple reason that he has a family to feed.

They are no longer satisfied with loyal, efficient workers. They want hostages.

That's when I decided to avoid marriage at all cost.

"You like reading, do you?" I was asked in another interview.

"I do," I replied. "Do you?"

"Yes, when I was young. But I'm afraid I no longer have the time."

They spend endless hours watching hockey on television and guzzling beer, but when it comes to reading, they do it in the toilet—mostly newspapers and preferably the sports section. Books, ideas, art, philosophy: they are bad habits you contract as an adolescent, and after experimenting with them for a year or two, you reconsider the matter carefully and reach the only sensible and pragmatic conclusion.

The local newspaper devotes an entire section (about 16 pages) every day to sports, and another to show business (mostly scantily clad Hollywood starlets, and rock musicians that look more like members of a savage motorcycle gang), and only *one single page a week* to literature—mostly short reviews of books about notorious crimes and scandals, biographies of personalities in politics and sports, how-to manuals, illustrated coffee-table books on such things as barns and antique cars, and, at best, texts on the native flora and fauna.

Once, many years ago, when as a naive newcomer—a sheep let loose in the jungle—I dared to say something remotely critical about life here, I was immediately reminded that beggars can't be choosers. And worse. I'll never forget the pale, timid blonde with baby-blue eyes and cherry lips, normally as sweet and gentle as a lamb, who suddenly turned into a viper and hissed: "If you don't like it here, why don't you go back where you came from?"

"To Russia," someone else snapped; "they know how to handle malcontents like you there."

There you have freedom of speech in action.

"After all, we are guests here," a fellow Armenian once pointed out to me, trying to teach me manners. "Don't you think we should make an effort to be more grateful to our hosts?"

"I have been insulted, cheated, exploited, humiliated, lied to. I worked in factories, lived in tenements—is that how guests are treated here? Is that your conception of hospitality?"

"All immigrants have been through that. If my dad were alive, he could tell you a few horror stories of his own. But we are better off here than anywhere else, right? Things could be worse."

"Compared to what? The interior provinces of the Ottoman Empire at the turn of the century? The Soviet Union in the grip of Stalin's Great Terror? Greece during World War II? Iran under Khomeini? Listen, just because Asiatic barbarians drove us out of our homeland and made of us starving immigrants, it doesn't necessarily follow that we should be eager and willing to accept—short of massacre—any other form of barbarism."

"Aren't you overstating your case? This, after all, is a free, democratic and civilized country. Live and let live, freedom of speech and action—"

"We obviously have a different conception of civilization too."

"Well, what is your conception?"

"I can tell you what it isn't: it isn't suburban wasteland, asphalt and billboard jungles, public-relation stunts, plastic gadgets, organized crime, political, moral, and chemical pollution, the apotheosis of sex and violence, music that is more a combination of deafening noise and primal screams, narcotics, television commercials, the fast buck, in GOLD we trust. Shall I go on?"

This fellow Armenian happens to be (appropriately enough) in the junk business—ruthless, hard-working, knowledgeable in the ways of the New World. When he decided to get married, he traveled to Los Angeles, Montreal, the Middle East, even Yerevan. "My dad used to say, if you want action, get yourself *odars;* but if you want a wife, nothing but an Armenian will do."

Action is a favorite word of his.

"How's business?" I said last time I saw him driving past in one of his trucks.

"Could be better," he said, "I expect more action next month."

"And the wife?"

"As big as a house."

"Again?"

"You bet."

A man of action. He already has seven children. "The more the merrier," he says. He was himself an only child.

When he got married ten years ago, he asked an Armenian bishop from a nearby city to come and perform the ceremony.

"And you? When are *you* getting married?" the bishop inquired at one point.

"Never," I said.

"Why not?"

"I'm a writer."

"Writers get married too."

"I'm an *Armenian writer.*"

"I know several Armenian writers who are married."

"Must be luck. They must have rich dead uncles or something. Because on my income, I couldn't even raise a couple of church mice."

I have a number of uncles too. They may not be rich, but they are certainly well off. Also very much alive. Generous? Yes, very much. Only with advice, however. Useless advice. And worse. Insults.

One of them pays us a visit. He has changed very little since I last saw him twenty-five years ago. Stentorian speech, ugly disposition, arrogant, rude, unschooled.

"I could have gone to Paris," he tells me.

"Listen to your uncle," my mother admonishes.

"I could have gone to London, Rome, Yerevan—"

"He has a very close friend in Yerevan," my mother says, footnoting his text. "They used to be as close as brothers."

"What do I do instead? I come in the middle of nowhere."

"Nowhere is right," my mother says.

She is a Negro audience; he, an inspired preacher.

"And do I come here for fun?"

"Not here."

"See old friends?"

"What friends?"—that's me, the considerate son giving his mother a chance to take a coffee break.

"Go sightseeing perhaps?"

"Sahara would offer better vistas,"—that's me again; I am beginning to get the hang of it now.

"Eat and drink in fancy restaurants?"

He waits. When no one reacts, he answers his own question: "*Of course not!* I come here to put some *sense* into your head."

"Bless you," my mother intones.

"You must get out of here," he says.

"Tell him, tell him!"

"Detroit, Montreal, New York City, Fresno, Los Angeles—anywhere is better than here," he says. He has been around. He knows. "At least there are Armenian communities there—"

"Human beings I can talk to and share my sorrows with," my mother adds. "Maybe even find you a nice Armenian girl."

"That's right," my uncle, who married a floozy, says.

"It's not for myself," my mother goes on. "How many years do I have ahead of me? Four, maybe five. I do not wish anything for myself—except maybe to die in peace."

That's a favorite line of hers. She has been using it for the last twenty years.

"We have a nice little Armenian community right here." I say.

The Armenian community here consists of about ten families: each from a different country, each with its own background, vocabulary, customs, and cuisine, hence hardly on speaking terms with one another. One Armenian is in the junk business; another, from Aleppo, has a restaurant; still another from Istanbul, a shoe-repair shop. They say there is even an Armenian psychiatrist, a recent arrival from Kalamazoo, Mich., who cannot speak a word of Armenian. And of course, there is also the inevitable rug merchant from Smyrna, likewise assimilated, and ferociously anti-Armenian to boot—he of the fly and elephant analogy. The only time I had a chance to talk to him, he immediately made it plain that he wasn't hiring any Armenian help— just in case I was entertaining hopes in that direction.

"You give an Armenian a job," he said "and next thing you know he goes into business on his own and opens a store right across the street from your own."

"You have something against initiative?" I said insolently. I have reached the conclusion that in this world one should make enemies with the same loving care as one makes friends.

"I have nothing against initiative," he said; "but I do have something against disloyalty."

Disloyalty, it will be remembered, is the crime Armenians committed against the Turks in 1915. It's always the same story.

When I refused to praise his last book, a well-known Armenian writer questioned my loyalty. Young Turks, Armenian rug merchants and writers: whenever you refuse to accept the subservient role they have assigned to you, you become their mortal enemy.

"When we first came," my mother says, "there were two Armenian families in the neighborhood. But after the old folks died, the young ones left. Everyone we knew here has left except us."

She is right.

I remember when we first moved in, it was a clean, respectable, lower middle-class neighborhood. It is more like a slum now. People from all four corners of the world—Portuguese, Yugoslavs, Pakistanis, Koreans, Germans, Greeks, Sicilians, Ukrainians, Hungarians, Vietnamese, Japanese, Turks. All of them recent arrivals—ill at ease, aloof, suspicious of one another. Communication between ethnic groups is minimal. Except for the Portuguese, everyone minds his own business. The Portuguese, in contradistinction, are like a breath of sea-breeze in the midst of the cold Canadian tundra. They paint their houses in bright colors, sit on their porches and play Latin-American music and *fados* on their tape decks; engage in loud conversation until the small hours of the night; saturate the air with the aroma of fried fish; and shout at each other from one end of the street to the other. And as soon as they make enough money, they return to their country—for which they are of course deeply resented by the natives. Though displaced, poor, overworked, and exploited, they (the Portuguese) seem to have more fun in someone else's inferno than the natives in the paradise of their own manufacture.

"In another year or two," my mother says, "this neighborhood will be a slum."

"What's the situation with the blacks?" my uncle inquires.

"I see more of them every day," my mother says.

"No more than three families," I say.

"One family alone has nine children," she says.

"They are well-behaved, decent children," I say. "And they are not Americans; they are Africans from Kenya."

Native children are the worst—especially teenagers. Sometimes they walk through the neighborhood after midnight, screaming profanities and vandalizing.

"You must move, and fast; I see no other solution," my uncle says.

"Move where? From one slum to another? I'm not a millionaire."

"You could have been," my mother says. "God knows you've read enough books to be anything you want." That's another one of her favorite lines.

"It was never my ambition to be a Gulbenkian," I lie. "I'm poor and proud of it." Another lie. "As long as I have bread and books, who cares for luxuries?"

"Luxuries?" my uncle snaps. "You don't even have a decent home. You call this a home? Looks more like a stable to me."

I reflect that if it weren't for the arrogance of the rich, most people wouldn't even notice their own poverty.

"Don't you care about what people are saying?" he demands, righteous indignation ringing in his voice like Russian cathedral bells in the finale of Mussorgsky's *Pictures at an Exhibition* as orchestrated by Ravel.

"What are they saying?"

"That you are lazy."

"These are not people who know me."

"That you don't want to work."

"Lies."

"That you are a failure."

"Success is relative."

"Success is success."

"The closer the relative, the greater the success."

"Failure is failure and it can never be a substitute for success."

"If by success you mean financial success, in my view, making money is a waste of time."

"And, I assume, what you do isn't."

"Of course not. If it were, I wouldn't do it."

"What have you got against money anyway? Maybe the whole world is crazy and you are the only smart one? Don't you have any ambition to improve yourself? To improve the way you live?"

"What's wrong with the way I live? I have food and shelter. What more could I possibly want? Except maybe a little peace and quiet in order to continue my work."

"Is your work of any use to anyone?—that's what I'd like to know."

"I think so, yes."

"You think so. Does anyone else think so?"

"Yes."

"How do you know?"

"I get letters."

"What about money? Do you get any money?"

"Sometimes."

"Once or twice a year someone sends him $50," my mother says. "Property tax alone is $780 a year; heating another $1,000. Everything is going up."

"How do you survive then?"

"I worked for fifteen years," I say. "I worked in factories, department stores, insurance offices. I have some savings."

"And how long is that going to last?"

"So far so good," I say.

"You are a worse fool than I thought."

"I never cared much about money."

"Never say that—do you hear?—never! *Think* it, if you must, but never *say* it out loud."

"Why not, if it's true."

"Why not," he says. "Because people will think you are *mad!*"

"Who cares what people think."

"I had a brother-in-law like you. A dreamer, an idealist, an *intellectual*. A poet he was—published poetry in newspapers. He had a roomful of books on art, philosophy, and he ended up in the gutter. I tried to talk to him a couple of times. But would he listen? Come to your senses, I said. You are a grown man. You have a wife, children. *What the hell do you know?* he said. *Mind your own business,* he said. My sister is my business, I said. My nephews are my business. What happens next? He starts drinking and one day they find him dead in the gutter, drowned in his own vomit."

I cannot help noticing that the memory of his brother-in-law lying dead in the gutter is not an image that is altogether unpleasant to him. There is a note of triumph in his voice. *I told him so!* And I have trouble getting rid of the suspicion that deep in his heart there lies a secret wish to live long enough to see me in the gutter too. *I told you so!*

"My situation is a little different," I say. "One, I do not publish poetry in the newspapers. Two, I have no wife. Three, I have no children. Four, I don't drink."

"He drinks," my mother says.

"Sometimes, after a hard day's work, or after I finish a major project," I explain, "I may take a drink, to celebrate rather than to forget—there is a big difference."

"I see no difference there. Before you know it," my uncle says, "one drink leads to another. I've seen it happen again and again. Writers, actors, artists: one cuts his ear off, another goes mad, another shoots himself, still another drowns in his own vomit."

"A friend of his, an artist, blew his brains out last year," my mother says.

"He wasn't exactly a friend of mine. I just talked to him on one occasion, that's all. Besides, businessmen, doctors, and lawyers kill themselves too. It seems to me everyone should be free to choose his own mode of life—" and I am about to add "death" when my uncle interrupts.

"You call this life? You should see your friends back home. That idiot Movses, the one that went to school with you, he lives in a mansion, he does. Compared to this dump, a veritable royal palace."

"Whenever company arrives," my mother says, "I feel so a-shamed I want to hide."

"Company? What company are you talking about?" I say. "Once a year someone may come to see me because he needs my help, or because he happens to be passing through and it is good public relations to be on friendly terms with someone who writes in the newspapers. I do not consider these people company. Others pretend to be your close friend, come into your home and before you know it they are trying to sell you something. You call these people company? Pickpockets, that's what they are. I have no friends and am proud of the fact."

That is not quite true. I do have a friend: a Catholic priest who drops in to see me once a month or so. I offer him a cup of coffee, some sunflower seeds and almonds. We talk about our respective congregations. We compare notes. We share our problems. It is not easy being a Catholic priest. Arsonists, vandals, rude parishioners who give him bad reviews ("Today's sermon was too long!"), winos and hoboes who drop in at the presbytery unannounced and insist on sharing his breakfast table; eccentric old ladies who telephone in the middle of the night in order to give him verbatim reports of their conversations with angels and demons. "Being a Catholic priest," I sometimes quip, "is almost as difficult as being an obscure writer—though nothing can beat being an obscure *Armenian* writer." He had a mental collapse last year and was hospitalized for four months. As for myself, I have come close, very close—on more than one occasion. I ask him to pray for me. He asks me to pray for him. I promise to do my best—though the last time I prayed with any degree of conviction was in 1947. Like poor Chinese housewives, we take in each other's laundry in order to make ends meet. Once, when I told him I no longer believed in God, he said:

"You may abandon God, but God will never abandon you."

"Armenian writers must be the exception that confirms that rule," I said.

He laughed.

We laugh a great deal when we get together.

"A happy man," my mother says after he leaves. "I like happy people. I used to laugh like that when I was young. My poor departed aunt Haiganoush used to say: May you never stop laughing like that for as long as you live. . . . It was not meant to be."

"That imbecile Movses," my uncle goes on, "has a summer place ten times as big as your house. He has a chandelier in his dining room as big as this room—had it made especially for him in Amsterdam. He owns two apartment buildings, one eight, the other eleven stories high; also three restaurants. He has a beautiful wife, four children—one of whom is studying medicine in Paris. You remember Movses, don't you?"

"I remember Movses very well, yes."

How could I forget that face of his—a puny version of the giant stone heads on Easter Islands. We were both students in the same boarding school in Venice. A depressing place run on a semi-seminary basis by monks. Italian nuns, most of them old crones, took care of our clothes and meals. But there was one—tall, young, beautiful, a ravishing creature—for whom we all had a secret passion. The regimen was spartan with sadistic overtones. Cross-examinations, public humiliations, physical punishments were constant companions. We rose every morning at 5:30, washed in icy water over long, soapstone troughs, prayers in the chapel, an hour's study, breakfast. Incoming and outgoing mail was censored. At night our dark, cold cells were locked. It was an educational institution only insofar as it taught us to survive under brutal conditions. Not all of us survived, however. Movses was one of those who couldn't make it to the end. After a year of this Ottoman regimentation, he cracked up and ran amok.

It happened on a cold, rainy night. We were studying in the classroom in complete silence, when he suddenly leapt from his bench, let loose a hair-raising primal scream, and made a dash for the door. It was like watching our own suppressed fears and fury assume a human shape and run out into the night, into the wind and rain, yelling like a Sioux brave on the warpath. He had been restless for days, pacing the back of the classroom like a caged tiger—unwashed, hairy chest exposed.

"We want normal boys in this school, *normal!*" the headmaster said in his uncivil farewell speech next day, as Movses, gentle Movses, his moist chin trembling and for once immaculately washed, combed, and dressed, stood by to be dismissed. This emphasis on normalcy sent chills down my spine. *Normal, loyal:* two words I loathe with every fiber of my being.

"All day long he does nothing but read and write," my mother says. "Where is this going to end, I don't know."

"Nobody gives a damn about things like that any more," my uncle says. "In the old days, maybe. But with television, radio, and movies, who has time for reading? Get a regular job, make something of yourself—a wife, children, a respectable home. When you grow old, who's going to take care of you? Your mother?"

"Sometimes he goes on reading until two, three o'clock in the morning."

"My brother-in-law all over again."

"And sometimes he starts writing four o'clock in the morning. Look how thick his eyeglasses are. When he reads his nose touches the page and his eyes move from side to side like that of an old man. I look at him and my heart is torn to shreds. But I say nothing. What if he goes blind? When you are alone, you think all kinds of things. I keep telling him to go and see a doctor but does he listen? He used to be such a sweet, obedient little boy . . . it's impossible to talk to him now."

They go on discussing me as if I were not there.

Blindness. I think about it often. Last week I watched a televised interview with the blind Jorge Luis Borges. He seemed contented. Smiled more frequently than his youthful American interviewer. And about a month ago, I had a talk with Earl—one of the retired old men on our street who went blind recently as a result of advanced diabetes. He used to be very active and energetic. Always working around the house—taking care of the flowers, watering the lawn, painting, repairing this and that. Seated on his driveway, under the sun, he now looked as serene as a lizard or a yogi in samadhi. I went up to him, touched his shoulder, shook his hand, told him who I was. He said only one thing: "I can see only shadows," and burst into tears, shaking uncontrollably. On the following day he was hospitalized. A week later he died. On my way to the library this morning, I had a talk with his widow. "In a way I'm glad he's gone," she said. "He suffered so . . . couldn't take it, you know . . . but I will miss him. I spent 59 years of my life with him—he was going to be 80 next month."

I will miss him.

Is there anyone in this world about whom I could say that?

I reflect that in life sometimes the best way to handle a problem or a crisis is not to resolve it (some problems have no solutions) but to accept it as a painful, educational process. Because if you stop and think for a moment, what is a crisis but the sudden revelation of an error of judgment on our part. In our efforts to deal with reality, we often simplify its complexities; we even pretend these complexities do not exist. But they are there. They conduct a life of their own, like certain viruses in the body; and suddenly, when we least expect them, they burst and poison our existence. What is my uncle if not a noisy personification, a stentorian metamorphosis of the horrible silence that has surrounded me ever since I decided to withdraw from life and dedicate myself to literature.

I also reflect that, whenever we undertake the task of understanding a fellow human being, we automatically assume that we share with him a common element which, for the sake of convenience, we call "humanness." Armed with that assumption, we then proceed to misunderstand him. It's always the same story. The instant we utter the word "humanness" we project in it our own set of obsessions, prejudices, projects, inclinations, tastes, etc., completely ignoring the other's set of prejudices, limitations, tastes, etc.—and here I speak not of those limitations and prejudices that we are aware of, but of those that lie buried in our subconscious.

To understand another is like immersing oneself in a totally alien element and dimension. To understand birds, a fish would have to sprout wings and feathers and spend some time soaring and riding the wind. To understand another is surely not as easy as we have been misled to believe. Every day I rediscover again and again how different people are; and how *different* the word "different" can really mean.

As for loving one's enemy: can one really love something one cannot understand?—I say some*thing* because an enemy, by definition, is a force whose purpose is to annihilate you: an impersonal, almost mechanical project rather than a human act.

"Company from out of town?" Fred Larsen wants to know. He is the observant one. The local oral historian. In his 80s, but extremely alert—short, wiry, thick eyeglasses, hearing aid, visor, sharp penetrating voice: there is something of the computerized toy and the robot in him. He is one of those indefatigable yaks who know everything about everybody, and if you let him he will walk with you almost as far as Alaska, telling you all the while about the history of the town, the biography of its notables, who quarreled with whom in 1922, who was mayor in 1915, the first execution by hanging in 1897, the name of the criminal, and a Capote-style re-creation of the crime. Once in a while he will interrupt his narrative and ask a discreet question, in passing and absent-mindedly as it were. By now, I suspect, he knows more about me and my family than I do.

"I guess you heard about Earl," he says. "Died of a broken heart, you know. Couldn't take it. He knew it was coming, but couldn't get used to the idea. Diabetes. I have diabetes too—a different kind, my doctor tells me. Earl was almost 80. Past president of the Horticultural Society. His brother used to be an important man around these parts, yes sir. Lawyer, alderman, ran for mayor in 1947, couldn't make it, tried again, made it. Died about nine years ago. A street was named after him. The two brothers didn't get along."

I seem to have a vague recollection of having met Larsen many years ago in the first pages of a Dostoevsky novel. At the public library this morning I finally decide to investigate this suspicion that's been lurking in the back of my mind ever since we had our first talk. After skimming over the first pages of *The Possessed* and *The Brothers Karamazov,* I at last come face to face with Larsen in the first chapter of *The Idiot,* which I remember to have read at the age of 13 or 14 in a Greek translation. "This sort of character," Dostoevsky writes here," is met with pretty frequently in a certain class. They are people who know everyone—that is, they know where a man is employed, what his salary is, whom he knows, whom he married, what money his wife had, who are his cousins and second cousins, etc., etc. These men generally have about a hundred pounds a year to live on and they spend their whole time and talents in the amassing of this style of knowledge, which they reduce—or raise—to the standard of a science."

My only pleasure these days comes from playing Bach on the organ and rereading Gostan Zarian. About a year ago, I wrote letters to several cultural foundations here and abroad to see if they would consider supporting the translation or publication of a book by Zarian—a giant of 20th century world literature who can stand comparison with such modern masters as James Joyce, Thomas Mann, and Jean-Paul Sartre. "However praiseworthy such projects may be," replied one Armenian foundation, "we must point out that they will have to depend on their own merit for reaching the necessary mass of readers. Our own limited pro- gramme of publications is based on erudite works authored by well-established academic personalities."

Another Armenian foundation did not even bother to reply.

A Canadian foundation on the other hand said: "We regret to say we do not offer any type of assistance for the translation of foreign literature. However, we may consider granting assis- tance for the translation of Canadian authored works written in a foreign language for translation into either English or French so long as the author is Canadian and the work in question is in the field of creative writing."

To Canadians, Zarian is an outcast because he was not a Cana- dian citizen. To Armenians, he is an outcast because he was that rare phenomenon—a genuine writer who stubbornly refused to be a peddler, a sycophant, and a political functionary.

"A collection of my poems is scheduled to appear later this year in Yerevan," writes an Armenian-American poet who is also a pros- perous rug merchant, "and shortly thereafter a Russian translation of this same volume will also appear in Moscow. A number of translators here have expressed the wish to translate my works into English, but so far I discouraged them because, in my view, none of them is in a position to do justice to the original. However, having read some of your translations from the Armenian, I am willing to reconsider my position."

No Armenian writer or merchant has ever written to me to say let us translate and publish Abovian, Demirjibashian, Charents, Gostan Zarian, Zabel Yessayan. It is understandable. Everyone wants to achieve his own immortality, and to hell with Armenian literature and culture. And who are these contemporary writers of ours? Insurance executives, rug merchants, businessmen, real estate developers greedy for both money and immortality. And what do they write about? What else but the eternal snows of Massis, the vision of Mashtots, the heroic stuggle of Vartan. After they accumulate a few hundred thousand dollars, they decide to spend one or two thousand on the printing of a book, which they proceed to distribute free of charge for the simple reason that no one will buy a single copy; and by this act they hope to change their image from that of mercenary peddlers to idealistic poets. And as if that weren't enough, they travel all over the continent, participating in symposia (to which they make generous contributions, of course) and deliver lectures on the crisis of contemporary Armenian literature in the diaspora. "We must encourage our young talents," is one of their favorite public statements. Elder statesmen formulating future cultural policy. In public, selfless servants of the community, dedicating their life to the preservation of its traditions and culture; in private, envious nonentities who care for no one but themselves. It's the old, familiar story of stealing privately and donating publicly. Times and environment may change, but tricks stay the same. ("But I'm not a writer!" one of these elder statesmen protested when I pointed out a contradiction in his lecture. A few weeks later he wrote a letter proposing that I translate one of his books into English. Instead of reminding him of his own assessment of himself, I told him I was busy. "Busy?" he retorted rudely. "I thought translating *was* your business!") And one day these shopkeepers die and their amassed fortune goes to the Church or to a museum in Yerevan. Not a single cent against the publication of our classics, let alone "our young talents."

"Zarian? Gostan Zarian?" a well-known Armenian-American writer and community leader said to me recently when I mentioned his name. "I knew him well. Very well, as a matter of fact. An extremely unpleasant character. Self-centered. Egotistical. Vain. Me . . . me . . . me! When I was in Paris, Picasso told me;

when I was in Madrid, Lorca told me; when I was in Brussels, Verhaeren told me . . . and Lenin, Marinetti, Mayakovsky . . . you name it and they were all his intimate friends. I must have met him at least 50–60 times. We had long talks. Have I written anything about him? No. Nothing. Neither do I intend to. Now then, the reason why I called—about translating a collection of my articles: there are several translators at work already, but I would prefer uniform translations handled by a single person."

Zarian was absolutely right when, writing about this type of imposter, he said: "For him the Armenian reader is nothing but a garbage can. Not a single principle. Not a single idea." And writing of his own fate, he said: "The street, the Stock Exchange, sordid scandals, the savage scorn for all disinterested intellectual labor, sensationalism, artificial novelties, the profit-motive, in short, all of moral syphilis, offer him 2½ piastres and send him on his way." Prophetic words which he wrote in 1922 in Istanbul. He could have written them in the United States in 1961—which is when he was indeed sent on his way to Soviet Armenia from Los Angeles.

Hundreds of Armenian books have been published in the United States since 1943, but not a single volume by or about Zarian. *Odars* like Lawrence Durrell, who could not even read any of Zarian's books, have written more about him than our own writers. *Amot!* And there are those who say: "I'll never understand why Zarian left for Soviet Armenia." Why? Because he chose to be a writer, in a world where only peddlers prosper; and he compounded that felony by choosing to be an *Armenian* writer, thus exposing all those imposters for whom the Armenian is nothing but "a garbage can."

An acquaintance from a nearby town telephones to inform me that after five years they have finally managed to persuade an Armenian priest, who happened to be passing through the neighborhood, to postpone his departure long enough to offer High Mass next Sunday.

"We need an organist. Can you help us out?"

I promise to do my best. I leave everything aside and on the appointed hour I enter the church.

The sacristy is in turmoil—*sargavaks*, altar boys, and singers by the dozen. And, inevitably, arguments with no end. Nobody agrees on anything. As soon as someone dares to say anything, someone else contradicts him, often in an unnecessarily offensive manner. There are five *sargavaks*—one from Aleppo, another from

Alexandria, still another from Beirut, and so on—all of them furiously eager to show their vocal dexterity and liturgical expertise.

"Which *badarak* are we singing?"

"Yegmalian."

"The Gomidas is better."

"We prefer the Yegmalian."

"It's almost the same, anyway."

"We are used to the Yegmalian here."

"It doesn't make any difference to me. I can sing both."

"We are ready. Start playing the *Khorhourt Khorin*," one *sargavak* orders me.

"No," another says. "I'll sing a *sharagan* first."

"What *sharagan* is that?"

"Today is the feast of *Sourp Khach*, isn't it?"

"So what if it is?"

"In Alexandria—"

"In Aleppo—"

"In Beirut—"

"Let him sing the *sharagan* if he wants to."

"Listen, if you don't want me to sing, I won't."

"Sing, sing, only let's get going—we are 55 minutes late already."

"I just saw a couple of people who got up and left."

"Those Egyptians," I hear someone whispering, "they are so smart . . . they think they know everything."

When I finally start playing, one of the *sargavaks* tells me to play louder. "If he plays louder," someone else says, "he'll drown us." Next, I am told I am playing too fast. "If he plays any slower, it will be Monday afternoon by the time we get out of here," another remarks. Someone complains that he is having trouble reaching the high notes and that I should transpose the accompaniment to a lower key. Whereupon he is reminded that as a baritone he should handle only the lower notes and leave the high notes to the sopranos and tenors.

One of the young women in the choir tells me; "If I were you, I wouldn't play at all. Let them do what they want." When I accept her suggestion, I hear someone say:

"What's the matter with him? Why isn't he playing?"

"Probably he doesn't know."

"Why couldn't you get someone who knows?"

"My niece plays the piano. If you had told me—"

"My wife plays the organ—"

"You should get together and practice once in a while," says the priest afterwards, his dark, hairy face twisted with anger and disgust. Practice for what? So that we shall have the privilege of singing the High Mass once every five years, if at all?

I ask him how our community compares with his last congregation. It is meant to be a harmless, conversational question, but he takes it seriously and answers with grim determination: "I have had congregations all over the world—Abyssinia, South America, France, Syria, Iraq, Jerusalem, California—but I have never seen anything like this. This is not a community. It is a mob. Everyone talks. No one listens. It will take more than one generation to give this crowd the semblance of a community." He goes on in this vein for some time.

Next, I am cross-examined by an elderly gent who wants to know where I come from, how long I have been here, and what I do for a living.

"On weekends," I reply, "I play the organ in a Catholic church, whose services, may I add, are less elaborate and better organized than the disaster you just witnessed."

"I noticed you had some problems with the *sargavaks*. . . ."

"I'm told you also do some writing," someone else butts in.

"Occasionally, yes."

"I used to write too."

"Interesting."

"But gave it up."

"Why?"

"A risky business—writing. They starve you to death."

"So what do you do for a living now?"

"I have a rug store."

"Wonderful."

We are joined by a third character, who says: "I hear you've written a book about Armenian history and culture."

I plead guilty to the charge.

"I would like to have a copy."

"I'm sorry, I don't have one with me at the moment."

"That's too bad. It's not for me, by the way, but for my grandchildren. I know all I need to know about Armenian history and culture. My son married an *odar*, you see. His children don't speak Armenian. But I want them to know something about their roots."

"I could let you have my publisher's address."

"No. I want a copy from *you*."

Shortly after the book in question came out, I remember, an old friend, whom I had not seen for a number of years, knocked on my door one Sunday afternoon, said he had heard about the book, and would like to have a copy. I gave him one. Next, he asked me to autograph it—he even dictated the wording of the dedication. I followed instructions. After which he took the book and left. (Did he say thank you? I don't remember and I couldn't swear to it.) A couple of weeks later he telephoned to inform me that he had not read the book yet, but a friend of his had and she thought it was biased. "Why couldn't you have written a more objective and impartial account?"

Shortly after my loud-mouth uncle leaves, my peace is disrupted once more: this time by an old friend of the family and his wife. Though in their late sixties, they both have the voracious appetite and furious energy of teenagers. They want to experience everything life has to offer before it slips away from their grasp permanently. We have not seen them for over twenty years. My mother is eager to speak about mutual relatives and friends, but all they want to do is talk about their recent trip to California where, it seems, they met an old, childhood friend from Smyrna, now a millionaire, and spent a fabulous weekend with him and his wife in Las Vegas.

"That man spent more money in two days than you'll ever spend in a lifetime," he says uncivilly, implying that "spending money" is the greatest and noblest act devised by man.

"First day alone he gambled and lost $55,000," she says.

"Without batting an eye—"

"And in less than an hour."

Listening to them completing each other's sentences is like following a game of ping pong.

"Once he took us to a fancy seafood place for supper—"

"You know how much it cost?"

"Don't tell him, let him guess."

"How can he?—if he has never been there."

"Go ahead and tell him then."

"$780."

"That's right. And what did we have?"

"A salad, a lobster, a piece of crab, a couple of drinks—"

"I didn't even drink—"

"He doesn't drink."

"Once I got drunk when I was a boy—"

"And was sick for a whole week."

"Alcohol doesn't agree with my system, I suppose."

"And since then he hasn't touched the stuff."

"Except for a glass of beer, once in a while."

"Yes. He enjoys a glass of cold beer on a hot day like this."

(Later, during supper: "You wouldn't have a bottle of beer, would you?")

"As for the lobster, he didn't touch that either."

"I just had some of the crab—I wasn't hungry, you see: we'd had a big lunch—"

"The lobster was delicious. It was served with a garlic-flavored butter sauce—it melted in your mouth—"

"We could have had the same thing at home probably for less than $10."

"Maybe, but the service! There were these beautifully uniformed waiters—so courteous, so eager to serve. As soon as they saw a cigarette in your hand, they were beside you with a lighter—"

"Of course, included in the bill was also the entertainment—"

"All famous singers, dancers, comedians . . ."

This goes on for quite some time with frequent divagations into autobiographical reminiscences, like the early encounter with alcohol cited above. Then the topic shifts to their millionaire friend.

"They live all by themselves, he and his wife, in a huge mansion—"

"They have a Japanese chauffeur—"

"Who drives a Rolls Royce of course—"

"Two black maids, a German gardener, a French chef, a full-time secretary—"

"But they are such friendly, unpretentious, modest people—"

"Very patriotic too."

"He has been awarded dozens of medals, including one from the Catholicos of Etchmiadzin."

When trouble comes, try to use it to your advantage, Solzhenitsyn says somewhere. I make an effort to follow that advice.

"Does he read?" I inquire.

"Yes, he loves to read—"

"He gets dozens of newspapers from all over the world every day—"

"He gets all the Armenian newspapers and magazines published in the United States, Canada, and the Middle East—"

"Also Soviet Armenia—"

"And books, records—"

"He had a painting by Aivazovsky on his living-room wall—"

"I don't remember how many thousand dollars he said he had paid for it—"

"$80,000 I think he said."

"Something like that, yea."

"And it is worth every penny. So beautiful. So real. Don't look at it too long, he told us, you might get seasick."

"A witty man—wonderful sense of humor—"

"Highly cultured, well-informed too—"

"He probably knows all about Gostan Zarian," I say.

"Who?"

"Gostan Zarian. One of our greatest writers."

"O yes! I think I've heard about him," he says.

"A familiar name," she says.

"For some reason," I explain, "so far no one has tried to translate him into English—"

"Probably because he is not easy to translate," she says, eager to parade her understanding of such matters.

"His books," I go on, "are filled with complex situations, fascinating characters and ideas that cover a wide range of topics— politics, sociology, philosophy, history, art, literature. The man has style, depth, originality, vision, even prophetic insight."

He yawns. She yawns. I continue:

"I would love to translate him into English if I found someone who would be willing to finance the publication of the book. I have asked a few cultural foundations without any positive results. Do you think your millionaire friend might be interested in such a project?"

Blank stares.

"A friend of mine, who works as a typesetter in a printing shop in New Jersey, tells me that printing and binding a small paperback volume shouldn't cost more than $800."

Icy silence.

"Do you think it would be a good idea to get in touch with your friend?"

Hostile stares.

"I'll write to him myself, of course, without mentioning your name."

"You'll be wasting your time," he says.

"It shouldn't take me more than five minutes," I say.

"It will do you no good," she says.

"Forget it," he says.

"He gets requests like that every day—"

"By the dozen—"

"Out of the question—"

"He gets letters like that by the dozen—all kinds of people and organizations—"

"If he were to say yes to all of them—"

"Forget the whole idea; put it out of your head," he says with real panic in his voice, as though I were about to commit a sacrilege.

And henceforth, their patriotic and generous millionaire is mentioned no longer. No mean accomplishment that in itself.

A week later, as they are about to leave, they give me the following piece of valuable advice:

"Forget this writing business—"

"No one amounted to much in our communities by writing—"

"It would be different if you were to join a political group—"

"They might let you edit one of their newspapers—"

"That way you may get a modest salary for your work—"

"But as long as you are on your own . . ." A sad, resigned shake of the head.

"That's the way it has always been with us—"

"Unfortunately."

To the poor everyone is generous with advice.

Whenever I read Solzhenitsyn, I wonder why it is that during the last three–four decades we, Armenians, have failed to produce a single noted dissident writer. Is it because an Armenian dissident (writing in Armenian of course) would be ignored by us and consequently by the rest of the world? And suppose he were lucky enough to be thrown out of the country (a privilege extended only to internationally recognized figures) what would he do for a living?

About ten years ago, a brilliant Soviet-Armenian composer whose symphonies, concertos, and piano sonatas had been praised by, among others, Shostakovich and Khachaturian, emigrated to the United States. He now works as a typesetter in a printing shop in New Jersey. Once in a while he telephones to tell me about his life in the free world. "Our cultural foundations," he once said, "are staffed by hooligans. You know what one of their secretaries once told me? 'Our foundation is not a charitable institution!' As for our aghababas: what do they know about art and music? Can a jackass appreciate the delicate aroma and sweetness of rose-jam?"

Solzhenitsyn had only the KGB to contend with. But how can one fight apathy? How can one ever hope to defeat ignorance and stupidity, against which—it has been said—even the gods are powerless?

I reflect that, long before Solzhenitsyn, in the 1920s, as a matter of fact, Gostan Zarian wrote a book *(The Traveller and His Road)* which contains a savage critique of Lenin and Marx and an exposé of the communist system. He wrote it after living in the USSR for three years. In its depth and brilliance, this book can rival any literary masterpiece produced in the West during the last eight decades. And yet, how many Armenians have read it? How many *odars* have heard about it? Decades passed before such eminent intellectuals as Gide, Silone, and Koestler wrote of their disillusionment with the Soviet system. More decades passed before Solzhenitsyn realized that there was something rotten in Marx's theories and Lenin's practice. If Zarian had been translated and read in the 1920s, none of these gentlemen could have said: "We were taken in. We didn't know. If only someone had warned us!"

Of today's two letters, one is from the USSR, the other from West Germany.

"I am 17 years old and my name is Natalia," I read in the letter from the USSR. "I am a student of jurisprudence at the State University of Yerevan and I am interested in literature, music, and the cinema. I would like to have a pen-pal in Canada. If you are too busy, would you be kind enough to give my address to someone who may be interested in having a pen-pal in the homeland? May I ask you for another favor? Could you send me a good picture of Paul Newman, please? He is my favorite American actor. I also like Alain Delon very much. I look forward to your reply with great impatience."

"It is my sad duty to inform you," I read in the letter from Germany, "of the sudden death of Dr. Paul Engelmann on October 11, 1980."

(Probably suicide, I think. He suffered from violent fits of depression and had already attempted suicide on a number of occasions.)

"As one of Dr. Engelmann's students," the letter goes on, "I was given the task of sorting out and cataloguing his manuscripts and papers, among which I found your novel titled *Semiramis*, which, as you probably know, Dr. Engelmann had begun to translate into German. Please let me know if you would like to have the manuscript returned."

"Good news?" my mother wants to know.

"Could be better," I say, and get ready for my daily walk to the library.

It is a mild, sunny, autumn day outside—yellow leaves ankle-deep on the sidewalks. The air is motionless, the sky blue. Someone nearby is burning leaves. I can't see the smoke (and the crow, whose receding shouts fill the air), but I can smell the fragrance.

"It's a lovely day, isn't it?" says Earl's widow with a sad smile.

"Yes, it is," I say.

If only it would last.

The Ambitions of a Pig

Well-being and happiness never appeared to me as an absolute aim. I am even inclined to compare such moral aims to the ambitions of a pig.

ALBERT EINSTEIN

THERE WERE ABOUT a dozen of us in the living room of a suburban house—young men and women in their twenties and thirties—smoking, sipping coffee, and talking. The subject was creative versus non-creative work.

"The manager of a department store, a bus driver, or a factory hand may drop dead or quit and no one will miss him—except family and friends of course—because he can be easily replaced," someone said.

"Psychologically speaking" someone else added, "creative work is more satisfying, fulfilling as well as challenging."

"I agree with you there. Routine work tends to degrade a man's spirit, stunt his growth and development, mechanize his responses."

"In my view," said a teacher, "the most creative work of all is teaching."

"Why do you say that?"

"Because a writer works with his ideas and a typewriter, a photographer with a camera, a painter with a canvas, palette, and brushes. A teacher, on the other hand, moulds the human mind and soul. His medium is not dead matter but live human beings—children, boys and girls—impressionable, sensitive to new ideas, unspoiled, pure."

That was four years ago. This morning, at the public library, I had a short talk with this same teacher.

"How's teaching?" I asked after we exchanged the usual greetings and how-de-dos.

"I don't teach any more," she replied. "I quit last year."

"What do you do now?"

77

"I am in insurance."

"Insurance?"

"Right. More money, less work."

More money, less work.

Some phrases stick in my mind and I repeat them mechanically a thousand times. Like a virus they enter my bloodstream, make me feverish and irritable. More money, less work.

Who but a jackass would refuse to see the overwhelming weight of that argument?

This morning the mailman delivers ten copies of my latest book.

"All right," my mother says. "You have now published seven books. Forget writing for a while. Try something else."

"Try what?"

"You could teach. You had a few offers recently."

"Yesterday I had a talk with a teacher who quit teaching and went into insurance."

"That's the way one should be in this world—change, experiment, try this and that. It's been ten years now that you have been writing and what have you accomplished? Nothing! Who reads these days? Even if you write like Shakespeare, who cares?"

"One does not write because people may or may not care, but to satisfy an inner need, to expose a scandal, to unmask a liar. Besides, what people think today may have nothing to do with what they'll think tomorrow."

"You mean *Kna merir, yegour sirem,*" she says, quoting a well-known Armenian saying meaning roughly: "Drop dead and I'll love you."

"*Oush lini, anoush lini,*" I retaliate ("Better late than never"). "Every occupation has its hazards and risks," I explain. "Businessmen go bankrupt, kings are assassinated, actresses grow old and commit suicide, prophets go unheeded, writers are ignored and insulted—"

"Lied to and cheated," she adds.

"That also."

"Starved."

"Sometimes."

"Always. Name a single Armenian writer who has amounted to anything in our communities."

"That proves only one thing: being a writer is difficult; being an Armenian writer—"

"Impossible!"

"All right, impossible."

"And knc wing this you persist?"

"Of cou :se. It is the only way I know of asserting my freedom. If I went into teaching simply because the community needs my services as a teacher rather than as a writer, then I would be doing what others want me to do and not what *I* want to do. I would no longer be free. I would be conforming. I believe there is only one luxury in this world, and that is *freedom*. Money in comparison is a form of slavery. The wealthiest man on earth is nothing but a slave to his capital. If you have a cow, a wise man once said, you milk the cow; but if you have seven cows, the cows milk *you*."

Speaking of cows, my mother thinks I am as stubborn as a mule. As for myself, I am fond of mules. They have character. We call them stubborn because on occasion they refuse to serve us and we lack the intelligence to understand the reason behind their refusal.

Mother and I have frequent arguments about literature. She thinks it is a waste of time. A racket. Sometimes I am inclined to agree with her, but I have committed too many years of my life to it to even consider the possibility of openly admitting that to her, or, for that matter, to myself. We all have our cross to bear. Literature is mine. I am hers.

"I'm not asking you to give up writing altogether," Mother is sometimes willing to compromise. "Go on writing, if you must; but try something else too. What have you got to lose?"

"No. Writing must be a full-time job. Art must become destiny. Who wants to waste his time reading the book of a part-timer? Would you trust your health in the care of an amateur physician? Besides, I don't believe in trying something simply because I've got nothing to lose. I *do* have something to lose: my time—that is to say, a fraction of my life, and my integrity—that is to say, my soul. A man can ruin his life trying everything there is to try in this world. I did that once and if I learned anything it's that you must choose what you want to do and go ahead and do it—and I mean do it with the single-mindedness of a maniac and a born fanatic— if you want to achieve anything in this world, that is. Otherwise you'll always end up doing what someone else wants you to do: work for someone else, fight in someone else's battles, and end up dying in defense of someone else's interests, privileges, and pleasures—a jackass of a martyr if I ever saw one."

Mother likes to maintain that traveling, meeting new people, seeing beautiful places, having new experiences, may make me a better writer. I am not sure about that. People are more or less the same everywhere. As for places: Hemingway went to Italy, Spain, Africa and Cuba, but his stuff on bulls, bells, and balls sounds phony today; he should have stayed home and written more stories like "The Killers." Maugham traveled to the Far East and all over the world, but he never wrote anything better than *Of Human Bondage, The Summing Up, The Vagrant Mood,* and *Points of View.*

"Aren't you tired of your surroundings?" Mother wants to know once in a while.

"I loathe my surroundings. I can't stand them! But they allow me to concentrate on my work."

"Work, work."

"Gandhi produced some of his best work in prison; Dostoevsky is unthinkable without Siberia; so is Solzhenitsyn. This place is my Siberia and my Gulag."

"There is more to life than work—reading and writing all day long, always the same people, always the same places."

She has a point there. Sometimes I get so depressed that to console myself I think of death. Death by suicide. Suicide by hunger. Slow, non-violent, natural.

"I have seen more places and met more people than I care to," I say, raising my voice (always a bad sign that. The Chinese are absolutely right when they say, "He who loses his temper has wrong on his side"). "I have also tried different lines of work—in factories, department stores, insurance offices, schools. I have taught Armenian, Greek, the piano. I have traveled around two continents, several Greek islands; I have lived and worked in about half-a-dozen cities. I wasn't born yesterday. I'm not the fool that I may appear to be. I know what I'm doing."

"You know *nothing!*"

One of the worst things that can happen to a man, my mother is fond of saying, is to say to himself that he is something. Not some*body,* but some*thing.* On that day his troubles begin. He loses all respect for others. He is filled with his own self-importance. He listens to no one, accepts no criticism, rejects all advice. Which may explain why my mother likes to remind me that I am *nothing.* For my own good. I am not complaining. I am even grateful to her. Humility is a rare virtue; arrogance a common malady; and vanity an insatiable monster.

"My wife is wonderful," an eminent writer once confided in a letter. "We speak the same language. I have always had her full support. I suppose I have been very lucky. If you ever decide to marry, I do hope and wish you will find a wife as understanding and supportive as mine has been to me. Because that's extremely important for an artist."

And one day they paid us a visit—the pair of them: the distinguished author and his exemplary consort. They stayed for four hours. He did all the talking. She said nothing. Not a word! On several occasions I tried to talk to her, asked her questions, solicited comments. She smiled, she nodded, but did not say a word. *He* answered for her. His instructions to her must have been direct and explicit: "Keep your trap shut!" And I began to see something that had not even crossed my imagination to suspect until then. He was a petty, envious, fiercely possessive, extremely narrow man—litigious, irritable, arrogant, authoritarian. He could not tolerate dissent. Anyone who had dared to disagree with him, or criticize his work, or refused to promote his career, was dismissed as a moron and a fraud. I am not particularly fond of my fellow men either, but he went to extremes. And I thought: What a cruel instrument of deception the written word is! A short face-to-face encounter can be more revealing than reams of correspondence and volumes of autobiographical reminiscences.

"Who was that man?" Mother wanted to know after they left.

"An able writer, an excellent craftsman, a hard worker. I admire him. But I never realized until today that he was also a mean little tyrant, an Othello with the temperament of a rattlesnake. If that man ever goes into politics, he will unleash World War III in no time. We should all thank the good Lord that he has gone into literature instead."

"And what kind of woman was that? She never said a thing."

"A woman? No. An angel. A saint. A martyr! She should be immortalized with a shrine, a cathedral, a dozen cantatas."

(Pam's definition of a rattlesnake: "A big fat worm with a mean poisonality.")

My mother does not think highly of writers. In her view, writing is not honest work. She doesn't read. "Books," she says, "have been the source of all our problems. You've ruined your eyesight, wasted away your life—and what do the people at the library say, I wonder. You go there ever day—"

"I go there to work."

"You call that work?"

"Writing is hard work. A scientist has calculated that a writer burns more calories than a construction worker."

"Do you see anyone else going there every day?"
"Of course."
"How many?"
"At least five."
Six, if you count the Korean.

The Korean is a newcomer—a perennially unkempt, unwashed, uncombed youth in blue jeans, green sneakers, and khaki windbreaker. With what looks like a large camera and a duffel bag slung over his shoulder, he saunters around with the asinine expression of an abysmally bored and disoriented tourist, occasionally muttering things to himself in his native tongue, and whistling as if he were walking down a dark, deserted alley.

And speaking of eccentrics: there is still another whom I see every day at the library—this one, however, is a new addition to the staff: a young girl who looks after the newspapers and magazines, and occasionally answers the telephone at the reference desk. Her name is Pamela Vecchione—Pam for short. Round face, beady, sparkling eyes—vivacious, cheerful, hoydenish. There is something of the chipmunk and the Bugs Bunny in her. Naive, phenomenally uncomplicated, direct, curious.

"How are you this morning?" she wants to know.
"Not bad, thank you. And you?"
"Rotten."
"Sorry to hear that."
"Oh! I always feel rotten in the morning," she says with one of the sunniest smiles you ever saw.
A little later:
"What are you doing?"—she speaks with her midriff touching my elbow, a hand on my shoulder.
"Reading, writing, a little of everything," I reply.
"Are you a writer?"
With some reluctance, I plead guilty to the charge.
"Are you very famous?"
"Totally unknown."
She couldn't care less and continues her cross-examination with undiminished zeal.
"Have you written any books?"
"Yes, I have."
"How many?"
"Written about forty, forty-five—I've lost count; but published about seven."
"Seven! Wow, that's a lot."

"That's nothing. At my age Simenon had already published 356 books."

"Who is he?"

"A Belgian writer."

"Is he good?"

"One of the best."

"What kind of books does he write?"

"Mostly short novels—60–70 pages long—mysteries, crime stories—"

"Is that what you write too?"

"No."

"What do you write?"

"Specialized works on history and culture, essays, annotated translations—stuff like that. I'm afraid you wouldn't find them very interesting."

"I know an old lady who has written a book but can't find a publisher."

"What's the book about, do you know?"

"A biography."

"Whose?"

"Her grandfather's"

"Who was he?"

"An inventor."

"What did he invent?"

"A farming implement, I think."

"Must have been a fascinating character, eh?"

"I also have a little cousin—eleven years old—who is writing a book."

"What about?"

"He wouldn't say. Last time I asked him, he said it was going to be a best-seller."

"Exactly what I thought too when I wrote my first book, and wasn't hurt so much, as shocked—scandalized!—when it was rejected by forty-eight publishers."

She laughs—a lilting brook, pine trees, blue skies, bird songs, a fox chasing butterflies. . .

"What are you working on today?" Pam wants to know.

"I'm translating a book."

"What's the name of the book?"

"The Island and a Man."

"What is it about?"

"A writer's impressions of an Italian island."

"Good?"

"You bet."

"Who is the writer?"

"Zarian. Gostan Zarian."

"In what language does he write?"

"Armenian."

"Are you Rumanian too?"

"Armenian, yes."

"I've never met an Aramaean before."

That makes two of us, I am tempted to say.

"We are an endangered species," I say instead. "No more than a dozen families in this area."

"Tell me something in your language."

"What would you like me to tell you?"

"How do you say *Hello?*"

"*Parev.*"

"And *Good morning*"?

"*Pari louys.*"

"*Parev!*"Pam says first thing this morning.

"*Pari louys,*" I reply.

"That's *Good morning*, isn't it? I couldn't remember that."

"*Pari louys!*" Pam says first thing this morning.

"*Louys pari.*"

"Didn't I say it right?"

"An Armenian couldn't have done a better job. Are you sure there are no Armenians perched in your family tree somewhere?"

She laughs.

"Don't laugh," I say. "Armenians have been living in Italy since the Middle Ages."

"Well, I'm not exactly Italian," she says, and goes on to explain that her father is only half Italian and that she also has some Indian blood (Cherokee, more precisely), German, French, Hungarian, Irish—.

"Listen, in the Middle Ages, Ireland was practically overrun by Armenian monks," I say, "they built churches there, taught the natives how to carve high crosses and a few other tricks. As for Hungary—we practically ran the joint in the 18th century."

I ask her if she speaks any of the languages of her ancestors.

"Are you kidding?" she says, and wants to know how many other languages I speak "besides English and Rumanian."

"Italian," I say. "I was educated in Italy. Lived there for six years."

"Where in Italy?"

"Venice."

"I've got a problem," Pam informs me. "There is a lady on the phone who wants to know more about a painting she bought in Venice recently."

"What's the name of the painter?"

"Here it is . . . she spelled it for me. Testa. How do you pronounce that?"

"Testadicazzo."

"I can't find him anywhere. Ever heard of him?"

"Many times. He's not a painter actually, but an obscenity—a common insult. Obviously the painting is a cheap fake."

"What do I tell her?"

"She should get a refund."

The Korean is now sporting a mustache—a Hitlerian quadrangle. And when he sits down, he assumes the pose of Rodin's *Thinker*. A perfect image of 20th-century anxiety. Once he tried to grow a beard but changed his mind because he couldn't get an even growth, only sickly tufts here and there.

"How come I never see you in the afternoon?" Pam wants to know.

"I stay home in the afternoon."

"What do you do there?"

"I work with my typewriter—I write, re-write, edit, correct, improve, read—"

"Read?"

"Read, yes."

"You mean to tell me there are books you haven't read yet?"

A little later:

"You work too hard," she tells me. "Why don't you take a coffee break? Shall I get you a cup of coffee? It's no trouble. I don't like the coffee here either, so I bring my own in a thermos. How about it? I can't have all of it. No? Sure?"

Damn it! She *must* have some Armenian blood in her veins.

"Do you write book reviews?" Pam wants to know today.

"Occasionally."

"I enjoy reading book reviews. Have you published any of your reviews in *Time* or *Newsweek*?"

"No, but a literary agent in New York once submitted one of my stories to *Playboy*, and I have several friends who have contributed articles to the *New York Times*."

"It's good to have friends like that. They can help."

"Are you kidding?" I say, making use of one her favorite replies.

"You mean they don't? But why?"

"You may not be aware of this, but writing happens to be a highly competitive business. More so than business. In business you risk only your capital. In writing much more is involved."

"Someday, if you get to be a famous writer and any of them asks for your help—"

"I'll say, *Are you kidding?*"

"Right!"

Now I feel like a Mafia don. I have a consigliere.

More conversations with Pam.

"How many books have you translated so far?"

"About fifteen, but published only five."

"I would like to read them."

"You like reading?"

"Very much, yes."

"What kind of books?"

"I like lots of dialogue."

"In that case you should read Saroyan—William Saroyan."

"Who is he?"

"Was."

"Dead?"

"May he rest in peace."

"Was he good?"

"When he was young."

"What happened to him when he got old?"

"That's the problem—he never did."

"Which one of his books should I read?"

"*My Name Is Aram, Mama I Love You, Papa You're Crazy.*"

"Is he a Rumanian writer?"

"American of Rumanian origin—I meant to say *Armenian.* There is a difference, you know."

"Is there?"

"Rumania is in Europe, Armenia in the Caucasus, as for Aramaea, I don't know where the hell that is—or rather was, because Aramaeans are extinct."

She gives me a sad, confused look, as if to say, The world is a complicated place, isn't it? To console her, I say: "There are those who maintain that in a few years we, Armenians, will join the Aramaeans." As if to say, That should simplify matters somewhat.

"I read one of your books last night," Pam informs me this morning, after the usual exchange of *pari louys/louys pari.* "It's not true that you are totally unknown, like you said. On the cover it says you are—"

"Don't believe everything you read on covers. People who compose blurbs don't, as a rule, take an oath. And I'll let you in on another professional secret. Very often, these blurbs are written by the writers themselves."

"No!"

"Yes."

"I don't believe you."

"On my honor."

"You're putting me on."

"Publishers, you see, can't afford to have someone else do the job, so they ask the writer—it saves time and money. I tell you it's a racket."

A little later:

"How's the translation coming along?" she wants to know.

"It's *finito*. All I have to do now is write the introduction and commentary."

"What are you going to work on after that?"

"I'm not sure. Maybe a novel."

"That sounds interesting. What kind of novel?"

"Probably something autobiographical—my daily existence, characters I meet, conversations I have."

"Am I going to be in it too?"

"Would you like to?"

"No."

"Why not?"

"Because I don't say anything smart."

"You say that because you haven't yet read Saroyan."

"Who else is going to be in the book?"

"My mother will probably play a prominent role."

"What about your wife?"

"I don't have one."

"Do you live with your mother then?"

"That's right."

"She must be proud of you, eh?"

"I am a constant source of embarrassment to her."

"Why do you say that?"

"She keeps telling me to give up writing and go into some other line of work."

"Like what?"

"Anything, anything—teaching, insurance, Oriental rugs, selling crap to shit. . . I meant, selling used cars."

"What made you decide to become a writer anyway?"

"Hard to say. Probably a combination of several factors, among them morbid shyness, an early contact with the 19th-century Russians, insatiable curiosity, utter poverty, masochism and assorted perversions."

The accomplishment that I value most, as a matter of fact, is not my literary work, but the fact that at the age of thirty, without anyone's help, and against the wishes of those nearest to me, I declared my financial independence and decided to devote the rest of my life to reading, writing, music, meditation, and similar unprofitable pursuits. I was able to do this not so much by saving money (of which I made very little) but by reducing my needs almost to zero. Since I have always detested waste, it was not difficult for me to accomplish that feat. I cannot to this day, for example, discard a piece of paper on which there is enough blank space to write a single sentence. Whenever, during my walks, I see a mangled stub of pencil in the gutter, I pick it up without a moment's hesitation. Pencil and paper: they are, after all, the sacred tools of my trade and I value them in the same way that a concert violinist values his Stradivarius. I am also aware of the fact that I am not the only writer on earth who goes to such extremes of frugality and fanaticism. Some of the letters I receive from fellow writers, mostly of Armenian origin, seem to have been written at a time when they had completely run out of regular stationery. I have even received hurriedly scribbled and hardly legible pencil jottings on torn newspaper margins and brown wrapping paper. And worse: I have received letters from prosperous merchants and rug dealers—some of them millionaires (according to my friend Shavarsh, who ought to know)—written on pilfered envelopes bearing the crossed-out letterhead of an insurance company or a bank.

Recently, I discussed this phenomenon with Shavarsh, and we decided that there may be a number of plausible explanations. Even when they achieve prosperity, Armenians cannot abandon their habits which were formed in exile and destitution. Wealthy Armenians don't like to flaunt their prosperity because they may become targets to all kinds of organizations and individuals, including writers (who have traditionally been poor and shameless beggars).

"I need your help," they mean to tell you, "but I warn you not to expect anything in return, because I can't even afford decent stationery." They are also afraid that if they treat you with the minimum of courtesy and respect, you may grow too big for your breeches. There is an often-used Armenian expression (probably of Ottoman origin): *martou degh trav,* literally, "he treated him as if he were a human being"—meaning, he flattered and spoiled him to death. Which may explain why whenever Armenians get together, they spend a good portion of their time and energy in insulting one another. It is their way of saying: "I love you, but I don't want to spoil you. You are good, but you can do better— provided of course you follow instructions."

Which is the greatest insult of all: the assumption that they know everything there is to know about you, they know better, they can solve all your problems in a matter of seconds, and only a hopeless ignoramus, an utter fool, or a stubborn ingrate would reject their advice.

We form cabals not so much against the world (most of which isn't even aware of our own existence) or against our enemies (who, fully aware of our weakness and fragmentation, can afford to ignore us, and they have successfully ignored us during the last seventy years), but against our fellow Armenians. When laboratory rats are enclosed within a cage, they bite, mangle, and maim one another. It is the same with us. Take a closer look at members of any one of our organizations (be it political or cultural) or even better, join one (provided you have the health of a horse, the vitality of an alligator, and the nerves of a hippopotamus) and you will observe that they all operate in a vacuum of anxiety compounded by a veritable mafia of conflicts, misunderstandings, fallacies, and prejudices. They become so absorbed in resolving these conflicts that they inevitably forget their ultimate goal. Whenever something is accomplished, it is done so against the will of the majority and through the initiative of a single individual (which may explain why so many of our schools, libraries, and community centers bear the name of a single individual).

7:30 AM. Another day has begun. I stand before the kitchen window with a cup of steaming black coffee in my hand. Outside, two black squirrels chase each other on the white snow and with satanic speed zigzag up the gray trunk of the neighbor's maple.

"Look at that man over there," I hear Mother saying from her corner in the living room. "Poor man has been waiting there in the cold now for over half an hour. His friend, who drives him to work every morning, is late today. He should have let him know he wasn't going to be on time. Some people are so thoughtless and inconsiderate. Animals! The poor man is freezing. Why is he waiting there anyway? Why doesn't he go back inside?"

Completely oblivious to this drama, a shaggy, dark-brown German shepherd patrols the street on a comfortable trot.

Our living room window is like a television screen to my mother. The least insignificant occurrence attracts her watchful eye and elicits her commentary. "Look at that!" she will say at least once a day. "Nobody. Nothing moves. A dead city. Cursed be the day we decided to settle here!"

The telephone rings.

"My name is Assadour Kilimian," the voice says. "I'm calling you from New York. Perhaps you've heard of me."

"Yes, of course," I lie.

The voice goes on to inform me that he is the author of a highly acclaimed novel about the Armenian Genocide (and here he mentions a couple of eminent critics who have done the acclaiming) and wonders whether I would be interested in translating it into English.

"Well, I'm not sure if I can" I say. "At the moment, I'm—"

"It is not for my own profit and glory that I ask you to do this," he stresses, "but so that odars will know what actually transpired in 1915. There has been some talk about a movie adaptation," he adds, dangling the inevitable carrot (I have had so many carrots dangled before my nose that any day now I will grow a long tail and ears). "But if that fails, a television series similar to Roots and Masada is a distinct possibility."

Next, he will try to impress me with his contacts, I say to myself.

"I have been in contact with a number of agents and producers here," he goes on, "and they are definitely interested. It goes without saying that a percentage of the royalties will go to my translator."

"That sounds great!" I say, assuming the stance and accent of a simple-minded yokel who has been bamboozled into buying the Brooklyn Bridge. "And you think I can do justice to your work?"

"Well, let me be frank about that. I asked a few people here and there before calling you and they were all unanimous in saying that if it is done, it should be done by you."

"How nice of them. And how good of you to trust their judgment."

There was a time when this type of call would annoy, irritate, and depress me for days. But no more. I can now handle them with the chilling nonchalance of a telephone operator and the cool apathy of a Sicilian hitman.

"By the way, have you read the book?" he wants to know next.

"I regret to say."

"I'll send you a copy."

"I'll look forward to it."

"Who was on the phone?" Mother says.

"A famous Armenian writer."

"*Another* one. What did he want?"

"The usual."

"Not again! And what did you tell him?"

"I considered it an honor and a privilege—words to that effect."

"Why don't you tell them to peddle their garbage somewhere else?"

In defense of her exploited and misunderstood son, Mother sometimes exhibits an extraordinary instinct for the jugular.

"Because I'm not a sadist," I say.

"But they have to find out sooner or later."

"Most of them are in their seventies and eighties. Maybe they'll drop dead and will be spared the pain. Besides, why should I be the bearer of bad tidings?"

Three days later, Kilimian's 786-page long Genocide novel arrives by special delivery. I read the first paragraph and put it aside.

Once, I remember, a writer called me from his deathbed. I couldn't even understand what he was saying. There were more rattles than intelligible words in his speech. Next day he died. I learned of this fact a couple of weeks later in the obituary column of our weeklies. He was ninety-eight years old. An insurance executive and an agha-baba of some eminence. It seems he wanted me to translate his last unpublished autobiographical novel, which I received shortly thereafter in a large box as heavy as a tombstone—over a thousand pages, small typeface, very narrow margins.

Until I reached the age of thirty, I hardly knew any writers. Once, many years ago, in the 1950s, I saw the Russian writer Ilya Ehrenburg in Athens, delivering an impassioned anti-imperialist speech to an audience of left-wingers, who cheered and applauded each sentence he spoke. "We are not against the type of hooligan who likes to put his feet on a desk," he said at one point, and after a dramatic pause added: "so long as it's his own desk." At this the audience roared. He spoke in Russian, with short, staccato sentences which a translator standing beside him on the stage rendered into Greek. It was a masterful performance. There was something lean, mangy, and aggressive about him. The soft-spoken, avuncular image he projects in his memoirs *Men, Years—Life* is totally misleading.

About this time I also had a glimpse of William Saroyan when he visited Athens, where, in our churchyard, he delivered a short speech (in excellent Armenian) with a booming voice, saying he was proud to be among fellow Armenians and thanking us on behalf of his children Lucy and Aram (who were with him) for giving them such a warm welcome.

To the names of Ehrenburg and Saroyan I could add those of Diego Valeri (a deservedly neglected Italian poet) and Irving Layton (a minor Canadian versifier), who delivered a lecture in our public library once—an informal, casual, almost improvised affair during which he reminisced, quoted Nietzsche, read some of his poems, made a few humorous and risqué remarks. (About a year later I saw him deliver the same lecture on educational television: the same poems, wisecracks, and Nietzsche quotations, down to the minutest detail. Saw Layton again last night on a talk show, in transit, for a second or two, as I was traveling from one channel to another during a commercial break, and I heard him say: "God has given all men assholes!"—an original as well as a poetic line that!)

In thirty years then, I met only these four writers. But during the last seven years—ever since, that is, I began contributing reviews and translations to a number of English-language Armenian weeklies in Canada and the United States—I have hardly met anyone who has not written or is not busy writing a book. It is no exaggeration to say that with one or two exceptions, all my correspondents are now writers—poets, novelists, historians, playwrights, biographers, scholars, journalists. They are all, as a rule, extravagantly generous with praises. Whenever I publish a book, I receive dozens of letters from them saying they enjoyed every single line. None of them says anything in print, however. But whenever *they* come out with a book, they expect, nay they *demand,* that I review it—make it, *praise* it. And praise it *highly.* Self-centered, ambitious, aggressive, ruthless, single-minded, Machiavellian.

My old friend Shavarsh Markarian drops in to see me. As an active member in a number of Armenian organizations, Shavarsh travels a great deal, and since I live not far from the highway leading to the United States, I see him more or less regularly. Well informed, shrewd, curious about his fellow men, he knows everybody who is somebody in our communities, in addition to a lot of nobodies, busybodies, gofers, hangers-on, and (to use two of his favorite expressions) parasites and *panchoonies* (literally, have-nothings). Mother likes him, because during his short visits he never fails to make an effort to convince me that my self-imposed isolation is harmful to my career and that I should be more active in our organizations, cultivate personal relationships, deliver speeches and lectures, interview celebrities, travel.

Immediately after we exchange salaams and the customary polite phrases, Shavarsh goes up to my bookcase—as is his habit—and spots Kilimian's Genocide novel.

"You've read this?" he demands.

"Only the first paragraph. You?"

"Not even that much. No one takes that character seriously. A pathetic old fool. The only reason he publishes books is that he doesn't know what to do with his money."

"What's his racket?"

"Retired. Used to be in oriental rugs. Big store on Fifth Avenue. Filthy rich. A millionaire. His sons take care of the business now. He sent forty copies of that book to our community center."

"Unsolicited?"

"Naturally."

"With a bill."

"Of course."

"Did you pay?"

"No way. We can't get rid of them."

"He called me last week. He wants me to translate it into English."

"I heard. And he's spreading the word you said yes."

"A misunderstanding on his part."

"I thought as much."

"Just because I didn't say no, he probably took it as yes."

"Did he offer you any money?"

"Yes, of course. A fraction of the royalties."

"You were touched by his generosity?"

"Almost to tears."

"Next time he calls make it an unequivocal no. Leave no room for doubt. Don't stand on ceremony. Say you're busy or something; you can't talk."

"Exactly what I've been trying to tell him," Mother says.

"And what makes you think he'll take no for an answer?" I say. "Most of these characters take me for a simple-minded farmhand living in a hick town in the middle of nowhere. Why disappoint them and make an enemy in the process? When one of them

recently made a series of absurd statements—the Nobel committee is a Jewish conspiracy, Solzhenitsyn is a Jew, Saroyan achieved
success because he married a Jew, Armenia owes its present
existence to the Russians and we should be grateful to them even
if they try to Russify, Sovietize, and sodomize us—that type of
thing—and I questioned his sources of information, he lost his
temper: *Who the hell do you think you are, talking to me like
that?*—words to that effect. These are Levantines: hard-nosed
businessmen, ruthless, tough, opportunistic, rude. They combine Oriental flattery and Byzantine complexity with Ottoman
cruelty. In a confrontation with them, I'm bound to emerge the
loser."

"Why do you think I keep saying you should play a more active
role in Armenian affairs? If we are at the mercy of people like that,
it's because people like you refuse to get involved."

"I refuse because I've got my own cross to bear. I can't give or
take orders. Pushing and being pushed around—that's not my
line."

"But if you have reason on your side, you don't have to do any
pushing. A few persuasive words should be enough."

"Listen, during the last seven years I have been trying very hard
to persuade my fellow Armenians that I deserve to survive as a
writer, and I haven't gone too far. While in America, Gostan Zarian
tried to persuade his fellow Armenians that they deserve to survive as a creative minority in an ocean of invisible, anonymous,
dollar-grubbing, sex-obsessed, and violent-prone interchange-
able units, and they bundled him off to Soviet Armenia—"

"You can't talk to him," Mother says to Shavarsh.

"I understand what he's saying and I know how he feels,"
Shavarsh says to Mother, then turning to me: "All right, let's forget
about politics for a minute; let's talk about literature, and more
specifically your work. Why do you allow people like Kilimian to
waste your time?"

"My time is not *that* valuable. Besides, I learn something from
them."

"Learn what?"

"Not to be like them. Sometimes they even amuse me. The way
they try to impress with their connections—dangle imaginary
carrots—brag. Kilimian, for instance, told me that the famous
Soviet-Armenian critic and academician Stepan Vladimirovich
Amirkhanian praised his book very highly—called it a masterpiece, a monumental achievement!"

"But how could he? Amirkhanian died three years ago. The

book came out last year. I'm sure Amirkhanian died in 1978 because I was in Yerevan that summer."

"I remember to have read about it in the papers too."

"Well? Did you tell him that?"

"Of course not. If I had, he would have said Amirkhanian (who
happens to be an old childhood friend of his, or perhaps even a
cousin) read the book in manuscript form. For each question,
these characters have a wide repertory of lies. Kilimian also told
me that Ardavast Der Zourikian, 'the foremost literary critic of the
diaspora,' called it the most important novel to be written outside
Armenia during the last twenty-five years, and comparable in
scope to Franz Werfel's *Forty Days of Musa Dagh.*"

"He may have said that and I wouldn't be surprised in the least
if he did. I know Der Zourikian well. Let me tell you a couple of
things about him. He's a born parasite. A shrewd wheeler-dealer
from Smyrna. He edits and publishes his own monthly periodical
in Aleppo. He can be bought. Very easy. Cheap too. I don't
exactly know his rates, but my guess is for twenty dollars he'll
review and praise the trashiest book; for another twenty he'll
compare third-rate verse to Byron, Baudelaire, and Verlaine; add
another ten or twenty and he'll say that if the Nobel committee
ignores you, that's because it is a Jewish conspiracy. You're laughing; you think I'm making all this up. Let me tell you more about
Zourikian, who deserves to be the central character of a satirical
novel, by the way. Beside him Panchoonie is nothing but a clumsy,
loud-mouth meddler. Once, a few years ago, Zourikian traveled
all over the Middle East and Europe in search of new talent—and
he found them. And by pure coincidence, of course, they all
happened to be young, attractive women. In the 1950s, the Central Committee sent him to Paris on national business. On his
return he handed in an expense account that included an entry
called 'Necessary masculine bodily functions'—"

"Trips to the bordello?"

"What else?"

"Soikhat chornar!" I hear Mother muttering in the kitchen,
where she has been busy with the coffee things—an untranslatable Armeno-Turkish curse on an unmentionable part of the male
anatomy.

"You're making that one up of course," I say.

"You wouldn't say that if you decided to come out of your shell
and meet some of these people."

"Afferim deghas!" (Bravo my boy), Mother says to Shavarsh.

"Go on with the Zourikian story," I say. "What happened next?

I'm interested. I may write about this."

"I wish you would. You *should!*"

"If I do, I'll probably be accused of negativism and cynicism. Some of my things have already been rejected because they lack a positive approach. Tell me, did the Central Committee pay up the bordello bills?"

"They threw him out of the party."

"But he maintains he resigned."

"Of course—'because of irreconcilable ideological differences.' "

"That's when he visited Soviet Armenia and wrote that book of his. What was it titled again?"

"*Prometheus Unchained?*"

"Something like that."

"*Lazarus Unleashed?*"

"No."

"*The Armenian Phoenix, Ararat Roars?*"

"Which was translated into Russian and published in Moscow—"

"And was awarded the Lenin Prize."

"Are you sure it was the Lenin?"

"May have been the Mikoyan Prize."

"Never heard of that one."

"It was created especially for him."

Later, on his way out, as we shake hands, he says: "My advice is, if Kilimian calls again, tell him to get lost. If he gets rough, hang up on him. I guarantee you, he won't bother you again."

"*That's it!*" Mother says in English, with a murderous glint in her eyes.

"I have a better idea," I say. "If he calls again, I'll tell him to talk with my literary agent here, *my mother!*"

We all laugh.

Sometimes I like to recount shocking anecdotes from my life in order to share my sense of outrage. Often all I get in return is cheap advice.

Another long-distance telephone call from an Armenian: this time an editor who has written a documentary history of the Genocide (actually a collection of articles that have appeared in the foreign press) and wants me to review it. "No hurry," he reassures me. "End of next month will be fine." When the book arrives, I don't even bother reading the first paragraph.

This editor, I remember, rejected one of my articles once because—in his words—"We prefer a more positive approach."

Whatever that may mean. A man of power does not explain. He dictates. He issues instructions and orders. Only the weak explain, justify, apologize.

A more positive approach.

What's positive about the Genocide? It makes people appreciate their small pleasures and privileges, of course. Remember the way things were in the Ottoman Empire and behold America the Beautiful!

Four days before my father died, the doctor said there was nothing to worry about. "Tell him it's just an infection that should clear up in a week or two," he said. "Tell him to think pleasant thoughts and remember pleasant memories." At the time, my father was in extreme pain and discomfort. His whole body shook uncontrollably. His teeth chattered. He was unable to swallow a single morsel of food. He was dying of starvation. And yet, the instant I translated the doctor's English words into Armenian, his face brightened. I shall always be grateful to that doctor. By lying he consoled a dying man. He gave hope to the hopeless.

Yes, one should lie to a dying man, because the truth may shatter him.

What about us? Is our situation so hopeless that I am urged to spread lies? Everything is just great. There is nothing to worry about. Think pleasant thoughts. Be positive.

But damn it, there *is* something to worry about. We are, after all, on the verge of extinction.

In one of our weeklies I see a photograph of half-a-dozen young men and women unpacking books from cartons. Everyone is wearing a big, contented smile. A happy occasion. The headline reads: BOOK ON ARMENIAN GENOCIDE A BEST-SELLER.

The Genocide has opened up a shop and is doing brisk business. They are interviewing survivors, producing plays, movies, documentaries, memoirs, novels, biographies, and polemics—as if being massacred by the Turks was our most noteworthy achievement. I can imagine the conversation between an Armenian author and the editor of an American publishing conglomerate.

AUTHOR: I'm translating a masterpiece of Armenian literature.
EDITOR: Verse?
AUTHOR: Prose.
EDITOR: Slow items both. How about a book on the massacres—that's where the money is now. Bedoukian's *Urchin*, Arlen's *Passage*, they have been doing real well.

AUTHOR: But I have no direct experience of that tragedy and I'm not a historian.

EDITOR: Maybe you can interview some survivors, pick an incident—something along the lines of the Smyrna fire—add a few dramatic touches, and a couple of footnotes here and there. We'll get a prominent academic to write an introduction and certify its authenticity. What do you say?

AUTHOR: Let me think about it.

EDITOR: I'm prepared to advance two thousand.

AUTHOR: Make it three and you've got yourself a deal.

EDITOR: Twenty-five hundred.

AUTHOR: Twenty-seven fifty.

EDITOR: It's a deal—you Levantine camel trader, you.

America is one vast supermarket. The trick is to find out what sells. After that all you do is mechanize, streamline, computerize, produce, and advertise.

Pam has been avoiding me. I wonder why. She looks grim. I should ask how come, but I don't. When the time comes, she will speak.

Pam decides to speak at last.

"I'm getting married next month," she informs me early this morning, eyes welled up, jaw trembling, forehead glistening with perspiration.

"Wonderful news. Congratulations!"

"You don't have to say anything if you don't want to."

"But I do. I wish you all the best. I'm sure you'll be very happy."

"How do you know?"

"Because I can't imagine you any other way. I think you have a talent for happiness, which is probably the rarest of all gifts. You are privileged indeed. Even when you feel 'rotten,' as you say, you radiate joy. I have known you for almost six months now—"

"Five months."

"—and during that time—"

"—and one week."

"—we never had a tiny disagreement, and I happen to have a mean poisonality—quarrelsome, argumentative."

"That's not true."

"Ask my mother. Very probably I'm the most argumentative person you ever saw. When I have no one to argue with, I argue with myself—fierce, savage arguments that last long into the night. Many times, when my mother comes down from her bedroom in the morning, she wants to know who telephoned last night. 'Nobody,' I tell her. 'Somebody must have called because I heard you talking,' she says. And since I don't want her to worry about me going cuckoo, I say, 'O yeah! that's right, somebody did call—an Armenian writer from Walla Walla, Washington, or Kalamazoo, Michigan, and he said things I didn't agree with so we had an argument.' And then, there is this Jewish friend of mine, a professor of Hebrew, who drops in once in a while to see me. We argue a lot. I contradict everything he says. Sometimes he gets so mad that he tells me, 'I'll never understand why the Turks didn't do a good enough job on you. In their place, I would have been more thorough.' "

"That's mean."

"And I tell him. 'The more I get to know you, the less I dislike Hitler.' "

She laughs. But it's no longer the same open, innocent, sunny laugh with pine trees, bird songs, butterflies, and foxes. There is something deep, dark, Russian, even Dostoevskian, in her expression. She must be in the family way.

Pam has been replaced by a gorgeous blonde—statuesque, Titianesque. Where did she come from? I wonder. Probably imported stock. Doesn't look like local talent. Somehow I can't imagine unspeakably drab surroundings like these to produce such marvels of Praxitelian harmony and symmetry. And what is she doing here? Slumming? She should be in Hollywood or in some principality like Monaco. First time I smiled at her, she looked past me; second time she smiled back—only a hint of a smile, mind you; cool, impersonal, no eye contact, as if to say, I don't mix with riff-raff; don't get any ideas; I'm trying to be civil, that's all.

"How is the protection racket?" I ask Margaret Peters (alias Makrouhi Hadji-Bedrossian), the former teacher and present insurance agent. She drops in more or less regularly at the library these days to do her paperwork.

A telephone call from a writer in Boston who informs me he has written a play that he would like me to translate into English.

"Has the play been published?" I inquire.

"Not yet."

"Produced?"

"No. Armenians won't touch it because it isn't the usual crap about Vartan Mamikonian, Mesrob Mashtots, and Mt. Ararat."

"What is it about?"

"Contemporary life—the new generation, violence, sex, drugs, Freud, psychoanalysis."

"Wonderful!"

"I'm sure you'll like it."

"And what do we do with it after we translate it?"

"Sell it to Broadway."

"You think they'll buy?"

"They'll grab."

"What if they don't?"

"What do you mean?"

"There is always the possibility, you know; I mean, you can never be sure about these things. My first manuscript was rejected by fifty-two publishers."

"Let me worry about that angle, okay? I have contacts. My brother-in-law is an off-Broadway director—Steve Anthony—you may have heard of him. I also have a cousin who is a professional actor—Mike Atamian. I'm sure you've seen him on TV. He has made a couple of commercials, one of which is with Peter Ustinov."

Armenian commandos have assassinated another Turkish diplomat. Headlines in the newspapers with the inevitable references to the "alleged" Genocide of 1915. Also professionally crafted letters to the editor by Turkish embassy officials seething with righteous indignation and charging the Armenians with the cold-blooded murder of as many as two million defenseless Turkish civilians (no, not two, but three million, states another authoritative Turkish source) during World War I. In another article, a young Turkish historian is quoted as having said that during the war, a limited number of Ottoman subjects of Armenian origin had wanted to emigrate and that the government had cooperated by providing them with an armed escort, but that during this mass exodus a small number of people had inevitably perished—mostly sickly old men and women who would have died anyway even if they had stayed home—and that Armenians all over the world were now exploiting these isolated incidents to publicize their absurd claim over territories that have rightfully belonged to the Turks and their ancestors, the Hittites, for over fifteen millenia. Also the inevitable letter by the born-again Armenian deploring terrorism, quoting the New Testament, and preaching forgiveness and love.

My Jewish friend (the professor of Hebrew) who likes to maintain that all Armenians are racists (because of their dislike of Turks) is outraged. "Don't they (the Turks) realize that by lying they are provoking more terrorist attacks? How can they be so naive?"

"They know what they are doing," I try to explain. "One should never underestimate the cunning of Turks. Besides, lying comes naturally to a nation with a genocide on its conscience—especially if it has no conscience in the Judaeo-Christian sense of the word. Because these are the type of primitive Moslems who think murdering giaours is a religious duty—something to brag about among themselves. And suppose for the sake of argument they were to admit their guilt: *that* wouldn't be the end of their troubles, but the beginning; because next, they would have to surrender vast territories and pay reparations in millions, perhaps even billions of dollars, and they are already on the brink of economic ruin. As for provoking more terrorist attacks: let's not get hysterical about this. Armenian terrorism is one big joke. Lurid sensationalism. Media blitz. Sixty victims in seventy years. Nickels and dimes. Peanuts. Mickey mouse stuff. Turks themselves kill more Turks in a single week. Sometimes the Israelis kill more PLOs and Arabs in a single hour."

"Whenever people find out I'm Armenian," Margaret (Hadji-) Peters tells me this morning at the library before I have had a chance to make a comment on the weather and inquire after the state of the protection racket, "they want to know why we are killing innocent people because of something that happened seventy years ago—people who weren't even born in 1915 for chrissake! What can I tell them? I am ashamed of being an Armenian. Those terrorists are ruining our image. Everybody now thinks we are a gang of bloodthirsty cut-throats, and I don't blame them. What the hell is the matter with our organizations anyway? Why don't they do something about it? If they can't stop it, why don't they at least make public statements to the media and let the whole world know once and for all that this small band of fanatics and crazy hoodlums from the Middle East do not represent the vast majority of hardworking and law-abiding Armenians?"

She goes on and on in this vein for quite some time. At one point I try to explain that *odars* in their own slums murder more people in a single week than all the Turks allegedly shot by Armenians during the last seventy years.

"Are you trying to justify the actions of this lunatic fringe?" she demands with a startled look in her eyes, as though I were myself a terrorist with sinister designs on her life and limb.

"I was just trying to point out," I say in an effort to reassure her, "that when it comes to terror, violence, bloodshed, and related atrocities, we Armenians are just a bunch of amateurs in a land of accomplished pros, and that as an Armenian, you have no reason to feel shame."

She is against terrorism because she thinks it is bad for business (at one point she spoke of a friend of hers who had refused to eat in an Armenian restaurant because, she had explained, she did not want to subsidize terror).

"Cheer up!" I tell her. "Now your clients may think twice before missing a premium payment. Who knows, we may even end up developing some kind of protection racket of our own."

"Very funny!"

The telephone rings. I answer it. Wrong number. After I hang up, I hear Mother's voice asking: "Who was it?"

"Nobody," I reply.

Then I go back to my typewriter—to kill time more than anything else. Because after a while, writing becomes a habit that is easier to keep than to give up.

The telephone rings again. I answer it.

"Wrong number again." I say to Mother after I hang up. And I reflect that even when, on those rare occasions, people know what they want, they don't always know how to get it.

Essays, Reminiscences
and Polemics

Portrait of a Genius

HE LOVED MUSIC, but he did not compose.

He loved books, but as far as I know he never wrote a single line for publication.

He was passionately interested in history, mathematics, politics, the sciences, but was not active in any of these fields.

His name was Vahe Esmeryan and he was a genius.

He himself never used that word.

Whenever he wanted to praise a man he admired, he would say: "He's a good man, a man you can trust."

"A hard worker" was another term of approval.

But a hard worker that could not be trusted was dismissed as "a mental masturbator."

I first met him when I was fifteen and he was in his early thirties. The wonderful thing about meeting a good man during one's formative years is that forever after you are not taken in by counterfeits.

Esmeryan taught me that it is easier to be honest than dishonest, because to be dishonest with any degree of success one must have an excellent memory and a mind that combines the functions of a calculating machine with those of a dictionary.

He himself was so removed from everyday, frivolous preoccupations like gossip, profit, greed, vanity, that evil ceased to be a temptation and became simply irrelevant.

He taught me that ideas are not abstractions invented by writers of books. Ideas, he said, surround our daily existence and animate our habits, and consequently each one of our acts, from the most petty to the most heroic. Wars, for example, are ideas in motion— bad ideas!

He taught me that even the most complex philosophical systems evolve from a vision that may last only a fraction of a second.

To understand a philosopher, however, it was not enough to share his vision, but to see the political actions that this vision aimed at.

When Charles Peguy said that "Everything begins in mysticism and ends in politics," he was saying the same thing.

But where Peguy saw corruption and degeneration in this process from mysticism to politics, and from ideals to concrete political actions, Esmeryan saw development.

If a writer's message was misunderstood or ignored, that was because it deserved to be.

A misunderstood message, he said, was like an important letter sent to the wrong man. One had no choice but to be as careful in writing the address on the envelope as the message in the letter.

The function, the *raison d'être* of an idea was to serve reality, and not to exist somewhere between heaven and earth, like a useless Platonic cloud.

But I think the most important thing Esmeryan taught me was to approach an idea, any idea, not with the question "Is it right or wrong?" but "Is it right for me?" or is it right for someone else (who may be my enemy) or some institution (the very institution that may be out to dehumanize and exploit me)?

In the many books that I have read from Abelard and Bachelard to Weil and Wittgenstein, I have never come across this notion expressed with the same directness and total absence of academic double-talk.

Esmeryan taught me other things, sometimes without having said a single word on the subject.

He taught me, for example, that one should never confuse fame with greatness.

Once Emerson boasted that most branches of learning were taught at Harvard. "Yes indeed," Thoreau is reported to have commented, "all the branches and none of the roots."

I suppose what Esmeryan did for me was to make me aware of the existence of these roots.

During our first conversation, I remember, he struck me as humorless and arrogant.

It took me several years to realize that the purpose of a conversation was not to flatter the other's vanity, but to eliminate falsehood and to take a step forward in the direction of truth.

Yes, I learned to appreciate him very slowly. He was so different from anyone I had known until then that my mind required a few years to adjust to the change.

In a letter he wrote a year before he died, he said: "The older I grow the more reasons I find for avoiding my fellow men. But I shouldn't complain. Things could have been much worse . . ."

Without him, I know, my life would have been unbearable—like a labyrinth without an exit.   (1975)

Intolerance

"THE TURKS," a well-informed friend of mine informs me, "are the transmitters of an extraordinarily rich cultural heritage—an admission made only *infrequently* by Western books of history, and *never* by Armenians, who ought to know better."

This well-informed friend of mine is one of those fierce liberals who cannot tolerate any kind of intolerance. He likes to boast of the fact that, though of Jewish background, he is fond of German music—in his own words: "I love Bach, Beethoven, Brahms, Bruckner, and all the rest of those Bs and sons of b.'s"

"The Turks," my friend goes on, "built a great empire which lasted over seven centuries."

As an assimilated American-Jew, he is more American than Jew, more pragmatist than idealist, more man of action than man of the Book. He has a secret preference for explorers, generals, empire builders, guerrilla fighters, statesmen, rather than prophets, preachers, mystics, and poets. On one or two occasions he has even gone as far as expressing pro-Palestinian and anti-Israeli views—all in the name of fair play and justice, of course.

"To call the Turks barbarians, as you do, is racist!" he concludes.

"You like music, do you not?" I ask.

"I do, yes. You know that very well. Would you mind explaining the non sequitur?"

"Please, indulge me."

"If you insist."

"What type of music do you like best?" I ask.

"I don't make distinctions; I like all good music—baroque, classic, romantic, modern, neo-classic, post-modern, atonal, jazz, avant-garde."

"That's very commendable of you."

"Get to the point, please."

"I assume you like opera also."

"Very much."

"Now then, name a single, good Turkish opera."

"No comment."

"Name a single Turkish symphonic poem, concerto, ballet suite."

". . . ."

"What about a piano sonata or an organ prelude and fugue? String quartet? A little waltz? A bagatelle? What, not even a little bagatelle?"

"Get to the punchline."

"Am I to assume that your knowledge of Turkish music is defective?"

"An expert in the field I'm not, obviously."

"You can say that again, brother. I hope your knowledge of Turkish literature is better. You must have read at least one good Turkish novel."

"I haven't, no."

"You disappoint me. What about a short story?"

"No."

"A little poem? Not even a little poem? Well, well, are we to assume that your knowledge of Turkish literature is not much better than your knowledge of Turkish music? Are you in fact acquainted with a single Turkish contribution to Western civilization—a painting, a scientific treatise, a mathematical formula, a philosophic theory, a political manifesto, a film?"

"Enough!"

"No further questions."

(1976)

Only in America

AT THE PUBLIC LIBRARY, where I spend a couple of hours every morning reading, researching, and writing, and where I am regarded as a harmless eccentric who keeps writing books that never get published, I am approached by a woman in her early thirties who wants to know if I am a writer. "The girl at the information desk told me you might be able to help me," she adds.

I promise to do my best.

"I want to write a book," she explains, "but I have no idea how to go about it, where to start—where do *you* start?"

Where else would anyone dare to ask such a question? Not that it is a bad question. Beginnings are never easy—and not just for beginners. Even Tolstoy had serious problems with the beginning of *Anna Karenina*.

"Sometimes you begin at the end," I tell her, "sometimes in the middle, but seldom if ever at the beginning." Make it Zen-simple, I say to myself. We live in a democracy where everyone has a right to know, understand, and make it to the top.

She nods. She wants more—straight from the horse's mouth.

"That's one of the fundamental laws of writing," I pontificate, feeling more like a jackass. "The important thing is to work, steadily, daily. When you contemplate the writing of a book, everything seems so impossible. But once you get down to work, difficulties and problems are overcome with astonishing ease. What kind of book did you have in mind, by the way—fiction or non-fiction?"

"Non-fiction."

"First, you read a few books on the subject—to find out what has already been written. I assume you are interested in making an original contribution to the field."

"There are no books on the subject."

"Choose a similar subject then—what is it exactly, may I ask?"

"The northern regions of Canada."

"Siberia."

"No, Canada!"

"I meant, read a few books on Siberia and choose the methodology that suits you best; devote separate sections to the history and exploration of the region, climate, flora and fauna, and of course endangered species, ecology—that's where the money is now. You can, if you wish, devote a separate chapter to individual species of birds, mammals, insects, also vegetation; and if you intend to write about the natives, I suggest you read a few texts on ethnology with particular emphasis on Indians and Eskimos. Above all, don't read a book on how to write a book—they are, as a rule, manufactured by complete mediocrities. Follow your instinct. Don't be afraid to break rules. The more rules you break, the better."

She nods, smiling. A born anarchist. She'll go far—mark my words!

"If you prefer the more immediate and personal approach as opposed to the comprehensive, academic treatment outlined above, I suggest you make it a travel diary or notebook. In that case Thoreau is your man. Read his diaries—he's generally regarded as the master of this particular genre. Don't be surprised, however, if you fail to find a publisher. Writing a book can be a lot of fun; but publishing it, that's a different ballgame—more like Chinese torture in fact—the death of a thousand cuts."

"How many books have you written?"

"About a dozen, maybe more—I've lost count; or rather given up counting."

"Fiction or non-fiction?"

"Both, also collections of plays and poems."

"How many have you published?"

"None."

"How come?"

"My stuff lacks commercial value—or so they tell me."

"They who?"

"Editors, publishers—"

"How many of them have you contacted?"

"Quite a few."

"You shouldn't give up!"

Great! She's giving *me* advice now.

"If you mean I shouldn't give up writing, I assure you, I don't intend to. What I was trying to convey is that there is more to writing a book than just writing it. That's only step number one—sometimes the easiest and most enjoyable, too. I remember when I went into the writing business, I thought all a writer has to do is write; the rest—meaning publication, fame, fortune—would follow as night follows day. Sometimes it does of course, but not always. More often than not you work for many years and all you end up with is a thick collection of rejection slips—mine is already as thick as *War and Peace* and *The Brothers Karamazoff* combined. But I do hope you'll have better luck. I'm sure you will!"

"What makes you say that?"

"Your approach, your manner of doing things. When in doubt, ask! I should have done that myself years ago, instead of going into it blindly, naively."

Some irrelevant chitchat follows. But I can tell she is anxious to leave.

She'll probably look for a published writer now, find him, pump him dry, go north and a year hence produce a best-seller and live happily and prosperously ever after.

(1976)

Fame and Fortune

A FRIEND OF MINE has written a story and wants me to read it. He is anxious to know what I think of it. I tell him it's good. (Like all first efforts, it stinks.) But I tell him it's okay because at this point he is in need of encouragement, not criticism. I also remind myself that once, shortly after a friend told me what he really thought of my first short story, I lost all interest in both his judgment and friendship. I decide therefore to sacrifice truth (which in cases like this is more or less relative anyway) on the altar of friendship—in short, to lie.

"It's surprisingly good!" I repeat.

"Don't you think it's too long?" he says, refusing to leave well enough alone.

"I don't think so, no," I persevere.

"Maybe it's too short?"

"Listen, there is nothing wrong with its length."

"I think so, too," he says. "As a matter of fact, I think it's a great story. I have read it many times and I can't believe *I* wrote it. I didn't know I had it in me. And I'm glad you agree with my assessment."

At this point I begin to feel like Dr. Frankenstein who has brought forth a monster with pronounced narcissistic tendencies.

"Tell me, I want your honest opinion," he goes on; "don't you think it's one of the best things you ever read?"

That's going too damn far and I try to put an end to the nonsense.

"Forget it," I tell him; "you wrote it, it's all right, it's done. Now, write another."

"I would like to have this one published first. Would you recommend an editor? You have been in this game longer than I have; you're familiar with the territory."

Game, territory—he's already speaking like a duke about to enter his domain. Very patiently I explain what sooner or later he's bound to find out for himself—namely, that editors are generally regarded by writers all over the world as scarcely human and that they belong to an entirely separate, undefinable species whose behavior is impossible to classify and predict. He and I and the rest of the world may love a story, but that doesn't necessarily mean that a single editor among a thousand will agree to publish it. "Submit the story to a few editors," I tell him, "and see what develops. In the meantime however, get busy writing other stories. Forget about this one—it belongs to [at this point, I check myself in time and replace the word *wastepaper basket* with] posterity." And for once I begin to feel some degree of empathy for editors (a development that until now I would never have thought in the realm of possibilities).

"Does it make any sense for me to start writing stories at my age?" he wants to know. He is in his thirties but has learned very little from life. He does not realize that to be a writer one must work as hard as a surgeon or a mathematician. Even insurance salesmen have to go through a period of apprenticeship.

"Do you enjoy writing?" I ask.

"Of course I do."

"Then write and rejoice!"

"But I enjoy doing a lot of other things as well."

"In that case you should do what you like doing best."

"I don't know what I like doing best."

"Wait until you find out then."

"I'm thirty-six years old. I can't afford waiting. That's why I asked you. What do *you* think I should do?"

"What I think isn't worth a damn."

"But I respect your views."

"*I* don't! and I don't think you should either. Important decisions like this one should be made in the solitary confinement of one's soul."

"But suppose I were to dedicate my life to literature; do you think I have a chance to succeed?"

"Now you're talking about something else."

"Am I?"

"From writing and literature you suddenly switched to fame and fortune—a complete non sequitur if I ever heard one."

"What have you got against fame and fortune?"

"Nothing, I assure you. They are lovely things to have, as a matter of fact. Sometimes I have the audacity to daydream about them myself. But if you're going to write with that end in mind, you might as well go into something else—"

"Like what?"

"Business, for instance."

"I hate business."

"How about politics?"

"I hate politics even more."

"Crime, then."

I'm afraid I can't tell you what happened next because shortly after this conversation my friend lost interest in both my judgment and friendship.

(1976)

Relevant Questions

I T TOOK ME fifteen years to find an answer to the following question: Can a man from the lower classes (make it lower depths) who likes reading, listening to music, taking long walks (as unprofitable an occupation as the other two), meditating (ditto), can a man who likes these things but who loathes business and what is generally known as making a living ever hope to get out of the rat race? To put it in other words: Is it possible for a slum-dweller who is indifferent to money to acquire enough of it to avoid the need for hard or unpleasant work?

To be accurate, although I was tormented by this question on an existential level—that is to say every single moment of my life—I never put it in so many words. I did not dare to.

I did not dare to because I did not think of it as a relevant question. In my view, to be relevant, a question had to have been asked, and thus certified, by an eminent thinker.

For fifteen years I was tormented by a question that I dismissed as irrelevant because neither Plato nor Tolstoy nor, for that matter, Buddha, Thomas Mann, Nabokov, and Wittgenstein had ever raised it. Books were my opium until I read Thoreau.

What I value in Thoreau is his love for commonplace details: things that happen every day to all of us—walking, eating, surviving in a hostile world without degrading oneself. Thoreau made me realize that the necessities of life can be obtained at a trifling cost. That wisdom consists in being independent. It was Thoreau who made me ask the relevant question "How much money do I really need?" I made a list of the things I needed, and to my astonishment I noticed that most of the items in the list were not necessities but luxuries. (What is a luxury? Answer: Anything that is not bread and books.) Also to my astonishment I realized that during these fifteen years I had saved enough money to be financially independent. The feeling of exhilaration I then experienced was similar to the one described by Molière in *Le Bourgeois Gentilhomme*, when Monsieur Jourdain suddenly discovers that he has been speaking prose all his life without knowing it. This happened five years ago, and during these five years I have lived happily, as in a dream, reading, listening to music, meditating, taking long walks, and sometimes writing.

If you want to know more on this subject, read Thoreau. He is your man. Not Tolstoy or Wittgenstein, for whom the problem of financial independence was irrelevant. Disgusted with their own wealth, these two gentlemen (like Buddha, another millionaire!) chose voluntary poverty. Not destitution, which is a curse, but voluntary poverty, which is a blessing and a luxury *only* the very rich can afford.

(1976)

Them and Us

G REEKS DIVIDED MANKIND into two camps: Greeks and barbarians. They still do. Some myths, like some habits, die hard.
Perhaps myths are nothing but mental habits, and almost always
bad ones. Greeks, however, are not the only people who suffer
from this type of egocentricity. Despite the frequency and ferocity
of civil wars, most nationalists divide mankind into two: them and
us. We all have our own unflattering descriptive terms—*giaour,
goy, gringo, gay*—to cover with contempt all those who don't
happen to be lucky enough to find themselves on our side of the
fence.

The French anthropologist Claude Lévi-Strauss in his *The Raw
and the Cooked* says that the human mind, whether it be Aristotle's mind or the mind of a Brazilian Indian, functions according to
the same laws and logic. Wittgenstein would have agreed. He
once said that philosophers went about their business like "savages, primitive people."

Following the example of Hegel, who divided men into masters
and slaves, Marx divided them into exploiters and the exploited.
We now know that when the exploited turn into exploiters, they
become the cruelest of masters—compare Stalin with Ivan the
Terrible.

Freud divided men into the well adjusted and the neurotic,
although he himself, having witnessed Hitler's New Order, must
have known that sometimes to be well adjusted means to adjust
oneself to an insane social order. Bertrand Russell once confessed
that of the reality or unreality of the mystic's world he knew
nothing. That did not stop him from writing *Mysticism and Logic,*
in which he viewed the scientific and mystical impulses in men as
mutually exclusive and contradictory, completely disregarding the
fact that some of the most outstanding scientists have also been
mystics: Pythagoras, Pascal, and Teilhard de Chardin are cases in
point. Wittgenstein himself, who was one of Russell's students,
was a mystic as well as a logician.

Koestler, in his *The Yogi and the Commissar,* divided people
into men of action and men of contemplation, ignoring the fact

that some of the most bloodthirsty men of action were men of contemplation: Muhammed, Shamyl of the Caucasus, the Mahdi of Sudan. Sartre's dictum "Hell is other people" is a late and acute case, a *reductio ad absurdum*, of this "them and us" attitude.

In our own day, Erik Erikson, one of Freud's most brilliant disciples, has gone so far as to say that all groups (nations, classes, tribes, or castes) are in fact dangerous "pseudo species" that maintain their own uniqueness by dehumanizing others. Each of these groups enforces a "normality" which may, in fact, be sick.

All efforts at dividing mankind into distinct camps are, it seems to me, disguised and unconscious attempts to avoid making the most difficult of all distinctions: between that which is good and that which is evil. The distinction is difficult because the moment we recognize and define evil we shall have to also recognize the evil that is within us, and *that* is the most unbearable of all confrontations.

(1976)

Satori

THE GREEK WORD *ecstasy* (literally, standing outside oneself) has lost some of its original meaning. *Satori,* its Japanese equivalent, has not yet suffered through long usage the same degree of distortion. *Satori* is an intense, blinding, white heat moment, totally unexpected, pure gold. The veil is torn away and the world rises before one's eyes as if out of nothingness, and one sees it at last in all its original, irresistible splendor. One understands, or, in the words of a contemporary scientist, one acquires "an intimate insight into a grand design."

To psychologists, it is a religious experience; to religious scholars, it is a mystic experience. It has been called many things by many people—oceanic moment, a state of cosmic consciousness, enlightenment, awakening (to emphasize the fact that ordinary consciousness, in comparison, is opaque, like a curtain of sleep), conversion (an act whereby "God turns a man inside out like a glove," in Jacques Maritain's beautiful phrase). It has been experienced by believers and non-believers alike.

There is a description of such a moment near the end of Dostoevsky's *Crime and Punishment.* It happens to Raskolnikov, a murderer: "It came over him like a fit," Dostoevsky writes. "Everything in him softened at once and the tears started into his eyes. He fell to the earth on the spot. . . . He knelt down in the middle of the square, bowed down to the earth, and kissed that filthy earth with bliss and rapture."

Though he lacked Dostoevsky's deep religious faith, Marcel Proust describes a similar occurrence at the beginning of his *Remembrance of Things Past.* "At once the vicissitudes of life had become indifferent to me," we read here, "its disasters innocuous, its brevity illusory. I had ceased now to feel mediocre, accidental, mortal."

And Jean-Paul Sartre, an atheist, in his first novel, *Nausea,* writes: "I had this vision. It took my breath away. When I believed I was thinking about *existence,* I was thinking *nothing,* my head was empty, or there was just one word in my head, the word *'being.'* " (My italics.)

119

It is the insight acquired in these extraordinary and marvelous moments that animates Proust's masterpiece and Sartre's magnum opus, *Being and Nothingness*. (Note how the three key words—*existence, being, nothing*—occur in the short passage quoted above.)

A similar experience, however, put a sudden end to the writing career of St. Thomas Aquinas, who is said to have declared: "Everything I have written seems to me straw—compared with the vision I have had."

Such visions give one a sense of being a privileged agent between the eternal and the temporal, of having the gift of prophecy, of understanding all mysteries, and of possessing all knowledge. It was such a vision that metamorphosed Muhammed from an obscure desert trader to a prophet, great political leader and warrior—the first of a long line of bloodthirsty Muslim prophet-warriors, two of the best known of whom are the Mahdi of Sudan and Shamyl the Avar of Dagestan.

Perhaps it is this dangerous, this sinister aspect of mysticism that has led some mystics to view their privileged visions with extreme caution, not to say skepticism. We are told, for instance, that the Sufi mystic Abu Yazid al-Bistami spent most of his life hiding in the mountain recesses of Tabaristan (Iran) in an effort to evade his followers. In his memoirs, *The Words*, where he takes a hard, critical look at his work and reaches the conclusion that it has been based on a misapprehension, Sartre dismisses mysticism as a mode of perception that "suits displaced persons and superfluous children."

"It is the humblest among you who are the most perfect, not those who are favored with ecstasies," said St. Teresa of Avila, herself one of the greatest mystics of christendom. And St. Paul, in his justly famous First Epistle to the Corinthians (chapter 13) states: *"And though I have the gift of prophecy, and understand all mysteries, and all knowledge; and though I have all faith, so that I could remove mountains, and have not charity, I am nothing!"*

There you have it: the noblest sentence ever written by man.

(1976)

On Solzhenitsyn

G REAT COUNTRIES PRODUCE great saints. Also great monsters. No other country has been more blessed and cursed than Russia. It is impossible to think of Solzhenitsyn without thinking of Stalin. They are brothers. To understand both men one must first try to penetrate the Russian mind: submissive to the point of masochism, cruel to the point of sadism, religious to the point of being intolerably dogmatic and self-righteous. It is this last quality—their deep and genuine faith—that has made Russians great moralists but poor political thinkers.

Dostoevsky's nationalism, anti-Semitism, and authoritarianism (the three pillars of fascism) make some pages of his *Diary of a Writer* unreadable, even repellent. Tolstoy, who had very little in common with Dostoevsky, shared with him a distrust of foreign influences, such as French liberalism. He saw them as setting Russian against Russian, and this at a time when Russian was already against Russian and the introduction of any type of liberalism would have been a breath of fresh air.

It is often forgotten that many of the greatest Russian writers as well as composers had a military education. Tolstoy preached non-violence but was, even in his old age, fascinated with violent men. One of his greatest novellas, *Hadji-Murad*, which was published posthumously, is about a fiercely proud and violent Caucasian warrior. Solzhenitsyn himself was a twice-decorated battery commander during World War II. After reading *August 1914* one emerges with the unmistakable impression that Solzhenitsyn is not so much against war as against an inefficiently conducted war.

Tolstoy, unlike Dostoevsky and Solzhenitsyn, never suffered imprisonment and deportation to Siberia. It is doubtful, however, whether such an experience would have altered his political outlook. It did not in the case of Dostoevsky and Solzhenitsyn; if anything it reinforced their strange, quasi-mystical love for Holy Mother Russia, the messiah of nations (try to call any other country *Holy Mother*), and their hope in a Christ-like, benevolent leader, notwithstanding the fact that from the days of Ivan the Terrible to our own, Russia has had no such leader.

During a 1974 televised interview with Walter Cronkite, Solzhenitsyn stated: "We just don't know our history. That's what's so frightful. Only the West knows our history, we don't. We have lost it." Perhaps it is this loss and the resulting innocence that led Solzhenitsyn to write, in his *Letter to the Soviet Leaders,* "It is not authoritarianism itself that is intolerable, but the ideological lies that are daily foisted upon us." Can authoritarianism function without lies? This question is never asked by Solzhenitsyn.

Again in the *Letter to the Soviet Leaders,* Solzhenitsyn calls the United States a "democracy run riot . . . in which once every four years the politicians, and indeed the entire country nearly kill themselves over an electoral campaign, trying to gratify the masses . . . in which a judge, flouting his obligatory independence in order to pander to the passions of society, acquits a man who, during an exhausting war, steals and publishes Defense Department documents."

At the height of the Watergate scandals Solzhenitsyn wrote an article, which was published in *The New York Times,* dismissing all the investigations and the hearings as a waste of time. Somewhat inconsistently he next stated that there is no *binding ethic* in the United States. No binding ethic! This from a writer whose sole aim from *Ivan Denisovich* to *The Gulag Archipelago* has been to document in great detail Russian inhumanity to Russian.

Solzhenitsyn's intensely introspective mind could not perceive that what was involved in Watergate was not simply the immorality of certain acts committed by a group of men at a particular "point in time," but the conflict of principles that have tormented mankind for thousands of years: whether a nation will be governed by *men* or by *laws.* And the heartbreaking, the tragic reality is that Russia has been one of the most spectacular arenas of that conflict.

(1976)

Teachers

WILLIAM SAROYAN TAUGHT ME to use words not to communicate other words or ideas, but myself.

Thoreau taught me to write not about imaginary creatures and situations, but about my daily struggles and doubts.

Thomas Mann taught me never to be ashamed to reveal that which is painful and embarrassing about myself, because only a liar and a fool will present himself as a noble specimen and expect others to believe him.

Montaigne reinforced this lesson by reminding me that it is truly profitless for me to get on stilts, for on stilts I must still walk with my own legs; and on the highest throne in the world, I am never seated on anything but my posterior.

J. S. Bach taught me that intelligence, talent, even genius are worthless if one does not acquire the habit of working patiently every day and finding in this monotonous and unadventurous regime a source of joy and exhilaration.

Einstein taught me that to aim exclusively at well being and happiness is to have the ambitions of a pig.

Plato taught me that knowledge may come after long study in the use of words, definitions, and images, but it does not come through them. It comes through some kind of direct insight into the essence of a thing.

Charles Péguy taught me that it is a writer's duty sometimes to displease his readers.

Paul Tillich taught me not to confuse loneliness with solitude: loneliness expresses the pain of being alone, solitude expresses the glory.

St. Teresa of Avila taught me that I should never submit my intelligence to one who hasn't much of it himself.

Hegel taught me that one does not have to be a slave in order to live and think like one, and that a slave is any man whose actions serve to further the interests of another.

Simone Weil taught me that freedom can be acquired only after one has lived at length in a state of total and extreme humiliation—but a humiliation that one has made every legitimate attempt to avoid.

Gandhi taught me that a truth acquires significance only when it is emotionally grasped and lived—that is to say, adapted, transformed, and developed.

I have had many other teachers. For everyone I have met has taught me something, including fleeting acquaintances, total strangers, and enemies. Yes, above all *enemies*.

Enemies more than friends, because by refusing to accept me as I am, they forced me to take a critical look at myself.

And if someone were to ask why it is that with so many illustrious teachers I haven't been able to make something of myself, I would say that I have been too busy learning, and that though I have learned much, I haven't yet begun.

No, it was not Socrates who taught me to say that but life—life: the wisest and harshest of all teachers that keeps reminding me every day that ignorance, the most innocent of all crimes, is also the most severely punished.

(1976)

Exile

I N 1934 STEFAN ZWEIG, an enormously successful writer of Jewish
origin, was driven into exile by the Nazis. After a short stay in
England, he emigrated to Brazil, where on February 23, 1942, he
committed suicide. In his suicide note he wrote: "After one's
sixtieth year unusual powers are needed in order to make another
wholly new beginning."

Thomas Mann, who was older than Zweig, (Zweig was born in
1881, Mann in 1875) was also forced into exile around the same
time under circumstances similar to Zweig's. He emigrated to the
United States, where he was to write two of his best books:
Joseph the Provider and *Doctor Faustus.*

Nabokov went further. He not only adopted a new country but
a new language and became one of the most brilliant writers in
English.

The same experience will destroy one man and develop another. Experiences in themselves are meaningless. It is what we
do with them that counts. Mann and Nabokov are no exceptions.
Twentieth-century literature has been essentially a literature of
exile. Writers like Conrad, Henry James, Joyce, D. H. Lawrence,
Kazantzakis, T. S. Eliot, Ezra Pound, Hemingway, Saroyan, found
life at home too stifling and went into voluntary exile.

A short list of well-known exiles from other centuries would have
to begin with the names of Dante, Machiavelli, Leonardo, Eras-
mus, Voltaire, Rousseau, Hugo, Marx, Herzen, Lenin.

And speaking of Lenin: let us remind ourselves that the overwhelming majority of Russian intellectuals spent their formative
years in exile in Siberia. Even writers who have not experienced
exile, like Sartre and Camus, have written extensively on the
concept of alienation, which is a form of spiritual exile. Sartre has
gone as far as to say that human life begins on the other side of
despair. But he has also said that if he were forced into exile, he
would probably share Zweig's fate. Sartre here was not talking so
much of exile, however, but the fear of exile, which is a different

thing. Fear is never good policy, especially fear of the unknown—which is the most crippling fear of all.

Once, recently, while I was visiting some relatives in the United States, I overheard an Armenian ask another Armenian—they were talking about a third person: "Is he *hai* or *odar*?"—that is to say, "Is he an Armenian or a foreigner?" And I thought: What a magnificent example of imperialism! The whole world belongs to us. We are not so much exiles as the true natives of the earth. Everyone else is a foreigner. We have not lost our motherland but gained the whole world.

On Being an Armenian Writer

EVER SINCE I gave up writing and publishing in Armenian, friends of mine never tire of letting me know that I am a turncoat and a renegade. On more than one occasion I have had to sit through sermons on the beauties of the Armenian language; love of country and sacred traditions; Apovian, Turian, and Charents. All I can say in my defense is that it is impossible to make a living in the diaspora by writing in Armenian. Whereupon I am informed that money isn't everything. At this point, I resist the temptation of asking my idealistic interlocutor what type of cut-throat business he is in. Taking advantage of my good nature, and perhaps mistaking my silence for tacit consent, he then goes on to remind me that some of our greatest writers were misunderstood, rejected, and nearly died of starvation—the implication being that any writer who is not in a state of complete inanition must be an impostor.

To him, this state of affairs is not a scandal but a given fact, a *fait accompli* imposed by *force majeure*.

Thus it was in the past, and thus shall it be in the future, *saecula saeculorum, amen!*

I make an effort to understand this outrage.

I look for an explanation, not necessarily a justification—for nothing can justify criminal conduct.

Why is it that we make such extravagant demands on our writers, demands that if we were to make on ordinary mortals, we would be accused of crimes against humanity?

Do we ask our doctors and lawyers, or, for that matter, plumbers and garbage collectors, to work for nothing?

If no, what is it exactly that makes us demand martyrdom from our artists? Is it to prove our worth?—if you love us, you'll die for us!

Or is it a symptom of an essentially shallow and materialistic approach to life?

Saroyan says somewhere that every Armenian is convinced that given the right combination of circumstances, he could be as good as Shakespeare. Perhaps we are not so much a nation of

127

shopkeepers (as Napoleon said of the English) or rug merchants (as the English think of us) as a nation of frustrated poets (as Surmelian suggests somewhere in *I Ask You, Ladies and Gentlemen*).

I am not sure.

I reject these generalizations because I suspect all generalizations. I search for an answer elsewhere. In myself. Not so much an accusation against my compatriots and brothers (which would be a projection in any case), but a self-accusation, a confession. And I search for an answer that will explain, in addition to our mistreatment of writers, our self-hatred, our fanaticism and factionalism, which are essentially symptoms of the same psychological malaise that continues to poison our social existence.

Toynbee says somewhere that civilizations are not killed, they commit suicide. The Turks did not, and could not, destroy us.

They tried but they did not succeed.

If we ever disappear from the face of the earth, it will be because of the Turk that we all carry deep within us like a curse. It is only after we accept this fact that we may hope to resolve our internal conflicts and contradictions.

Until then, preaching and exhortation will only add hypocrisy to our previous list of vices.

(1976)

The Art of Writing

BOOKS ON WRITING and books about other books are my favorite reading matter. Writers writing about the act of writing itself: its mechanics, rules to follow, pitfalls to avoid, temptations to resist.

I read such books with a pencil—underlining passages, adding marginalia, making notes.

Here are some of these notes, which after a long period of trial and error, have become quasi-commandments.

After finishing a story or an essay, delete the first and last paragraphs.

Use familiar tools: the kitchen table instead of an expensive desk; a ballpoint pen or a pencil instead of an electric typewriter; the back of an envelope instead of an immaculate notebook.

Read good writers as well as bad ones. A bad writer will teach you how not to write. A good writer will teach you how to live. For writing well is a by-product of life, a reflection.

Can a bad man write a good book?

A best-seller, perhaps; but a good book *never*.

That's because a scoundrel can master only one art: that of cheating other scoundrels, and ultimately himself.

More important than reading is the act of writing itself. The habit of sitting at a desk every day and writing a few pages. *"Those who are good at archery"*, says a Chinese proverb, *"learnt from the bow and not from Yi the Archer."*

It has also been said that we have been given two eyes in order that we may observe the greatness of the Almighty with one eye, and with the other to contemplate our own worthlessness. To write well (or live well, for that matter) one must be two persons in one: one person deeply involved, committed, emotional, the other cool, detached, critical. One must build, the other destroy. If you don't destroy, your critics will. And if critics fail to do the job, time will.

To be original means to remember rather than to experiment. We were all born original. It is education and social pressure that force us to conform, to be like everyone else. To be original means to go back to the origins. To remember. What was it like to confront evil and injustice for the first time? To experience fear, shame, and rage, to fall in love.

And speaking of love:

To create does not mean to make something out of nothing—to erect a monument, to write a book, to compose a symphony, to paint a masterpiece. To create means to touch another's heart. A smile can be as creative as an epic poem, a tragedy in five acts, a philosophical system.

Who will not willingly exchange the smile of the person one loves with the contents of a thousand libraries and museums?

And never—*never!*—say: If I had the time, I could create a masterpiece. Because in your case, *creating time* is the real, the authentic, the *only* masterpiece.

(1977)

In Macondo

A FTER THE ARGUMENT, I remember to have said to myself: We are all inhabitants of Macondo. Macondo is everywhere.

The argument was about the concept of loyalty. But first, let me tell you about Macondo.

Macondo is the name of a mythical town in South America. Many extraordinary things happen in Macondo—for more details see Gabriel Garcia Marquez's *One Hundred Years of Solitude*. At one point, for example, we are told that the inhabitants are ravaged by a mysterious plague a result of which is that they begin to lose their memory. This forces them to label objects in order not to forget what they are. With an inked brush they mark everything with its name: *table, chair, clock, door, wall, bed*. The animals and plants get the same treatment: *cow, goat, pig, hen, cassava, banana*. But soon it becomes evident that this can be only a temporary solution. When they study the infinite possibilities of a loss of memory, they realize that the day might come when things would be recognized by their inscriptions but that no one would remember their use. A sign is therefore hung on the neck of the cow: *This is the cow. She must be milked every morning so that she will produce milk, and the milk must be boiled in order to be mixed with coffee.* "Thus they went on living," the author tells us, "in a reality that was slipping away, momentarily captured by words, but which would escape irremediably when they forgot the values of the written letters." Marquez does not tell us how the people of Macondo set about dealing with abstractions like love, goodness, justice, beauty, loyalty.

Loyalty. Now about the argument I mentioned at the outset. I dislike all arguments. But what I dislike even more is avoiding them. This one began when my interlocutor, a rug merchant, a self-made man, complained that Armenians had no sense of loyalty. "Interesting," I said, meaning something quite different. He explained that once, after hiring and training an Armenian, he (the Armenian) had decided to go into business on his own. That struck me as an example of enterprise rather than disloyalty.

"What have you got against enterprise?" I demanded to know, somewhat uncivilly. He had nothing against enterprise, he said, and reminded me that we had been talking about loyalty. "Let's change the subject," I said. "Let's talk about enterprise." He said he had lived long enough to know the difference between dis-loyalty and enterprise. After reminding myself that one should make enemies with the same care and diligence as one makes friends, I said: "What about exploitation? Would you be inter-ested in talking about that?" With suppressed anger he replied that he did not exploit any of his employees. Maybe not, I said, and invited him to agree with me that *that* was only *his* side of the story, at which point our conversation degenerated into an ex-change of insults. It must have been a situation of this type that prompted Heinrich Heine to observe that he had never seen an ass who talked like a human being, but he had met many human beings who talked like asses.

On another occasion, I remember, a friend of mine, to test my loyalty to Her Majesty's Government, asked me the following question: "Suppose Canada were to declare war against Ar-menia—"

"Impossible!"

"Suppose."

"Okay, have it your way."

"Would you then be willing to fight against your own people?"

I told him he ought to be ashamed of himself. Was that a decent way of judging my loyalty? What was the matter with it? he said. What gave him the idea, I asked, that to have a bloodthirsty disposition to massacre my own brothers would be a proof of loyalty to Her Majesty's Government, or for that matter to any institution or person or organization that had any claim to being civilized, Christian, and humane?

In a 1972 interview John Ehrlichman told what President Nixon expected from his appointees: "When he says, 'Jump,'" Ehrlichman said, "they only ask 'How high?'"

That's loyalty for you: the loyalty of dogs for their masters. But there are other forms of loyalty: loyalty to a set of principles, to ideals, to truth. Lord Acton once said that power corrupts people. He should have gone further and said it also corrupts the meaning of words, and through them the whole fabric of social relations. George Orwell expressed an awareness of this when he wrote: "One ought to recognize that the present political chaos is con-nected with the decay of language, and that one can probably bring about some improvement by starting at the verbal end."

Alfred Korzybski, the leading prophet of general semantics, has gone as far as to write that the verb "to be" is a dangerous and frequently misused word that has been responsible for much of mankind's semantic difficulties. (For example, one should never say "I'm not good at math," but "I didn't receive good grades in math.")

Twenty-five centuries before Korzybski, Confucius (551–479 BC) had this to say when asked what he would undertake to do first were he called upon to rule a nation: "To correct language. If language is not correct, then what is said is not what is meant, then what ought to be done remains undone; if this remains undone, morals and art will deteriorate; if morals and art deteriorate, justice will go astray; if justice goes astray, the people will stand about in helpless confusion. Hence there must be no arbitrariness in what is said. This matters above everything."

Confucius failed to carry out his political reforms and in despair went back to teaching and writing. Unlike Confucius, Chuang-tzu (4th century BC) had no political ambitions. According to one story, when invited to become prime minister, he declined and said: "Instead of an ox richly decorated only to be sacrificed in a temple, I prefer to remain a lowly pig."

But like Confucius and Korzybski, Chuang-tzu knew that men's thinking was confused, prejudiced, and superstitious because their language, in addition to being vague and inaccurate, was burdened with the delusions and misconceptions of an ignorant past. He is said to have declared once: "Where can I find a man who has forgotten words, so that I may speak to him?"

Where? In Macondo, of course.

(1977)

An Armenian Tragedy

When you see a good man,
think of emulating him;
when you see a bad man,
examine your own heart.
                              CONFUCIUS

IN WAITING FOR GODOT, one of Beckett's *clochards* says to the other: "Let's ask each other questions. Let's contradict each other." A critic has remarked that the rituals by which Beckett's characters combat silence, emptiness, despair and nothingness are "elaborate and original." As an Armenian, I see nothing original and elaborate in that particular ritual; I do it all the time. I go further: I become argumentative, vociferous, even offensive. But I do it, it seems to me, not so much to combat silence, emptiness, despair, and nothingness, but to get rid of the poison of hostility from within my system. I am after all the offspring of men who for seven centuries lived under Ottoman terror. I say this not to justify my conduct—there is not and cannot be any justification for uncivilized conduct—but to explain it.

"I dogmatize and am contradicted," Samuel Johnson once said of himself, "and in this conflict of opinions and sentiments I find delight." Delight? Not quite. For while I may dogmatize and do so frequently, I have an extremely low tolerance for contradictions.

I said *as an Armenian* because I have observed a similar inclination in most of my relatives and friends: the same innate drive not only to dogmatize and contradict, but to inflict injuries on those who take positions different from one's own. It is not my intention here, however, to speak of the mote in their eyes, but of the beam in my own.

I don't know the formula of the potion that metamorphosed gentle Jekyll into hideous Hyde, but all *I* need to turn from a timid, introspective Armenian into a terrible Turk is an insignificant quibble, a minor disagreement, a harmless contradiction. I see in such contradictions an overt insult to my intelligence and a

134

covert threat to my very existence. I go to extremes, I know. I am morbidly oversensitive. I know, I know. But I become aware of that only afterwards. And the more I say to myself that I loathe and despise that aspect of my character and that I must do my utmost to avoid arguments, the more frequently I find myself in the eye of the storm. And many times, during an argument, I have caught myself defending a position with the same zeal and fanatic single-mindedness, with which I attacked it on a previous occasion. Every man is his own hell, a wise man once said. In that sense perhaps I am my own civil war.

"Let's ask each other questions. Let's contradict each other." Why, I used these exact same words once when I couldn't have been more than twelve or thirteen. That's when I discovered Greek philosophy. The Sophists. Socrates. Plato. Philosophy to me is not so much the expression of a world-view, but a technique, a tool with which to demolish my opponent. I quoted Samuel Johnson on himself. Now let me quote a contemporary on Samuel Johnson. "When in an argument, his pistol misses fire," this contemporary said, "he [Johnson] knocks you down with the butt-end of it." That's more like it. Once, I remember, to prove that all men were brothers, I made an enemy of a friend. I quoted the Sermon on the Mount, St. Teresa of Avila, Albert Schweitzer. I quoted Gandhi: "Hatred injures the haters, never the hated." I quoted St. Paul: "And though I have the gift of prophecy, and understand all mysteries, and all knowledge; and though I have all faith, so that I could remove mountains, and have not charity, I am nothing!" *Nothing!* NOTHING!! I shouted several times with menace and hatred in my voice, as though I was about to kill my interlocutor. Consider the horror and absurdity of the situation. To prove that all men were brothers, *I made an enemy of a brother.* There, ladies and gentlemen, you have the making of an Armenian tragedy.

(1977)

Enemies

"ARMENIANS WILL NEVER amount to anything," I once heard a wealthy, fat matron say with an expression of stupid self-satisfaction on her heavily made-up face. "They'll never amount to anything because all they do is quarrel among themselves."

She spoke as though she belonged to a different and superior species.

"Whenever an Armenian comes to me and asks for my support," she went on, "I always tell him: Stop the quarreling among yourselves and you'll have my full support—and you won't even have to ask for it either."

"She is saying that," I heard someone whispering, "because she knows that Armenians will never give up their quarrelling."

On another occasion, I heard a young Armenian woman say to another: "Join your group? I know all about Armenian groups. All they do is fight. I get enough of that at home. No thanks!"

We all agree that we must agree, but we all disagree as to who will do the agreeing.

"Even if the other side compromises and agrees to all our terms," I was told by a partisan once, "I would refuse to have anything to do with them."

"Why?"

"Because that would be just a tactical ploy on their part—a trap. I never trusted those guys and I never will. All they want is to infiltrate our organizations and take them over—and that's exactly what they'll do, too, if we let them. Mark my words. How can anyone trust fanatics who stop at nothing, including the use of terror and assassination?"

"May I remind you that you are talking about fellow Armenians and not Turks."

"I know what I'm saying."

"And don't you think you're being a little unfair? After all, there are extremists and fanatics in every cause and organization, and to say that the whole organization is rotten is like saying that all of Italy, including the Pope, is one big Mafia family."

"Before we continue with this argument, let's put our cards on the table, okay? Are you willing to admit that you are a card-carrying member of the other party? Because if you are, it's useless to go on. You'll never see my way, and I'll never see your way. We might as well stop here and now. We are wasting our time."

"Will you believe me if I tell you that I'm not a member of any party, or for that matter of any cultural foundation and editorial board?"

"Frankly, no."

"Why not?—may I ask."

"Because if you were non-partisan and objective about this thing, you wouldn't take their side."

"*Objective!* That's what *I* am trying to say; let's be fair and objective."

"You practically condoned terrorism and assassination; you call that fair and objective?"

"I don't remember to have condoned any such thing. I may have said, however, that—"

"Listen! what you said, I heard. You don't have to play the same record all over again. I already told you, you'll never see my way and I'll never see your way. I know what I know."

"*I know what I know!* Now, what the hell does *that* mean? You have a closed mind? You know everything there is to know on the subject? You are infallible? And I am a liar and a spy?"

"Well, it was nice talking to you, but I have to leave. I'm sorry. Maybe we can continue with this discussion some other time."

"And if we do, do you think we'll ever reach any kind of agreement?"

"It will be up to you, my friend."

His finals words were "my friend," but there was such heavy sarcasm in his voice that he might as well have said "my enemy." Because we may have begun as friends, but it was as enemies that we parted.

(1978)

The Art of Organizing

I T IS A SUBTLE ART. It requires some degree of depersonalization, coordination, discipline, renunciation, acceptance of authority. We are suspicious of all authority.

Like all mountain people, we have learned to be self-sufficient and skeptical of outsiders—be they representatives of *nakharars*, governors, kings, or emperors.

It is different with people living on flatlands—Americans, for instance. Even little boys here know how to break down an event into its component parts, assigning to each a number of possibilities and unforeseen variables: if step one of plan A works, we'll proceed with step two; if it fails, we'll try plan B.

We Armenians, on the other hand, function under the illusion that all it takes to succeed in this world is enthusiasm, perseverance, and cunning—all of which are important, of course. Important, yes, but not sufficient! Our history proves that. Our present malaise proves that also.

It is common knowledge that when two irresistible forces clash, they cancel each other out. Likewise when two invincible enemies meet and fight, neither will emerge victorious. They will either kill each other or continue fighting forever. There can be no other outcome. Unless, of course, one of them says to the other: "Instead of continuing this senseless fight, which is bound to have consequences tragic to both of us, let us coordinate and organize ourselves. That way we may conquer the world."

Conquer the world!

Isn't that what the Americans have nearly succeeded in doing?

As for us: it is as though having been fragmented and dismembered by the dark forces of history, we proceeded to blind ourselves and we are now making preparations to commit suicide.

I am not saying we *will* commit suicide.

I am just saying, let's try plan *B* for a change.

(1978)

138

A House Divided Against Itself

A N ARTICULATE LADY from a nearby town calls me on the telephone and after a short introduction informs me that Armenians are a disorganized lot and that it is high time that we do something about it.

"Armenians know nothing about the democratic system and the way it works," she goes on. "I didn't either," she adds, "until I got involved in the American electoral process in Washington, D.C. a few years back. The secret code is *compromise*. Compromise to the point of *conspiracy*. You make deals. If you do this for me, I'll do that for you. It's as simple as that. And Armenians know nothing about making deals. They are inflexible fanatics. They cling to outmoded and useless principles. They inhabit a world of dreams and completely ignore realities. The end result? Impotence, fiasco, defeat! Look at the Jews, the Palestinians, the Arabs. The whole world is talking about them. Who knows anything about Armenians? Whenever I say anything about Armenians, they think I'm talking about Rumanians and Aramaeans— and I don't even know who the hell *they* are. Even Turks have a weekly television program in my town," she concludes with seething outrage.

"Same here," I say.

"What's the matter with us anyway? What kind of people are we?"

I ask her if she is involved in Armenian affairs.

"I went through that nightmare once," she replies, "and I swore never to repeat it. Thanks, but no thanks."

About a month later, I get another call. This time it is a man, but equally articulate and knowledgeable. He tells me he would like to drop in for a chat. I am in the middle of four projects with as many deadlines, but since I have not yet mastered the art of saying no gracefully, I say he is more than welcome.

He comes. In his sixties. Bald. Shrewd, bloodshot eyes. Mustache. Restless, no-nonsense type. Frank to the point of being rude. What he has to tell me has a familiar ring.

"We are politically naive," he begins. "All words and no action. Good at rhetoric but lousy vis-à-vis live issues and flesh-and-blood situations. Am I right or wrong?" he demands.

"So far so good," I say. "Now, let's get to the solution."

"The solution is in the development of some form of consensus. We must get together. We must get organized. We have no more use of ideologues and partisans. What we need is technicians. Organizers on the grassroots level. Our churches and political parties—we can no longer rely on them. What are they up to anyway? It seems to me all they're trying to do is finish the job the Turks started. At least the Turks had a pragmatic reason for doing what they did to us."

"Harsh words."

"I'm giving you the facts as I see them."

"I know some very good and able men who are active in our organizations."

"Yes, but who listens to them? They don't set the policy, they only carry them out. We are at the mercy of small-minded, vindictive men—"

"You seem to know a great deal about Armenian affairs," I say.

"I should. I used to be active for a number of years."

"But you are no longer?"

"I couldn't take it."

In the opinion column of a weekly, I read of a student who, after several years of involvement in Armenian organizations, has decided to get out for good. His reasons are easy to guess. I don't even read them.

If we have survived for several thousand years, it's because we didn't have to depend on quitters. Maybe so. If certain ladies and gentlemen can't take the heat, let them get out of the kitchen. Perhaps. But let us also be modest enough to admit that *we could have done better*. Whoever says "let the quitters quit, who needs them?" knows little about human beings and nothing about community work. As a matter of fact, in the long run, he may turn out to be worse than a quitter. He may be a *dedicated* Armenian, not necessarily a *friend*. It would be no exaggeration to say that some of our most dangerous enemies are dedicated but misguided patriots who, in their efforts to serve an *abstract cause*, forget that their primary concern should be *human beings*.

I know many dedicated Armenians who spout superpatriotic slogans in public, but in private they are filled with bitterness and resentment against their brothers. They feel more at home in abstractions. Human beings—with their frailties and imperfections—they cannot deal with. These Armenians think being an Armenian gives them the right to dislike, mistreat, and perhaps even hate their fellow Armenians with impunity.

After listening to such a character recently, I could not help saying: "You don't like Armenians, do you?"

"I *love* them, I don't have to *like* them. As a matter of fact, I know very few likable Armenians."

"You love them so much that maybe you even hate them?"

"How can I hate them if I am myself Armenian?"

"You may hate yourself, and by extension your fellow Armenians."

"I didn't know I hated myself."

"Only self-centered narcissists don't hate themselves."

"I'm glad you think I'm normal."

"I never said you weren't. What I was trying to point out was that perhaps being a perfectionist, you may make unreasonable demands on your fellow men. And when they fail to come up to your expectations, you may become harsh and intolerant. Am I right in assuming that you can't suffer fools gracefully?"

"I plead guilty to that charge, yes."

"Then perhaps you shouldn't be involved in community action."

"Why do you say that?"

"Because you may alienate others willing to serve the same cause."

Our conversation and probably friendship, ended on that note. I say *probably* because he looked deeply hurt and I haven't heard from him since. Which goes to show you that even in our efforts to preach tolerance and compassion we may act in an intolerant and harsh manner. In other words, while trying to serve a just cause, one may end up serving injustice. St. Paul is absolutely right: *"And though I have the gift of prophecy, and understand all mysteries, and all knowledge; and though I have all faith, so that I could remove mountains, and have not charity, I am nothing!"*

(1978)

Toynbee and the Armenians

ARMENIANS ARE PRESENT in almost all of Toynbee's books. From the first three, which he wrote as a young man during World War I—*Armenian Atrocities: The Murder of a Nation* (1915), *Documents Relating to the Treatment of Armenians and Assyrian Christians in the Ottoman Empire and Northwest Persia* (1916), and *The Murderous Tyranny of the Turks* (1917)—to his magnum opus, *A Study of History,* in twelve volumes (1934/1961), and to his last two major works of historiography—*Constantine Porphyrogenitus and His World* (1973) and *Mankind and Mother Earth* (1976).

The Armenian genocide, Toynbee tells us in one of his autobiographical books, *Experiences* (1969), made an indelible impression on his mind; it gave him an insight into human nature; taught him the meaning of "original sin." In his own words: "There is a vein of diabolical evil in all human nature. Our 'Original Sin' may be overlaid by layer upon layer of civilizing habits, yet no one can go bail for the moral integrity of any individual human being or any human community. No one can guarantee that anyone will be proof against all temptations. Under temptations the volcano may suddenly erupt, even when its fires have been dormant for so long that they have been deemed to be extinct."[1]

In other words, we may not be guilty today, but we may be guilty tomorrow. This line of reasoning, by the way, is uncannily close to the one used by the Turkish Minister of the Interior who, in 1918, replied to American protests against the atrocities by saying: "Those who are innocent today might be guilty tomorrow."

In another autobiographical book, *Acquaintances* (1967), Toynbee tells us that after he wrote the book on the treatment of the Armenians in the Ottoman Empire in 1915, he could not dismiss its contents from his mind. "I was not only haunted by the victims' sufferings and by the criminals' deeds," he writes, "I was exercised by the question how it could be possible for human beings to do what those perpetrators of genocide had done." To answer this question, Toynbee decided to learn the Turkish language, and in the process, acquire Turkish friends. "If I was to get to know human nature in Turkish embodiments of it," he writes, "I must get to know live Turkish men and women individually, and I must meet each of them as one of my fellow human beings of like passions with myself. . . . My first step was to start to learn the Turkish language."

In *Acquaintances* Toynbee devotes a whole chapter to these Turkish friends, for whom, he tells us, he had a great deal of affection, even admiration.[2]

Of their language, he has this to say: "I have been educated into seeing in French a vulgar deformation of Latin, and in English a barbarous substitute for it. But I also have a rational ground for finding these Western vernaculars inferior to Latin and Attic Greek, and also to pre-Ataturk Ottoman Turkish (of which I have a smattering)."[3]

There is some degree of reckless daring, not to say inconsistency, in bracketing Turkish with Latin and Attic Greek, for elsewhere we find Toynbee quoting Sir Charles Eliot on pre-Ataturk Ottoman Turkish. "The Turkish language," we read here, "copious as it is, contains no equivalent for 'interesting.' The ordinary Turk does not take an interest in anything. . . . A natural want of curiosity, and a conviction that their own religion contains all that man knows or needs to know, keep the provincial population in a state of ignorance which seems incredible and fantastic."[4]

It is relatively easy to point out contradictions and inconsistencies in Toynbee's vast *oeuvre*. Toynbee himself has observed somwhere that "There is a mixture of motives and a tangle of contradictions in the conduct and character of even the most single-minded and self-consistent human being." Hundreds of articles and dozens of books have been written on Toynbee's indifference to hard facts and details. In his efforts to reconcile some of these inconsistencies, Toynbee wrote one of his longest, and in many ways most fascinating, works entitled *Reconsiderations (A Study of History,* Volume 12). He explains here that in order to understand and answer the questions set by history, one must be more than a historian. One must be a *metahistorian*— that is to say, a philosopher, a theologian, a metaphysician, a sociologist, an anthropologist, a psychologist, a moralist. Yes, above all a moralist. For, in whatever Toynbee writes, his subject is not this or that civilization, event, or personality, but *man,* that is to say, *himself.* Toynbee's *oeuvre,* and more particularly his *Study of History,* is essentially a confession, an *apologia pro vita sua.* And Toynbee is his own severest critic. Listen to his criticism of all those Western intellectuals (like himself) who, at one time or another, have been attracted by exotic and primitive cultures (like the Ottoman Turkish): "In repudiating our own native Western tradition of art and hereby reducing our aesthetic faculties to a state of inanition and sterility in which they seize upon the exotic and primitive art . . . we are confessing before all men that we have forfeited our spiritual birthright."

And: "There is to me something grim and horrible in an essentially mature civilization playing at savage immaturity when it knows better."

It is therefore wrong to say with H. R. Trevor-Roper that "Toynbee detests Western civilization because it is basically liberal and rational. On its ruins he envisions . . . the religion of Mish-Mash, of which he is the prophet and Messiah."[5] Because Toynbee's loathing of the West is essentially a form of self-contempt. His efforts to understand "the criminal deeds" of the "perpetrators of genocide" are nothing but efforts to understand and accept the potential evil that is within him. Like all moralists, Toynbee is incapable of distinguishing *sinful* from *criminal* conduct. And he is so absorbed in examining his soul and its relations with God that objective reality loses its primacy and is seen as the projection of a psychological malaise. Toynbee has no interest in justice, only in his own spiritual salvation. He wants first and foremost to establish his own innocence before God and men by confessing his sins—not only sins of commission and omission, but sins of intent. Viewed from this perspective, Toynbee's inconsistencies and contradictions, like his excessive interest in the tormentor at the expense of the victim, are not results of duplicity but confusion. Toynbee is not wicked, just perplexed.

(1978)

NOTES

1. Toynbee, *Experiences,* p. 36.

2. Toynbee, "Some Turkish Friends," *Acquaintances,* p. 231.

3. Toynbee, *A Study of History, Volume 12: Reconsiderations,* p. 589.

4. Toynbee, *A Study of History, Volume 10,* p. 8.

5. H. R. Trevor-Roper, "Arnold Toynbee's Millenium," in *Encounter,* Vol. 8, no. 6 (June 1957): pp. 14–28. Reprinted in his *Historical Essays* (1966).

A New Phenomenon

THERE IS SOMETHING of the ape in all of us. We shouldn't be surprised therefore if, after *Passage to Ararat* and *Roots*, we now have among us a generation of Armenian-Americans who have suddenly discovered their *identity*. These hitherto assimilated prodigal sons, who until very recently were ashamed of their nationality as if it were some kind of family skeleton, now infiltrate our organizations and become not only active members but dedicated leaders. In this land of instant coffee, these instant patriots and leaders like to believe they are also instant experts on Armenian affairs. After reading a couple of articles in newspapers and illustrated magazines (mostly about the massacres), and after talking with someone who has visited Yerevan, they think they know all about our history and culture. What culture? As Michael Arlen says on the final pages of *Passage to Ararat*, "One hears of 'Armenian culture,' at least, from Armenians—but it is surely not that!"

It is *surely not that!*

What is it then?

What else but a confused jumble of dreams, pride, and madness. Yes. That's right. It's all there in black and white. Reread the book, please.

And what is to be done?

The answer is very simple.

Assimilate.

Take a bath every day. Use underarm deodorant. Avoid foods with garlic. Watch a sitcom on TV. Dig a swimming pool in your backyard. There are so many things you can do. Buy a new car. Keep up with the Joneses. Buy another car. Buy, buy, buy!

The whole world, including Americans themselves, may express disgust at their own moral decline, political corruption, opportunism, materialism, commercialism, in gold we trust, the apotheosis of sex and violence; but we, remnants of a wretched Oriental tribe, are expected to believe that Americanism is the latest word in human progress and civilization.

I not only don't believe in these instant Armenian-Americans, I don't believe they believe in themselves. As a matter of fact, they

145

remind me of doctors who pour drugs of which they know little, to cure diseases of which they know less, into human beings of whom they know *nothing*.

The order these psuedo-Armenians create around them is a new chaos—the chaos of Babbitts on Main Streets, the chaos of TV commercials, billboard and asphalt jungles, public-relations stunts, plastic gadgets, suburban wasteland, organized crime, and the melting pot. I began by saying that there is something of the ape in all of us. I should have added: and something of the fool in too many.

(1979)

Horatio Algerian

W E HAVE ALL MET the Armenian-American whose sole ambition in life seems to be to prove that he is as good an American as the next John Doe and Joe Smith. To this type of Armenian, Americanism is a new religion with its own gods, tenets, and decalogue.

I may have a strange last name—this Armenian seems to be saying (assuming of course he has not already changed Hampartsoumian to Hammer or Koeroghlanian to Kerr); my parents may come from a strange little village in the Ottoman Empire (a dismal little place, hidebound, torn by prejudice, washed with blood); I may be the offspring of wretched, penniless immigrants, persecuted in the Old Country and exploited in the New (but never mind about that) but lo and behold! I've arrived in the land of the brave and the free; I speak impeccable English (make it American); I have completely forgotten my mother tongue (he lies: he can speak and understand not only Armenian, but Turkish as well); I have a swimming pool in my backyard, two cars (latest model), an attractive wife (native born), three wonderful teen-age kids (thoroughly assimilated). That's not all. I take a bath every day; I have a martini before supper; I avoid foods with garlic (shish kebab and pilaf? never touch the stuff; steak and potatoes—that's my cup of tea).

Ask this individual what his contribution is to his country of adoption, and he will automatically assume you're talking about cash and reply: I contribute regularly to the church and to a number of charity organizations, and more important, to the economy by buying all kinds of gadgets (made in USA of course) that I don't need.

It never occurs to this bald-headed, pot-bellied loud-mouthed Oriental Horatio that he is not the envy of the world and the latest word in human civilization and progress, but just a vulgar, jazzed up imitation of a character that's been around for centuries, and that his brand of second-hand Americanism ("America's business is business," "What's good for General Motors is good for America") is just third-rate Levantine mercantilism.

147

He thinks what counts in life is not so much wealth, but the appearance of wealth, the outward trappings and rituals—conspicuous consumption, keeping up with the Joneses. He explains selfish aims with altruistic motives and calls it public relations. He steals privately, donates publicly, and calls that free enterprise. He thinks culture consists of a bookcase with the latest best-sellers (unread) and *Time* or *Newsweek,* maybe even *Playboy* (which, as everyone knows, publishes some first-rate fiction by reputable contemporary authors, not to say in-depth interviews with statesmen and other important personalities); a stereo set with Tchaikovsky's *"Swan Lake"* and Strauss waltzes (classics) or Mantovani and Bing (semi-classics); walking through a museum once every two years (if at all).

His definition of well-being: a bottle of beer in one hand, a cigar in the other, and a baseball game on TV. "You like Sartre and Bach," I was told by such a specimen one day; "I like baseball and hockey. It takes all kinds. To each his own."

His speech is a succession of clichés. He is himself a cliché. Originality? The word has a bad smell in America. It is, as a matter of fact, un-American. *Conform*—that's commandment numbers one to ten in the decalogue of his new, synthetic religion of plastic. If you don't conform, you'll be an outcast in a world where the supreme virtue is to be like everyone else. In the land of the brave and the free, he is neither brave nor free, but a slave to social pressures, prejudices, greed, and ignorance.

(1979)

What's Your Racket?

LONG AFTER I began to devote my full time to writing (that is, at least eight hours a day, six, sometimes seven days a week) I would hesitate to call myself a writer. But now, with a few published articles and a handful of books to my credit, I have acquired enough daring to declare myself a writer—which has invariably led me into a new set of difficulties. Last week, for instance, when a civil servant wanted to know what my occupation was, I said: "Writer."

"Writer?" he said.

"Writer," I said.

"What kind?"

"A little of everything."

"Articles in newspapers?"

"In magazines too."

"Plays?"

"About half-a-dozen."

"Staged?"

"Broadcast."

"Books?"

"Three so far; another coming out soon."

"How come I've never heard of you then?"

Popular conception dictates that if a writer is not a hard-drinking, best-selling, and headline-making celebrity, he may safely be dismissed as a harmless charlatan.

"Maybe because I don't write the kind of stuff you like to read," I tried to explain, without managing to convince him however.

"What's your racket anyway?" an old friend, whom I've not seen for years, wants to know. We are at a wedding banquet. He has had one too many. So have I.

"I write," I reply.

"A writer, wow! You must make a lot of money."

"Not much, I'm afraid."

"I bet, a hell of a lot more than *I* make."

"I doubt that very much."

149

"You're putting me on."

"Do you really want to know how much I made last year?"

"How much?"

"Less than a thousand."

"A week?"

"A year!"

"No!!"

"I know some writers who don't even make *that* much."

"Impossible."

"I know still others who lose money."

"How can they lose money?"

"Expenses—printing costs, postage, typewriter ribbons, repairs, stationery."

"I bet I can guess what their problem is," he tells me.

"You can?"

"They don't write what the public wants to read."

"Which is?"

"Thrillers and porno. What kind of stuff do *you* write?"

"Anything *but!*"

"See what I mean?"

He feels wonderful. He has not only established his superiority over me, but has also solved all my financial problems.

"Do you write in English or Armenian?" an inquisitorial old man demands to know when he is informed that I am a writer.

"In English," I reply.

"You are an Armenian, are you not?" he persists.

"You bet."

"You should write in Armenian then."

"I did—for a while."

"Why did you stop?"

"No one seemed to be interested."

"That happens to all writers."

"Besides, there isn't any money in it."

"Money isn't everything—as a writer you should know that better than anyone else."

"I do. Money, as a matter of fact, is *nothing*—provided of course you have other sources of income. But you see, I do not belong to the privileged classes. I must work for a living—"

"Like the rest of mankind."

"And I did for a number of years, I assure you—in factories, department stores, insurance companies—until, that is, I realized that if a writer has any respect for his profession, he must devote his full time to it."

"I've known many great writers who worked for a living and wrote in their spare time—Nartuni was a doctor, Shahnour a photographer, Oshagan a teacher—"

"I have no doubt in my mind that all these gentlemen could have been better writers had they decided to devote their full time to writing—you disagree?"

"You may be right; but the fact remains that we don't live in utopia."

"I never said we did."

"But your demands are utopian."

"Come, come. A garbage collector gets paid for his services; so does a plumber; why is it that when it comes to writers, we dismiss their demands as utopian?"

"Listen, my friend. I didn't make the rules. If it was up to me—"

"Please, no explanations are required. I understand. You were trying to make a point. So was I."

"The point I was trying to make, however, was that so long as you write in English, you'll never be remembered as an Armenian writer and you'll never be part of Armenian literature."

Why is it that whenever I recall this conversation, I feel slightly diminished and excommunicated?

(1979)

Vartan Mamigonian:
An Armenian Archetype

Human behavior is governed by the limitations of man's
mental processes.

CLAUDE LEVI-STRAUSS

Man should learn that he is not the master in his own
house and that he should carefully study the other side of his
physical world, which seems to be the true ruler of his fate.

C. G. JUNG

W E HAVE BEEN TOLD and retold the story of Vartan Mamigonian
and the Battle of Avarair so many times that it has become an
integral part of our consciousness.

Soon after we adopted Christianity as our official religion, we
read in our history books, the Byzantines and the Sassanid Persians began to fight one another for the possession of Armenia. In
438, several Armenian provinces came under the control of the
Persians, who watched with alarm the rapid expansion of Christianity—which also meant the expansion of the Byzantine sphere
of influence. Christians in Persian territories were massacred.
When entire villages began to disappear, the massacre was re-
stricted to priests, monks, and nuns. Next, an effort was made to
introduce Mazdaism (Zoroastrianism or the worship of Ahura
Mazda) into Armenia. This led to revolt under the leadership of
Vartan Mamigonian, and in 451 the Persians invaded Armenia. At
the cost of heavy losses the Persians won. Vartan Mamigonian was
among the slain, but his heroic resistance against a much more
powerful army (66,000 Armenians against 220,000 Persians, reinforced by squadrons of armored elephants) convinced the Persians of the impossibility of uprooting Christianity from the hearts
of the people. The Battle of Avarair was a military defeat but a
decisive moral victory.

What are the hard facts behind this moralistic tale with an
ambivalent and almost, but not quite, happy ending?

My teacher of Armenian history, an iconoclastic Mekhitarist scholar, was fond of saying that the Battle of Avarair was very probably an extremely minor border skirmish whose importance had been exaggerated by our historians who, in the manner of poets, confused fact with factoid and fancy. Persian records, it seems, don't even mention the incident—which is unusual, since nations are prone to boast of their military victories no matter how costly.

In an interesting footnote in Jean-Pierre Alem's *L'Armenie* (Paris, 1959), we are informed that the Mamigonian dynasty was very probably of Chinese origin.

Well, no matter. As they say of so many good things, *Se non vero, ben trovato* (If not true, well invented). Or as professor Hamalian in his review of Derenic Demirgian's famous novel *Vartananc* says, "If Vartan Mamigonian had never lived, Armenians some day would have had to invent him."

Whatever its historic authenticity, the Battle of Avarair is an event of great importance for the subsequent development of our collective psyche, and Vartan is much more than a hero and a saint: he is an Armenian *archetype*—I use the word in both its Platonic (as the original pattern or prototype from which copies are made) and Jungian sense (as the collective equivalent of the personal complex). More specifically in Jungian terminology, an archetype is a psychological structure or pattern of instinctual behavior, an inherited mode of thought, if you wish, derived from the experience of the race.

Now the question that comes to mind at this point is this: Why is it that we as a nation have identified ourselves with, or projected our destiny onto, a loser? Brought down onto a more mundane, pragmatic level, the question could be rephrased thus: To what extent do we allow ourselves to undertake a task, to solve a national problem, to confront a crisis or an enemy, with the foreknowledge that the final outcome will be ambivalent and perhaps, on a pragmatic level, a *defeat*? As we now face the possibility of ultimate defeat—that is, assimilation or collective annihilation—this unanswered question or conflict in our collective psyche acquires added relevance and significance. We may fail to resolve it completely, but we must attempt to discuss and understand it, because in Jung's own words, "When an archetype is not consciously understood, one is possessed by it and forced to its fatal goal."

(1979

He Who Gets Slapped

M Y MOTHER HAS a favorite saying: "To the underdog, everyone is generous with advice." I was able to ascertain the veracity of this saying soon after I decided to become a writer.

"Indiscriminate reading!—that's what did it," I heard our parish priest say to my father. "You should never have allowed him to read so many books. I warned you."

An uncle of mine, who had never committed the sin of reading a single book in his life, was more to the point: "What's wrong with honest labor?" he demanded to know.

A friend of the family, a dentist, who occasionally contributed articles and short patriotic poems to the local daily, wasn't much help either: "He should learn a trade first," he said. "Get a degree if he can. He can do his writing on weekends."

My father summed up the situation in the following manner. "It's not easy being a writer. As long as you are alive, even if you are good, no one bothers with you. After you are dead and buried—*maybe*, provided of course you were not just good, but very good."

After I wrote my first book, a hundred editors said: "Your stuff is good but not good enough yet. Keep trying."

After I published my first book, I was dismissed by an American critic as a chauvinist, a racist (for my dislike of Turks), and a crypto-fascist war-monger.

A friend said: "You write too much about the past—history, ideas, books. You should write more about life, people—*now.*"

An Armenian who ran a pizzeria, said: "You should write in Armenian."

"I did, for a while."

"Why did you stop?"

"There is no money in it.

"Money isn't everything!"

Some of our staunchest idealists are in either the rug or pizza business.

A Canadian friend said: "What's all this nonsense about Armenians and Turks? Who the hell cares? This is 20th-century America. We are confronting other enemies now—pollution, nuclear contamination, discrimination. If you want to be read, you must be more relevant."

Another friend said: "You should write fiction, original stuff. Journalism, reviewing, translating—they belong to the dustbin of literature."

A writer whose book I had praised, with one minor reservation, accused me of having reviewed his book without reading it. Another writer, whose book I had praised highly, wrote to inform me that I was wasting a great deal of valuable time by translating, reading, and reviewing a bunch of mediocre works written by nonentities, and that in the future I should write about him in greater detail. He suggested that after I did that, I dedicate the rest of my life to spreading his message. When I ignored that suggestion, he accused me of all kinds of loathsome and unspeakable crimes. Some of our ablest writers are as narrow and greedy as shopkeepers.

Whenever I am asked "What's your line of work?" I try to change the subject. This evasive tactic doesn't always work. After some harmless chitchat, the stranger comes back with, "What did you say your line of work was?" "Well," I am tempted to reply "it's not so much a line as a vicious circle."

(1979)

The Crisis of Contemporary Armenian Literature in the Diaspora

T WO YEARS AGO, at a seminar whose theme was the crisis of contemporary Armenian literature in the diaspora, I met an established and prolific Armenian poet, playwright, and author of over a dozen books, who interrupted one of my arguments to say that he did not regard himself as a writer. How so, I wanted to know. "Because I'm not a writer," he replied simply and unequivocally, as though the whole world had been aware of this fact all along. There was no humor or irony in his voice and expression. He meant what he said. For a long time I couldn't understand what had motivated him to make that absurd statement, but I think I know now—or at least I have a theory. Though he had devoted many years of his life to writing, this author had no pride in the result because it did not represent his profession. He was in some other line of business—I no longer remember which (it may have been insurance or pharmacy). He regarded himself only as an amateur writer—a gifted amateur perhaps, but an amateur nonetheless.

Now, it is said that a gifted amateur can easily surpass an average professional. But that's like making rules out of exceptions. *As a rule*, all professionals begin as amateurs. But whereas a professional perseveres and concentrates, an amateur continues to operate under the illusion that he can serve two masters at once. In psychological parlance, he is a case of arrested development. He is a promise that perpetually postpones its fulfillment, a swimmer forever afraid to leave the security of the beach and plunge into the unknown waters. His sense of safety, or rather the pleasures and comforts of a bourgeois mode of existence, mean much more to him than the agony, ecstasy, despair, and uncertainty of a life dedicated exclusively to writing. He likes to believe

156

that his love for his art is so intense that even if he devotes a small fraction of his life to it, he will satisfy its requirements and demands. People who speak in defense of amateurs would be the last men on earth to seek the services of an amateur lawyer or surgeon in time of trouble. These same people, however, seem to be unable to grasp that, like law and medicine, literature demands full-time dedication—eight hours a day, not just a couple of hours a week.

The crisis of contemporary Armenian literature in the diaspora originates not in some nebulous political, ideological, or psychological realm compounded by inevitable historic forces, but in the much simpler fact that our writers are part-time amateurs who function on a small fraction of their potential; they are, in other words, only pale shadows of themselves.

"There is no future in literature," my father used to remind me whenever I told him I wanted to be a writer. "Learn a trade first in order to hold a bread-winning job, after which you can, if you still want to, write in your spare time."

I refused to take his advice, but it seems that several hundred other Armenians who shared my dreams and ambitions accepted it willingly and followed it to the letter. As a result they are now successful teachers, lawyers, doctors, and executives who relegate their literary labors to weekends—some of which are also dedicated to delivering lectures (on, among other topics, the crisis of contemporary Armenian literature in the diaspora), attending testimonial dinners in honor of fellow writers, participating in seminars and sundry other more or less worthy cultural activities. Add to this an indifferent public who is perfectly content in the knowledge that Armenians like Khachaturian, Saroyan, and the Arlens have made contributions to the arts, and you'll have a full-blown crisis (or anti-crisis) that won't be dispelled even by a thousand conventions, study groups, seminars, editorials, and articles like this one.

I said *anti*-crisis because the word crisis presupposes some kind of ferment, whereas the situation of contemporary Armenian literature in the diaspora is marked by apathy (on the part of the public) and absence of commitment (on the part of writers). We are facing not so much a contradiction that demands resolution, but a war on two fronts, and history tells us that such wars are notoriously easy to lose.

(1979)

As Armenian as Pilaf

EVER SINCE A NUMBER of alleged—repeat *alleged*—Armenian ter-rorists in America and Europe allegedly (ditto) murdered a number of Turkish diplomats, we have been exposed to a verita-ble orgy of statements in the Armenian-American press to the effect that revenge is wrong and that terrorism is intolerable, and that we—Armenians living in this great country of America—should not condone indiscriminate murder and bloodshed, and so on and so forth.

Whenever I read these politically naive and morally self-right-eous declarations, I want to ask, whom are we trying to impress, the Turks or our fellow Yankees? Are we trying to say to the Turks: We may dislike you for what you have done to us (after all, who wouldn't), but please stay assured that henceforth we will do our best to express our feelings toward you only *verbally*. You see, unlike you, we are a civilized, Christian nation, fond of delivering speeches and sermons, writing letters to the editor, singing lam-entations, reading Narekatsi. All verbal, you see. You may not wish to talk to us, and for the last 65 years you have consistently refused to acknowledge our demands; but we trust your sense of fair play and goodwill, and we shall continue asking, asking hum-bly, even begging if necessary, that you come and sit around a negotiating table with us; and while we wait, we shall continue writing poems, articles, and books about our million and a half, publishing documents, eyewitness accounts, and interviews with survivors—just to remind the world—because, as Hitler said, the world has a short memory, it forgets; everybody after all has problems of his own. . . . All verbal, you see. No harm in that. Even children in this part of the world know that sticks and stones may break bones, but words will not even harm a defenseless worm.

This indeed is the kind of talk the Turks would like to hear. They love it. It is what they want. It is what they *need*.

What about our fellow Americans? Let's forget the Turks. Let's consider instead the Americans and what they'll think of us. After

158

all, we live in a civilized country. We are no longer in the Middle East. We are not barbarians.

Maybe not, but in a single week more people are murdered senselessly in New York City and Detroit than all the Turks murdered by Armenians during the last 65 years.

Violence, it has been said, is as American as cherry pie. I suspect Americans have never felt the need to be reminded that we, Armenians, are not a bloodthirsty, murderous bunch. Consider their history and ours. In a relatively short span of time (two centuries), Americans have declared war and fought against practically anyone you care to mention—including the British and even Americans themselves (in a savage Civil War that is reputed to have been one of the bloodiest conflicts in world history). Against how many nations have we, Armenians, declared war during the last twenty, make it thirty, centuries?

If violence were taught in universities, Americans would write the textbooks and Armenians wouldn't even qualify as students, because they would be told to go to a seminary instead. Why there? Because we love to preach. And preach what? Tolerance and forgiveness—forgiveness not of our *misguided brothers*, but of our *enemies*. You might even say that *preaching is as Armenian as pilaf*.

End of sermon.

(1980)

Occupational Hazards

YOU HAVE AN overwhelming experience; you go through a crisis; you are shattered and rebuild yourself: you rebuild yourself from foundation to roof, brick by brick, after which you wish to share your discoveries and insights with your fellow men. You write a book. You condense the book into a 10-page essay. You go further: you condense the essay down to a single beautiful, accessible, insightful, deep, pearl of a sentence. At which point you suddenly realize that what you have really produced is a popular saying that's been around for centuries, perhaps even millenia.

All in a day's work.

You throw the manuscript into the wastepaper basket and get back to work—knowing full well that the final result may turn out to be an Albanian proverb, a maxim by la Rochefocauld, a Confucian adage, or a quotation from Mao's Red Book. And you console yourself by saying that kings, after all, get assassinated, businessmen go bankrupt, politicians lose elections. It comes with the territory.

It comes with the territory.

Another cliché. And yet, an undeniable fact of life—like death. A universal phenomenon applicable to life in the jungle as well as the city.

I am beginning to suspect that perhaps originality consists not so much in avoiding clichés (which, in a way, would amount to trying to avoid the human condition) but in *experiencing* them. What counts is the authenticity of the experience rather than the verbal dexterity with which one disguises a familiar cliché by a brilliant aphorism, essay, or philosophical treatise. Isn't that why four clumsy lines written by an honest man are more readable and satisfying than 500 pages of empty verbiage written by an erudite, academic nonentity? Isn't that also why the most frequently quoted words in the world are neither by Plato nor Shakespeare, nor for that matter Marx and Freud, but *"Our father who art in heaven. . . ."*?

(1980)

160

Encounters with Authors

L AST WEEK I met a best-selling novelist in her thirties who was so attractive, polished, articulate, and blonde that she could have passed for a Hollywood starlet. And yet I was disappointed, perhaps because I want my writers to look more mysterious and remote, like creatures of the night, with something of the owl, the wolf, and the scorpion in them.

There is some truth in the dictum that writers should be read, not seen. I've met many writers—both the published and the unpublished varieties—and with minor exceptions I have found them all disappointing. A published writer will almost always speak of mercenary agents, narrow-minded publishers, ignorant masses, philistine critics, careless distribution, poor advertising. An unpublished writer, on the other hand, will either compose elegies on the decline of the West (on the grounds that so far the West has failed to appreciate his genius) or try to impress and dazzle you with his particular brand of jargon. When I was much younger, I remember, I met a representative of this last species who spoke to me at great length about his personal vision of reality, of his mythos and identity, and of the dichotomies that were tearing him to pieces. Though he looked comfortable enough to me, I was disturbed and for some reason or other I felt cheated. I too wanted to be tormented and torn asunder by dichotomies; but damn it! I didn't even know what they were. Maybe I had been on the wrong track. The only reason I didn't develop an inferiority complex then and there was that I already had one.

I was reminded of this incident recently while reading Jimmy Cagney's autobiography, where he states that what motivated him to act was simply the urge "to put groceries on the table."

That of course isn't quite accurate. Cagney went on acting even after he acquired enough capital to buy a dozen supermarkets. Perhaps what he was trying to say was that a creative person does not and should not feel the need to cross-examine his unconscious.

And yet I can't give up wondering what it is exactly that makes me want to write. I have come up with a hundred reasons none of them satisfactory. As a matter of fact, every time I ask that question I come up with a different and often contradictory answer. I like to be read, sure! Fame and fortune? Perhaps, but not quite. I suspect I write because writing is an activity that makes me feel comfortable with myself and my surroundings—and comfortable in the physical as well as metaphysical sense of the word. No other activity (and I have tried several—from factory hand to insurance clerk), except perhaps playing Bach on the organ, gives me as much pleasure. In that sense, I suppose, like most of my fellow men, I am more like Sancho Panza than the Don. I am motivated by love of comfort and not by hunger of martyrdom, adventure, and heroics.

(1980)

On Universality

UNIVERSALITY IS THE characteristic that makes a writer's work accessible to all men regardless of class, language, nationality, and culture. Shakespeare is the quintessentially universal writer; Russians admire him as intensely as the English. But only Germans fully understand and appreciate Goethe. To appreciate Dante, one must not only understand archaic Italian but also be familiar with medieval Italian symbolism, history, and culture. It is impossible to appreciate Somerset Maugham's or Aldous Huxley's conflicts and crises without being familiar with the class structure of British society. It's different with Shakespeare. His kings and princes are men with flesh and blood, and when they bare their souls—when they suffer, despair, love, hate, and thirst for revenge—we recognize them as brothers.

The same could be said of Anton Chekhov. When Chekhov writes about an unfaithful wife, a dentist, or an impoverished landowner, we no longer think of them as characters in a Russian setting at the end of the last century, but as men and women we have known—or *could* have known. That's true universality.

Another short story writer whose characters have such an immediacy that they seem to belong to our own circle of friends is Guy de Maupassant. It is universality that makes Chekhov and Maupassant the two greatest short story writers in world literature.

By contrast, the characters of Hemingway's "The Killers," which is generally regarded as one of the greatest short stories in American literature, seem to be stuck to their particular time and place. Though masterfully depicted, they remain nonetheless specific phenomena; that is to say, they no longer exist, and they would have been totally incomprehensible to 19th-century readers.

The same could be said of Ambrose Bierce's "An Occurrence at Owl Creek Bridge," Erskine Caldwell's "Kneel to the Rising Sun," and J. D. Salinger's "For Esmé—with Love and Squalor"—to mention only three representative works regarded as masterpieces.

Generally speaking, American literature, indeed all of American culture, is too dependent on consumption—that is to say, on the laws of fashion, popularity, and the marketplace. American writers like John Updike and Salinger may be very popular in the USSR today, granted, but so are ballpoint pens, rock music, chewing gum, and blue jeans. One may be justified in suspecting that as soon as the Soviets develop the know-how to produce these items themselves, a very large portion of American literature will become obsolete there.

(1980)

Words of Wisdom

IGNORANCE (WHICH, ACCORDING TO SOME, IS BLISS) has always seemed to me the outcome of a cold-blooded and premeditated decision *not* to know. A wise man once said that all you need to acquire wisdom in this world is to keep your eyes and ears open. If you can't afford traveling a thousand miles in search of knowledge, don't worry about it, because knowledge itself will eventually travel ten thousand miles and fall on you like manna. Because knowledge abhors ignorance as much as nature abhors a vacuum.

Once, in Venice, I was taught how to phrase a Bach fugue by an African diplomat. I was practising on the piano ("slaughtering" would be the more accurate verb) and he happened to be in the next room. Unable to endure the horror, he rushed in to prevent further bloodshed. This may sound like a very simple explanation or coincidence, but consider the fantastic aspects of it. The son of an Armenian immigrant from the Middle East meets, in an Italian city, a dark-skinned bureaucrat from another continent and is taught how to play an 18th-century German composer on the piano.

Another thing that I have noticed: frequently words of wisdom are spoken by total nonentities. "Never trust a man in power." These words have haunted me ever since I heard them spoken by an old man who was not widely recognized for his wisdom. I disagreed with him. I maintained that there were good men and bad men and that power could not change a good man into a bad one. He said even the best man in the world should not be trusted with absolute power. He was right. It took me years to realize that not to be tempted by the evil that is inherent in power, one must be a saint. Which may explain why no saint has ever run for political office. It must have been this very fact that led Plato to remark: "The truth is, and must be, that social life is the happiest and most harmonious when those who have to rule are the last people who would choose to be rulers and is least happy and least harmonious when the rulers are of the opposite disposition."

165

Another sentence that has haunted me for many years: "Never give advice—it's a waste of time." These words too were spoken by a total mediocrity. Some insights, I suppose, are inaccessible to great and wise men. A man in power, for instance, will never admit that power corrupts, because this admission would undermine his own authority. Likewise, a preacher would condemn himself to silence if he were to suspect that giving advice is a complete waste of time and that words of wisdom, even when heeded, are almost always distorted and misunderstood. Organized religions from Christianity ("the opium of the masses") to Marxism ("the opium of the intellectuals") attest to this fact. Christ spoke in very simple parables, and he was not only misunderstood but crucified—he still is, according to Dostoevsky, Tolstoy, and more recently Kazantzakis. Marx, in contradistinction, spoke in highly detailed, almost scientific terms, and he brought forth the nightmare of Stalin and the Gulag. The Chinese are fond of saying that he who knows does not speak, perhaps because when truth is spoken, it turns into a lie.

(1980)

Notes from a Journal

W HEN WE FAIL to appreciate the fantastic complexities of life, we take refuge in our own fantasy.

Goodness is a coward's favorite mask.

It is relatively easy to suffer one fool at a time, but very difficult to suffer two of them at the same time; perhaps because one fool represents only one vote against our own sanity, whereas two fools place us in the uncomfortable position of a minority.

Never turn the other cheek: you may be mistaken for a masochist, or you may be encouraging a sadist.

Weakness is an invitation, strength a threat.

Sometimes your enemy's courage is nothing but a reflection of your own fear.

The Chinese are fond of saying that a journey of a thousand miles begins with a single step. The reverse is also true: sometimes we must travel a thousand miles in order to cover a single step.

John Stuart Mill once said: "Better to be a dissatisfied Socrates than a satisfied pig." Alas, we live on a continent where pork is much more widely consumed and valued than books of Greek philosophy.

The law of the jungle says: Never stand between a hungry lion and his kill. Likewise between a man and his injured vanity.

When punishment comes at last, it is more often than not as a result of carelessness rather than the commission of a crime.

Those who refuse to learn from history will repeat its errors? Not very likely—unless of course they happen to be in full control of events. It is more accurate to say that those who cannot foresee the consequences of their acts are like blind men walking on the edge of the precipice. They don't have to be destroyed by historic forces but by a much more universal and fundamental law: that of gravity.

167

Time: a universal and indiscriminate killer.

A man of cunning views others as either victims to be exploited or ambushes to be avoided. This naturally restricts the gamut of his perceptions and experiences. A man of cunning is a man limited by his own calculations. Even as he manipulates people and events, he is in turn manipulated by his lower instincts. His victories are nothing but defeats in disguise.

Sometimes, in the heat that is generated by a controversy, we tend to forget that the most effective weapon against noise is silence.

There are many ways to teach a man a lesson. Sometimes the most effective way is not to teach him at all. Let him find out for himself. The hard way.

Juvenal writes: *No one ever reached the depths of wickedness all at once.*

Or the heights of sainthood; or greatness; or mediocrity, for that matter. It has always seemed to me that to be mediocre one must constantly, relentlessly, daily, reject the temptation to be original, unique, great.

To be truly, genuinely mediocre is no mean trick.

What is wisdom? Adopting this or that religious doctrine or philosophical system?

No. That is simply mimesis.

Following the Ten Commandments or the Golden Rule?

No. That is obedience, regimentation. True wisdom must have originality, daring. Pure wisdom is pure invention. It is the highest form of creativity.

Literature should teach us new ways of dealing with reality.

But these ways (or styles) should come to us as shocks. They should be alien to our temperament.

The difference between a good writer and a great writer is that a good writer makes us see something we had been aware of only vaguely, whereas a great writer makes us aware of a world, of a mode of existence, of an inner dimension, we had not even suspected existed.

Suffering is an instrument of discovery. That is why happy people, generally speaking, lack originality and depth.

What prevents us from being understood by our fellow men is a constant effort on our part to be misunderstood in a way that is flattering to our vanity.

It is always an error to allow the intensity and violence of another's opinions to cloud our own judgment.

Intensity and violence, like war and murder, are in themselves completely devoid of meaning.

When a group of young Armenian demonstrators recently pelted the Turkish Embassy in Ottawa with eggs and tomatoes and in the process broke a couple of windows, some Armenians were outraged. "That's vandalism!" I heard an Armenian lady say. "We are guests in a civilized country and we should make an effort to behave in a civilized manner. Where do they think they are—in Lebanon? Things like that aren't done here."

Good manners are important of course. But so is justice.

We live in a tough world where no one has yet been able to concoct a political omelette without breaking a couple of windows—and sometimes heads.

To act like a barbarian under certain circumstances is the only civilized thing to do. The barbarism of civilization consists in exaggerating the importance of etiquette at the expense of justice.

What is history but the dialogue of conflicting interests whose medium of communication has been and continues to be violence?

If history were made by well-mannered individuals, dancing masters would be the most influential people on earth.

If you seldom think of your enemy's fear, that's perhaps because you are too busy with your own.

Greed has many faces. A thirst for immortality is one of them.

Love is an arrow, marriage a boomerang.

To understand is to forgive?

Not always. Sometimes it is understanding that leads us to intolerance and hatred, and misunderstanding to forgiveness and sympathy.

Disgust defies eloquence; that's why the worst on man has not yet been expressed.

Even when you have good grounds to be afraid, you should behave as though you were not afraid. Not because cowardice is bad and courage good, but because fear is *never* good policy.

Need makes us short-sighted. Necessity, blind.

Enemies and critics have their uses. They reveal what is base in us—if not actual then potential. One should cultivate enemies with the same care that one cultivates friends.

In a conflict, a coward will undermine his position by exaggerating not only his own weakness but his enemy's strength.

Some errors of judgment (like the one above) are like avalanches: we cling to them until we are buried.

Talent is a spark, genius a conflagration. Talent is a gift, genius a curse.

Some virtues are not only irrelevant but dangerous—like tolerance in the midst of a massacre.

If your enemy is weaker than you, try to understand him; if he is stronger, try to survive him.

It is easy to forgive an isolated act, but a way of life?—never! Such forgiveness would tend to degenerate into encouragement.

Avoid apologies and explanations. If the other trusts you, no explanation will be required; if he doesn't trust you, no explanation will seem satisfactory.

I suspect the visions of prophets, the inspiration of poets, and the fireworks of orators—all of which may tend to arouse the enthusiasm of crowds and the loyalty of disciples. I feel diminished in crowds, and disciples remind me of mules with only a limited understanding of their rider.

I no longer waste valuable time trying to persuade others that we live in an ocean of mediocrity. Surely, the best way to punish mediocre people is to let them drown in their own mediocrity.

When a man is forced to live like a dog, all his energies are concentrated on a single goal: not to die like a dog. What is the accomplishment of such a man in the eyes of posterity even when he succeeds? Nothing! And yet, he deserves a monument.

Life has its own way of reminding us that ideas, insights, even philosophical systems and faith itself are instruments of limited application and scope, and that if we want to understand life (or rather, not to *misunderstand* it), we must constantly doubt, question, reject, and deny—that is, think *against* ourselves.

I am beginning to suspect that one of the most important things in life is to instill doubt in the minds of men. Love thy neighbor, if you can, certainly; but at the same time doubt the efficacy of love; doubt also your neighbor's need of your love; and above all, doubt your ability to love.

America is the only country on earth where it is possible to make a fortune by writing a book on the virtues of poverty.

I like to read a writer in whose books life speaks louder than art.

You can never persuade a man that what he believes is wrong. The best you can hope to accomplish is to seduce him into considering the possibility of alternative beliefs—and *this,* only after assuring him that his own brand of idiocy is the greatest wisdom between heaven and earth.

Only crooks deliver brilliant sermons on morality. Honest men are, as a rule, too busy trying to make ends meet to have any time for oratory.

When fear becomes intolerable, courage asserts itself.

Objectivity may be desirable in a court of law, but not in art, in friendship, or in anything else that is dependent on feeling. No one has yet been able to compose an objective symphony. For myself, I would prefer to be rejected violently rather than be judged objectively.

As for fame, so many fools have it that it is no longer as attractive as it seemed in my younger days.

Armenian saying: "It is safer to shed tears with a wise man than to laugh with a fool."

If you believe in God, you can always ask Him to forgive you.
   If you don't believe in God, you can ask forgiveness only from your fellow men or yourself—a transaction that is seldom as easily arranged.

The most popular topic of conversation? Little triumphs—carefully edited and embellished anecdotes from which the speaker invariably emerges victorious.

When in doubt, I contradict, hoping to discover the truth in the heat of the argument.
   I have discovered many things that way, but truth has consistently eluded my grasp.

The moment I decide that I know more than he does, I condemn myself to learn nothing from him.

Armenian saying: "If going in is easy, make sure so is coming out."

While listening to certain individuals, I am constantly tempted to say: "If you know something I don't know, please tell me. Don't make me wait; because the longer you make me wait, the more of your defects I shall notice."

It is not enough to voice lofty principles. One must earn the right. For myself, I shall always be grateful to Judas for not writing an ode to loyalty.

When midgets are in control, giants become outlaws.

Great accomplishments produce great monsters—men who say: "I did this alone and I can do it again. Everyone needs me, but I need no one." In the end, such men destroy more than they build.

Every day I discover how different people can be. Every day I also discover how different the meaning of the word *different* can be.

When we speak of ourselves, we hide ourselves. It is when we speak of others that we confess.

You achieve success in one field only at the cost of failing in a thousand others.

Sometimes two men fight because one of them saw fear in the eyes of the other. The law of the jungle says: If you don't want to be chased, stand still!

It has been said that God loves the poor and helps the rich. It could also be said that God helps the man of courage and abandons the coward.

Just because a man is a complete fool, it doesn't necessarily follow that everything he says is wrong. Even a broken-down clock will show the correct time once every twelve hours.

That which is acquired by luck may be lost by accident. Example: life.

Is it a sin to be rude to people who are in need of a rude awakening?

When I say: "All men are selfish," I justify my selfishness without admitting it.

All statements that begin with "All men are" or "Everyone is" are nothing but disguised confessions.

People who take nothing seriously, take themselves seriously—their health and disposition, their image, their prejudices, likes, dislikes; that is to say, they take a great many things seriously.

The anxiety of failure, the exhilaration of success, the joy of inspiration and discovery—these are all impediments. To achieve anything of lasting value you must work slowly, soberly, methodically. You must build, demolish, until what you have built even *you* cannot destroy.

It is not enough to have faith. Faith may remove mountains, but only sober judgment will tell you what to do next.

A topic that has been neglected by psychologists: the role of vanity in our phobias and troubles. By exaggerating our self-importance, vanity promotes disappointments and bitterness in us and hostility in others—hence fear of retaliation. In everyday parlance, vanity tells us we are better than we in fact are, and when others fail to accept us on our own terms we are disappointed; we become irritated and offensive. We make enemies. We are hated. We experience fear. We suffer. To say that modesty is just a virtue is to underestimate its pragmatic importance and significance. By restoring a more balanced view of ourselves, modesty may turn out to be the only key to serenity and health.

When a coward decides to fight he always chooses a weak or defenseless person as his opponent.

Armenian saying: "His cunning is such that he even knows where the devil sleeps."

Action without contemplation is destructive and ultimately self-defeating. So is contemplation without action. To know how to balance contemplation with action is to have mastered the greatest balancing trick in the world.

Why do I write? Because I have no one to talk to.

I am grateful to all my friends who have chosen to live in distant places. I am also grateful to my surroundings for failing to provide me with a single friend.

When two bad men strike up a friendship, we must either redefine the word "friendship" or call their relationship a conspiracy.

Many speak but few make sense. It's always the same story. I have myself heard numerous sermons and speeches delivered by men who have invariably reminded me of cannibals preaching vegetarianism to an audience of starving men. And what has always astonished me is that at the end, audiences have applauded these impostors instead of stoning them to death.

In the Soviet Union, writers form a government within a government—that is why the real government has to censor and occasionally even silence them. In the West, writers are either dismissed as entertainers or simply ignored. For myself, I can never give up dreaming of a country in which writers will neither be feared nor ignored, but *needed*—just like plumbers and garbage collectors. But perhaps that's too much to ask.

> Once, I began to write an ode to silence—
> its complex eloquence,
> noble austerity,
> enigmatic beauty . . .
> But I changed my mind
> and left it unfinished.
> Silence, I thought,
> should be praised with silence.

When in doubt, do what comes easy.

If you are strong, you can choose your enemy. If you are weak, you are chosen—and quite frequently too.

To touch the ceiling, one must try to reach for heaven.
   Likewise, to achieve goodness, one must strive for sanctity.
   To write a decent line, one must aim at the Nobel Prize.

When logic cannot justify an act, our emotions provide all the justification we need.

The most effective revenge, like the most wounding insult, should be unintentional. To premeditate, carefully plan, and execute a revenge is in itself an admission that one has suffered an injury—that is to say, that one is weak and vulnerable.

I distrust the generosity and refinement of a man who can afford being both generous and refined. The virtues of such a man appear to me not so much reflections of his soul but of his income.

Anatole France: "How majestic is the equality of the Law, which permits both rich and poor alike to sleep under the bridges at night."

Only after I confront and overcome the fear of solitude will I be able to distinguish a friend from a sycophant.

What you love today you may loathe tomorrow. And vice versa.

To inject some degree of indifference in your emotional life is therefore not only a sign of wisdom but also of prophetic insight.

Don't tell me what you want because you'll bore me.

Tell me instead what you are doing in order to acquire the ability to get what you want.

It is the selfish man, more than anyone else, who is constantly reminded that he is not the center of the world; and yet, he stubbornly and with increasing despair clings to his egocentric view of life.

The avaricious man tends to be generous with advice.

To be loved for qualities one does not possess is almost to be hated.

It is easy to contradict one aphorism or proverb with another. It is more difficult, however, to discern the different levels on which these apparently contradictory statements move, and the particular type of situation to which they apply.

There is a degree of authenticity in the most casual of our offenses that even heartfelt apologies cannot emulate.

(1975–1980)

My Hero

WHEN A NATION loses a war, it loses much more than a series of battles.

An assistant professor of history from a neighboring university, whom I shall call Ashot Yergatian, telephones to inform me that he has just completed an essay on terrorism.

"Congratulations!" I say.

"Yes, but I'm not sure what to do with it," he goes on.

"Do you mention Turks and Armenians?"

"Yes, I do."

"There are several Armenian weeklies that might be interested in publishing it."

"I realize that, but what if some hot-blooded, fanatic Turk reads it?"

"They don't read Armenian weeklies."

"Who says?"

"Do you read Turkish weeklies?"

"Do they have them?"

"*If* they had them?"

"I don't read Turkish."

"Make it English-language Turkish weeklies."

"All right, I wouldn't read them."

"No further questions."

"Not so fast, pal. These Turks are out for blood. For all I know they may get their marching orders from Ankara, where, I'm sure, everything we say is carefully monitored."

"Are you trying to tell me that some bureaucrat in Ankara will read your essay, send an order to some Turkish terrorist group here, and they'll come and burn your house down?"

"Why not? Now, I'm not saying they'll do it; I'm only saying they may—"

"Tell me, in this essay of yours, do you advocate terrorism against them?"

"Nothing like that, no. Actually I don't even express personal

176

views; I merely quote statesmen, historians, sociologists. I present the evidence in as objective a manner as possible."

"What makes you think then you will be singled out as a target for counter-terrorist action?"

"Well, you know how hot-blooded Middle-Eastern people are. They may read between the lines and draw all kinds of conclusions that were not meant to be there."

"If it's any consolation to you, I have published several articles and books on the subject and my home hasn't been bombed or burned down yet."

"Maybe I won't be as lucky. Besides, we have a fairly large Turkish community in this town."

"We have them here too."

"They are organized here."

"Same here. They operate a radio station, they have a club, a community center, an anti-defamation league . . you name it."

"Are your Armenians organized there?"

"A couple of them may belong to the Hamazkain."

"In that case you're better off than I am. Because my Armenians are not organized."

"Organize them!"

"That may take years."

"You've got a point there. I'll tell you what: Why don't you publish the essay under a pseudonym or just your initials?"

"Initials are no good. They may guess my identity. In this town I'm the only Armenian with my initials."

"Name a different town then—Walla Walla, Washington; Kalamazoo, Michigan. And if you want to throw them off the scent even further, sign with a pseudonym—Mamigon Kachaznouni, Antranik of Sassoun, Kevork Chavoush."

"That's not a bad idea. Let me think about it. Anyway, thanks for your help."

"Any time."

When a nation loses a war, sometimes it may also lose its manhood.

(1981)

Writers, Readers, Critics and Related Atrocities

A RMENIAN WRITERS FROM such population centers as Istanbul, Paris, Los Angeles, and New York write letters to ask if I would be willing to help them with the distribution of their books. Some of them enclose long bibliographies ranging from translations of Goethe to commentaries on *Narek*. "As a man dedicated to literature and ideas," they say, "I am sure you will do whatever you can to help a colleague" ("pen-brother" in Armenian).

In my reply, I try to explain that the handful of Armenians who live in this godforsaken Siberian town are hard workers without intellectual pretensions. Most of them don't even know that I am myself a writer, and those who do tend to make a big joke of it.

"So, tell us then, how's the writing business?" they say whenever we meet in the street.

Or: "Have you come up with a best-seller yet?"

"Of course, we expect a great deal from you," says an older man with total indifference, assuming the air of a statesman. "I wielded a fiery pen myself in my younger days, and I am familiar with all the problems and difficulties. The main thing is to persevere and be patient." He is now a maintenance man in the head office of an insurance company.

"Someone told me you write," another said recently. "I didn't know you were a writer."

I pleaded guilty as charged.

"So what kind of stuff do you write?"

"A little of everything."

"Thrillers and mystery novels?"

"I'm afraid not."

"Pornography?"

"Sorry."

"No sex? No violence? What then?"

"History, culture, translations of classics, and garbage like that."

"Is there any money in that?"

178

"No money."

"So how do you survive?"

"You may well ask."

"So how do you survive?" a well-fed Armenian priest wanted to know, too, after a short cross-examination.

"Barely," I replied.

"May the good Lord give you strength and perseverance."

If it's not advice, it's blessings.

This story with the priest has an interesting sequel.

Less than a month later, I read in the newspapers that the church of this same priest was in the business of selling Oriental rugs at wholesale prices. I wrote him a letter asking if his church would also consider selling books dealing with Armenian history and culture. His secretary replied, saying they had tried to sell books at one time but they had given it up because there wasn't enough money in it.

In his letter of rejection, an editor explains that though he likes my style, he cannot accept my novel because it is a first-person narrative and he no longer publishes autobiographical fiction. He then goes on to say that I should learn to use my imagination. "With material like this, why should I?" I am tempted to reply. "Can there be anything more fantastic than reality?" and I'm not excluding editors like himself. But I have discovered that one gains nothing by insulting editors. The more mediocre the man, the more impervious to reason, the more limited his understanding, the more trashy his perception of art. There was a time when I thought of mediocrity as an absence of intelligence combined with poor taste. I am beginning to suspect, however, that mediocrity is a powerful and aggressive force. It is a state of mind rather than an attribute: a state of mind that must be constantly cultivated, reinforced, trained, nourished, encouraged. And the most effective way to deal with mediocrity is to let it be devoured by time.

"Why don't you write something like *Roots, Shogun,* and *Masada?*" a young whippersnapper demanded to know once, explaining how I should go about producing such a tome. "All that stuff about the massacres, Mount Ararat, Lake Sevan, and Mesrob Mashtots," he went on," I mean, who cares, man!"

As soon as people find out I am a writer, they give me advice on what to write and how to go about writing it—what books to read, whom to interview, where to go.

"You should write a book about your uncle," an aunt of mine (who hasn't read a single book since the time of Gutenberg) told me during a recent visit. "He witnessed the burning of Smyrna."

"Did he really?" I said, to be polite more than anything else.

"I was there from beginning to end," he said indifferently, to further whet my appetite. "So many people have asked me to write about it," he went on, "but who has the time? I tried once or twice, but always something happens."

Everyone complains about his lack of time; no one complains about his lack of ability. If they can write a letter, they can write a book. If they can write one page, they can write two hundred. The logic is elementary, the illusion widespread. Saroyan may have been right: every Armenian thinks he could be as good as Shakespeare. Which may explain why Armenians like to starve their writers—to punish them for not being better than Shakespeare.

"A book about the burning of Smyrna has already been written," I said to my uncle.

"Probably by someone who wasn't even there," he said.

"That's right, but the book is based on eyewitness reports and interviews with survivors."

"Maybe, but I saw things that nobody else could have seen."

"Atrocities?"

"Horrible beyond anyone's imagination."

Yes, there may be money in that. An American professor has written a book in which he maintains that people like to read about atrocities because it makes them appreciate the small pleasures and privileges of life. Never say, therefore, that suffering is meaningless, because someone somewhere may write about it and make someone else very happy. And I reflect that victims are always victimized twice: first by sadistic barbarians, second by a well-meaning imbecile who uses their suffering in order to enhance the pleasures of his readers.

"A writer, a genuine writer—and I think perhaps you have a chance of being one," a reader writes, "—should be above such petty details as you have been writing about recently. A writer should deal exclusively with lofty ideas. He should inspire his readers, urge them toward higher goals."

"Easy to say," I write in my reply. "I too would like contemporary composers to write music like Beethoven and Brahms. I too would like to see my contemporary philosophers produce dialogues like those of Plato. And who would not prefer to write about noble princes, elegant princesses, and beautiful sunsets? If

I write about scum, it's not because I enjoy it but because I am drowning in it. And if you think you are not as vulnerable as I am, you must be an extremely lucky fellow. By the way, what's your racket?"

I doubt very much if I shall hear from him.

"Do you know this character?" I ask a widely traveled and well-informed friend of mine.

"Who doesn't," he says.

"Tell me about him."

"What would you like to know?"

"What's his racket?"

"He's a retired millionaire."

"How did he make his money?"

"Selling rugs."

"Oriental?"

"What else?"

"That figures."

I read today that a noted French philosopher (Louis Althusser) strangled his wife in a fit of rage and is now locked in an insane asylum. A demented philosopher for a demented age. I wouldn't be surprised if a future biographer concludes that strangling his wife was this philosopher's most daring and original praxis.

I like to invent sayings. Things like "living is like trying to cross a river infested with piranhas" (Brazilian saying).

Someday, if and when I decide to write my memoirs, I may quote that "saying" at the head of page one.

(1981)

A Note on Saroyan

AN ARMENIAN PERIODICAL where William Saroyan began to publish his youthful stories boasted in its pages recently that Saroyan had never asked for any money and had never been paid a single cent for his contributions, implying (perhaps unintentionally) that had it been up to them, Saroyan would very probably have starved. When he began to write, Saroyan was not a financially independent person. Most of the stories of this period speak of destitution and hunger. Saroyan survived and died a millionaire because his talent was easily accessible to the average American reader. There were others, less fortunate than Saroyan, who were ignored and thus silenced as effectively as Charents and Bakounts under Stalin, simply because their style and worldview were not easily accessible to the general public. In Russia they get rid of *dissident* writers. In America they ignore *unpopular* writers. The result is the same. To serve American popular tastes can be as repugnant to an authentic artist as to serve the Kremlin. An artist should serve only God (if he believes in Him) or Truth (if he doesn't). The moment he decides to serve a particular audience or political platform, he degrades himself and turns into an entertainer, a propagandist, a clown. And when that happens, even the audience he chose to entertain will ignore him. Isn't that what happened to Dikran Kouyoumdjian (Michael Arlen)? And wasn't that the reason behind Saroyan's own gradual decline as an artist?

(1982)

The War of Images

LIKE ALL POLITICALLY FRAGMENTED PEOPLE, we are addicted to talk. Among ourselves, we argue. From outsiders, we expect nothing but flattery. We fail to take into account the fact that we live among pragmatic, practical men—achievers without a past—who judge us not by what we say, but by what we do. Not by what we may or may not have accomplished in the past, but by what we are capable of achieving today.

For several decades now, we Armenians have been trying very hard and without much success to persuade the rest of the world that Turks are savages and Armenians a creative minority that has been unfairly treated by the West. It is true that after reading the evidence, some academics have expressed sympathy for us and sometimes, with the financial aid from Armenian foundations, have produced books favorable to our cause and flattering to our vanity. These books, however, have been read mostly by Armenians and have had very little influence on world opinion. Who else but Armenians and a certain English professor who has had the financial support of the Gulbenkian Foundation—one of the wealthiest foundations in the world, it is said—would call Armenia "the cradle of civilization"?

The Turks, in the meantime, have not been sitting idly by, allowing us to corner the academic market. They too have been offering their financial support and cooperation to young English and American professors, who have produced many texts in which their side of the story is told with the inevitable bias. As a result, the world goes on thinking of Turks as a fiercely proud and warlike people, and of Armenians as servile and crafty traders who probably got everything they deserved. Next time you enter a public library, take a look at your average text on the history of the Middle East, the Ottoman Empire, the Turkish Republic, Ataturk, and related atrocities. In the acknowledgments of these books you will be informed that most of them were penned with the financial assistance of the Turkish government and the cooperation of the Turkish academic establishment. (In the first edition of my book *The Armenians: Their History and Culture—A Short Introduction* [Toronto, 1975], I discuss half a dozen of these books and expose some of the absurdities they disseminate.) Even such prestigious reference works as the *Encyclopedia Britannica* have begun to tone down their treatment of the Genocide of 1915 (which is now described as "wartime deportations") and have nothing but praise for such Turkish "statesmen" as Talaat Pasha (our Hitler/Himmler)—perhaps because more copies of the *Britannica* are sold in Turkey than in Soviet Armenia.

In election years, American presidential candidates offer moral support to our cause and, immediately after they are elected, military and financial support to the Turks.

"You have books about Indians, Eskimos, Turks, and Kurds, but not a single volume about Armenians," I once said to a librarian in a small Canadian town (pop. 35,000).

"Our collection reflects the interests of the community we serve," he replied. "Are there many Armenians in this area—do you know?"

"A handful of families," I said, adding, "probably no more than Kurds, Turks, and Eskimos."

"Perhaps, but your average reader has heard of Eskimos and Turks. Not many people know much about Armenians," he said.

I was tempted to say at this point that *that* proves only one thing; namely, your average reader is an ignoramus and an imbecile, and that the function of a library is not to reinforce the prejudices and limitations of its readers but to educate them and broaden their perception of the world. If you give them what they want, if you repeat that which they already know, what have you accomplished? But I kept my peace. You don't advance your cause by insulting those who may be in a position to help. I tried instead to explain that unlike Kurds, Turks, Apaches, and Eskimos, Armenians have made many contributions to the civilization of the West—first nation to adopt Christianity, Romanesque architecture, music, Aivazovsky, Mikoyan, Saroyan, Khatchaturian, Arshile Gorky—

"I thought Gorky was Russian."

"You're thinking of Maxim, the Soviet author. I was referring to Arshile, the modern American painter—his real name was Adoian, actually, Vostanig Adoian: born in Van (Armenia), spent most of his life in the United States, where he also died."

"Interesting," he said, without trying to disguise his boredom and skepticism; then, after casting a quick glance at his wristwatch, he added, "you should have a talk with Miss Joyce Some-thingorother—she handles our acquisitions. Prepare a list of books, if you like. We'll be glad to consider them. Suggestions are always welcome."

And I imagined him entering his office, calling Miss Some-thingorother on the phone, and saying: "Some Aramaean or Rumanian nut may get in touch with you complaining we have no books about his particular tribe. You know what to do."

We like to brag about our past achievements without realizing that *that* will prove only one thing: we have degenerated into a bunch of windbags. Many *odars* think of us in those terms already. "I used to work for an Armenian rug merchant—a Mr. Art Tulumian, perhaps you know him," a Canadian said to me one day, adding: "Quite a character he was. Proud of his heritage. Bragged a lot. I never knew how much of what he was saying was true." (Anglo-Saxon understatement for "The man was an unmitigated liar.")

Most of us are naive enough to think that we can impress others with verbiage. Do you think your average American gives a hoot about Arshile Gorky's background or whether or not we were the first nation to adopt Christianity? Even most books dealing with the history of Christianity do not mention that curious fact; and some art historians continue to assert that Arshile Gorky's background is Jewish, Russian, and even Greek and Turkish. And in some Turkish textbooks, such eminent Armenians as Mesrob Mashdots and Gomidas Vartabed are identified as Turks, in the same way that in many reference works Saroyan is identified as an American author and Khachaturian as a Soviet composer.

I was myself irritated with a Canadian recently when she tried to convince me that a certain American economist (or was it a Hollywood starlet) was in fact of Canadian origin. How would you react to a man from Kenya or Kamchatka who came up to you and insisted that a certain internationally recognized celebrity was in fact born in the same obscure village as he? I'll never forget the loud-mouthed Pakistani who kept bragging about his nation's past achievements and military might. He went on and on, and when I could take it no longer, I said: "What happened to you?"

"What do you mean, what happened?"

"How did you manage to squander all that might and glory? Why are you in such a political and economic mess?"

"History moves in cycles," he lectured, assuming the resigned air of a guru facing an unruly disciple. "A thousand years ago we were strong; now we are weak. Where do you think your Americans and Russians will be in a thousand years? The American colossus, my friend, will collapse as surely as the Roman Empire. The walls of the Kremlin and the Pentagon will crumble just as surely as the Akropolis in Athens."

I should have guessed. People prefer to put the blame on others (including some dark force they call history) rather than themselves. But historians tell us that empires and civilizations are not killed, they commit suicide. Greed and corruption are more lethal than the mightiest and cruelest of enemies. In our case it is fragmentation. It has always been fragmentation. And is not fragmentation a species of greed? Greed for power. At one time Armenia was subdivided by men who said: "If I cannot be king of the land, I'll be prince of my province, *nakharar* of my district, ruler of my mountain." In our diaspora today, we have men who say: "If I cannot be the head of all Armenians, I'm willing to settle for a fraction." Something is better than nothing.

Conquerors and colonizers know how to divide and rule. We make ideal subjects because we do not even allow foreign conquerors to divide us. We divide ourselves. Even the Ottomans were aware of this peculiarity of ours. That is why they regarded us as their favorite and most loyal ethnic minority.

Am I advocating one-man rule? Not at all. What I am saying is that if we are going to have two, or even twenty leaders, we would be better off if these leaders cooperated with one another. Wouldn't we all benefit if our leaders decided to fight against our real enemies rather than against one another? Because if we fight our enemies, we may survive. If, on the other hand, we fight one another, we will be doing nothing but carrying out the policies of Sultan Abdulhamid and Talaat Pasha.

Arlen's Passage: A Post-Mortem

"I T IS NOT A MASTERPIECE," a friend of mine warned me, speaking of Jacques Hagopian's play *The Call of the Crane*, "but I think you ought to see it. It raises some relevant questions. Its approach may be one-sided and melodramatic, but it is worth seeing."

So I went along. When we entered the theater, we found standing room only. I was surprised. How long had it been since I had seen so many Armenians under the same roof? The performances were not bad either. The plot, however, held no surprises. Disgusted with the indifference of his compatriots, an Armenian poet changes his name to Jackson (from Hagopian—a friend of the author assured me during the intermission that the play was indeed autobiographical) and tries to write in English. When an Armenian patriot shows up and urges him to be more active in the local Armenian community, the poet tells him to get lost. "I'm leaving now," the activist declares, assuming the haughty air of a retreating general, *"but I shall return!"*

The son of this assimilated poet eventually discovers his true identity, falls in love with a dark-eyed Armenian beauty, promptly ditches his dizzy Anglo-Saxon blonde, and walks out on his renegade father.

"We have lost our son," says the mother tearfully, her head on her husband's shoulder.

"Our loss is Armenia's gain," says the father.

The curtain falls. Deafening applause. Here and there, tears.

The plot reminded me a little of the Arlens.

Dikran Kouyoumdjian changed his name to Michael Arlen, married an *odar*, produced some very popular novels in English, acquired fame and fortune, gave his son the best English education money could buy, and warned him to stay away from Armenians. After his father died, however, Arlen Jr. eventually discovered his half-Armenian background, went through an identity crisis, sought out Saroyan in California, had a long heart-to-heart talk with him and, taking his advice, traveled to Armenia. Upon his return to America he wrote *Passage to Ararat*, which became a best-seller. At the end of this book he urged his fellow Armenians to follow in his father's and his own footsteps by forgetting all about their tragic and dark past ("Armenian problems . . . starving Armenians . . . distant and repellent events"), their nationalism ("madness and pride"), and their non-existent culture ("One hears of Armenian culture—at least from Armenians—but it is surely not that"). His work and mission thus concluded, Arlen Jr. went on to write a book on television commercials—a topic on which he is generally regarded as an authority. Same plot, different endings.

Passage must be viewed first and foremost as an act of understanding and exegesis. By exploring the past of the Armenian nation, Arlen tried to understand and explain his own father—a complex and ultimately tragic man who was rejected by the aristocracy of the very people he tried to entertain (in this connection, see Harry Keyishian's informative biography *Michael Arlen*, published by the Wayne State University Press).

Arlen Sr. was a man of contradictions. By resolving these contradictions, his son tried to exorcise and overcome them. America is the land of well-being and happiness. In America, happiness is a civic duty. If it cannot be found, it must be manufactured. If there is a scarcity of the real thing, a synthetic substitute must be mass-produced, widely advertised, and marketed. Nothing must remain unexplained, unresolved, unavailable. If Arlen Sr. was unhappy, that's because of some kind of misunderstanding between himself and the world or his fellow men. With Yankee ingenuity, the son would clear up this misunderstanding, and with it all the problems that haunt the Armenian-American community. America is strong, healthy, open, normal. Armenia is a dark obsession, a nightmare—blood, massacres, tyranny. We must forsake the incubus of our past and embrace America with its wide open spaces, clear blue eyes, gleaming white teeth, big friendly smile. The open spaces may be polluted, the clear blue eyes nearsighted, the teeth capped, the friendly smile vacant. But never mind about that. Beggars can't be choosers.

What interests me here however, is not Arlen's motivations in writing *Passage*, but the unreserved enthusiasm the book aroused among Armenian-Americans. And *Passage* became a best-seller not because it acquainted the American public and the world at large with a nearly forgotten Genocide (several competent and well-documented books had already been written on the subject) but because it flattered American vanity and assuaged the guilt of an already half-assimilated Armenian-American community by providing them with a clear rationale. Even dedicated Armenian-American intellectuals and patriots are now willing to concede that there is no future in being an Armenian in America. A couple of generations and *that* may well be the end of our diaspora. Can anyone say that this is a pessimistic prognosis? What assimilationists like Arlen Jr. try to do is accelerate the process. Why wait for another forty or sixty years? Let's dissolve and vanish now. The sooner the better.

In the name of Christian ethics and humanitarian principles, assimilationists may be willing to expose the red massacres of the Ottoman Turks without realizing that they are advocating the American Melting Pot and its euphemistic variant, the Canadian Mosaic. They like to speak of tolerance, compassion, equality, freedom of choice; but they seem to be incapable of conceiving a society wherein man may live side by side without conducting some form of repression and ultimately cultural genocide—or, as our fathers used to say, "white massacre."

The citizens of a mighty empire must serve that empire; adopt its goals as their own ("America's business is business"); forget temperamental and cultural differences, which belong to the Old World.

A man is no longer a man but a producer and a consumer. A pair of hands and a mouth. The human brain, that which distinguishes us from the rest of the animal kingdom, has become an obsolete organ. One must produce and consume as much as possible. Anything that does not contribute to these all-important functions must be regarded as undesirable.

When businessmen advertise a product, they prefer to deal with a homogeneous audience—people with the same tastes, inclinations, outlooks. Because that way they can reach and seduce more people.

The Old World declined because it was torn by internecine wars, religious intolerance, nationalism, lack of mutual understanding, further enhanced by a wide diversity of languages. The New World dissolves all these differences, eliminates misunderstandings. One language, one culture, one ethos.

These were the aims of the Ottoman Empire, too. The Turks failed because their system was autocratic, backward, corrupt, warlike. America has its problems too, of course. The apotheosis of violence, sex, money. Racism. Political corruption. Poverty, unemployment, crime. Military and economic aid to dictatorial regimes. Moral support to Armenians, dollars and missiles to Turks.

America and Turkey: Is it possible that these two powers speak a language we are not equipped to understand? The language of geopolitics. An ethics of territorial rather than moral imperatives. Human rights, traditional concepts of justice and morality: these are regarded as useful topics for preachers and professors with verbal diarrhea. In places like the Pentagon, the White House, Wall Street—wherever, that is, the fate of nations is discussed and foreign policy formulated—the primary consideration remains the preservation of the Empire. One must endure at all cost. Even mighty empires think of survival, and all empires feed on the flesh and blood of minorities. Some empires behave like cannibals, others like vampire bats. Different approaches, same result.

In the 19th century, in the Ottoman Empire, we had among us men who foresaw the coming catastrophe and warned us. They were not believed. In progressive America today we are at the mercy of men who advocate assimilation or are willing to concede that we don't have much of a chance to survive. Without knowing it these men advocate genocide. They pretend to have our interest at heart, but they are our worst enemies. Beside these confused and gullible men, Sultan Abdulhamid and Talaat Pasha were shrewd operators. Pragmatic. Machiavellian. Far-sighted. Direct. They didn't beat around the bush. They knew what they wanted.

Millions of people today worry whether or not an obscure species of fish or bird known only to a handful of scientists will manage to survive our century. But does anyone care whether or not a unique and priceless cultural heritage will survive? Or whether a language (which, after all, is a mode of perceiving and expressing the world) and its literature (most of which remains untranslated and buried in obscure and defunct periodicals) will ever be read and known by the so-called civilized nations of the world?

But Armenia and Armenian culture are not dependent on the Armenian-American community, you'll say. There is after all an Armenia where writers continue to write in Armenian, and where the intricacies of our language are carefully taught in schools and universities. And yet, some of the greatest masterpieces of modern Armenian literature have not yet been published in Soviet Armenia simply because they do not conform with the doctrines of Marx and Lenin. Occasionally English translations of Armenian literary works appear in Moscow—actually retranslations from the Russian, handled by impersonal translators with little affection for and no affinity with the original work. The results are very often so disappointing that one wonders why the Russians don't give an end to the whole program. Could it be because the mediocrity of their own official literature is such that the mediocrity of our own writers goes unnoticed?

No. We cannot and should not rely on others. If something is worth doing, we must do it ourselves. And if we cannot do it with all the academic freedom and vast financial resources at our command, why should we expect our brothers in Armenia to do it under vastly more difficult conditions?

In the New World, we are being Americanized. In the USSR, Sovietized and Russified. To what extent will Armenia still be Armenia a hundred years from now? When Armenian-Americans speak Armenian, they use more English words than Armenian ones, and the Armenian words they use are twisted out of shape and hardly recognizable. Don't think things are better in the USSR. Some of our greatest writers and scholars there prefer to think and write in Russian. Aram Khachaturian himself, writes Rouben Zarian in his recently published memoirs, spoke Armenian with great difficulty. Even Armenian professors, writing in Armenian and teaching in the University of Yerevan, prefer to use Russian words and expressions. Confronted with this question, a visiting Soviet-Armenian author retaliated: "Instead of criticizing us for our use of Russian words, you [Armenian-Americans] should mind your own language. The Armenian spoken here isn't exactly pure either." He meant: If, in your freedom, you abuse and besmirch the purity of our language, how dare you criticize us who live in oppression?

Our *freedom*. What is it exactly? The relentless promotion of vulgarity, ignorance, sports, trivia, sex, and violence can create an atmosphere wherein freedom turns into oppression as surely as day into night and life into death.

Anti-intellectualism in
Armenian Life

IN OUR PUBLIC LIBRARY today, I came across a recently published English-language reference work on contemporary world literature. Like all such works, it is a collective effort put out by a university press. The literature of every nation in the world is discussed. Separate entries are devoted to noted authors. There is a fairly detailed article on Turkish literature and several entries on eminent 20th-century Turkish novelists and poets. But Armenia and Armenians are not even mentioned. Not a single entry on any of our writers.

There is a literary quarterly published by the University of Oklahoma called *World Literature Today* in which books in all languages and published in many countries (from Japan to Brazil) are reviewed. Whenever I can, I contribute reviews of Armenian- and English-language books published in Armenia and the diaspora. But whenever I can't, no one else does. I note, however, that in every issue without fail, several reviews of Turkish books written by Turkish critics (mostly professors in American universities) appear. To the editors of this particular periodical, Turks are more interested in their own literature than Armenians. To the readers of this periodical, Turks produce more literary works than Armenians. Perhaps I should add here that *World Literature Today* does not pay its contributors. I am not implying that Armenian scholars and critics are greedier than their Turkish counterparts. I am sure there are other reasons; one of which is that there are many more Turks than Armenians; another being that more Turks read and understand Turkish than Armenians read and understand Armenian. Turkish writers, moreover, very probably enjoy the full support of their government. (I say "very probably" because I don't know any Turkish writers and I have not talked with one about this matter). It is different with Armenian writers. (And here I speak from experience.) As a reviewer and translator, I have had little or no support from Armenian foundations, mis-

192

cellaneous cultural institutions, and our government in Yerevan. The few cultural foundations I have written to have either failed to respond or informed me that my work is outside their scope and that I should get in touch with other foundations (and more precisely the ones that failed to respond). President Truman was right when he said: "You want a friend? Get a dog!" Except that on my income as an Armenian writer, I couldn't afford even a churchmouse.

"Forget Armenian literature and the Armenian press. Write instead for a Canadian and American audience. Our people have no time for literature." How many times have I been given this piece of advice by well-known and well-meaning Armenian intellectuals, poets, and party functionaries—or what I like to call "professionial Armenians"—men who are fond of delivering grandiloquent speeches in public, publishing fiery editorials and letters to the editor, pretending to serve a noble cause, but in private are willing to admit that this cause no longer exists. With a little encouragement and after a couple of drinks, they may even go further and expose others in their own line of work as impostors, frauds, and parasites. "Don't trust that man," one professional Armenian said to me recently, speaking of another. "He is a liar, a plagiarist, a fool, and a child molester to boot." A busy man indeed. Resourceful. Versatile. Energetic.

The Armenian communities are on the verge of extinction and at the mercy of Levantines in whom the Armenian *voki* is buried under thick layers of resentment, envy, and malice. Take ten of these leaders, put them in the same room, and the result will be a Hamidian massacre. We have been hating the Turks for such a long time that without realizing it we have acquired many of their characteristics—among them intolerance, cruelty, envy, ignorance.

A philosopher once said that to love means to hate the same enemy. Instead of providing us with a common purpose, our hatred of the Turks has fragmented us, damaged our perception of the world, mutilated our judgment. When one hates intensely and over a long period of time, one may gradually forget the meaning of compassion and lose the ability to understand, let alone forgive. Such a man usually ends up hating not only his friends and members of his own family, but himself as well. Such an Armenian can be as merciless and dangerous as a Turk.

I have a friend who hates his father so much that without knowing it he thinks and behaves like his father. His father (now dead) was an intolerant man. His son is tolerant with a vengeance—that is to say, he is fiercely *intolerant* of all those who do not advocate total license and anarchy. Duty and discipline he dismisses as totalitarian tools. "Anarchy and license may lead to perdition," he says, "but at least it will be perdition on my own terms, and I'd rather burn in my own hell than be condemned to listen to someone else's harp music for ever and ever." But a slave to his own instincts is still a slave. Our aim should be liberation, not slavery; salvation, not perdition.

In our diaspora today we publish dozens of newspapers and hundreds of books every year—from Beirut, Aleppo, and Paris, to Montreal, New York, and Los Angeles. And yet, can you name a single memorable title? Can you name even a single writer whose dedication to his art is such that he has devoted his entire life to it? Or, for that matter, a single writer who can support himself as a writer? And why not? Is it because we are few in number? Of course not. Is it because we are poor and weak? We are neither! The truth of the matter is, we admire and look up to successful writers, composers, artists, and actors only when they acquire their fame in foreign circles. We don't trust our own judgment. Or perhaps we have no use for intellectuals and artists, only celebrities about whom we may boast to *odars*.

"He isn't worth much, can't be," an Armenian poet once confided to me, speaking of another Armenian poet. "He began his literary career by writing in Armenian, then changed his mind and tried to contribute to foreign journals; couldn't make a name for himself, and is now writing in Armenian again." For him, that indeed is irrefutable evidence of total failure and moral bankruptcy.

If an Armenian had written the New Testament, the father in that well-known parable would have insulted the returning prodigal son and kicked him out of his house. Same plot, different endings.

Reviews, Interviews and Views

Reviews

Alexander Pushkin

A Journey to Arzrum

ORIGINALLY PUBLISHED IN 1836, *A Journey to Arzrum* is Pushkin's account of his travels from Moscow through Georgia and Armenia to Erzerum (the generally accepted spelling) during the Russo-Turkish war of 1828–29. This is the first English translation, although substantial portions of it appeared in Henri Troyat's magisterial *Pushkin* and Lesley Blanch's *The Sabres of Paradise*.

In his *History of Russian Literature,* D. S. Mirsky rightly remarks that in *Journey* Pushkin "reached the limits of noble and bare terseness." Pruned of all irrelevant ornament, precise, lucid, Pushkin's prose is pure delight. In a short span, we encounter an astonishing range of characters: a Persian poet, a noseless Tartar bathhouse attendant ("a master of his trade"), a hermaphrodite ("a man with a woman's breasts, underdeveloped testicles, a small and boyish penis. We asked whether he had been emasculated. God, he answered, castrated me"), a pipe-smoking Caucasian beauty (the conversation with this "Circe of the Steppes" is more detailed and piquant in Troyat's version, which leads me to the conclusion that Ms. Ingemanson based her translation on a bowdlerized edition), several Russian generals, a Turkish pasha, a young Armenian soldier from Kars, who eagerly volunteers to be Pushkin's guide. "In half an hour I rode out of Kars," Pushkin writes, "and Artemy (that was my Armenian's name) was already galloping beside me on a Turkish stallion, with a supple Kurdish javelin in his hand, a dagger in his belt, and dreaming about Turks and battles."

Particularly poignant is the description of his meeting with the small company from Persia transporting the body of Alexander Sergeevich Griboedov, who had been massacred by a mob in an anti-Russian riot while trying to save the life of an Armenian.

(Translated by Brigitta Ingemanson)
Ardis, Ann Arbor, 1974.

199

Two oxen harnessed to a cart were descending the steep road. Some Georgians were accompanying the cart. "Where do you come from?" I asked them. "From Teheran." "What do you have on your cart?" "Griboed." This was the body of the slain Griboedov, which they were taking to Tiflis.

There follows a short but unforgettable memoir of this great playwright and ambassador to Persia, whose best-known work, *Wit Works Woe*, the most important Russian play with the possible exception of Gogol's *Government Inspector*, was first performed in Yerevan. "I got to know Griboedov in 1817," Pushkin writes:

His melancholy character, his caustic wit, his good nature, his very weaknesses and vices, those inevitable companions of mankind—everything in him was unusually appealing . . . I do not know of anything more enviable than the final years of his stormy life. Even his death which befell him in the midst of a valiant, unequal battle, held nothing terrible, nothing agonizing for Griboedov. It was instantaneous and beautiful.

The final chapter is devoted to a description of Erzerum. Originally an Armenian city and an important commercial and military center since antiquity, Erzerum was shuffled back and forth between Byzantines (who called it Theodosiopolis), Arabs (who renamed it Arzar-Rum, i.e., the Armenian country that had previously been under Roman sovereignty), Persians, and Turks. The Russians captured and temporarily occupied Erzerum in 1829, two years after the liberation of Yerevan (which event was to inspire the first Armenian novel, Apovian's *Verk Hayasdani*). Erzerum was eventually retaken by the Turks and again liberated by the Russians in 1878 and 1916. It is now in Turkish hands.

If you are interested in seeing 19th-century, war-torn Armenia through the eyes of a writer of genius, or if you are simply interested in Russian literature, this book is a must. In addition to the translator's notes—some of which are helpful, but some of which strike me as redundant ("Circe: Famous sorceress in Greek legend") or curiously irrelevant (about Griboedov we are told that "Griboed" means "mushroom eater," but we are given no details concerning his death, about which the reader will have to turn to Lesley Blanch's *The Sabres of Paradise*, a fascinating work and a neglected masterpiece)—there are several illustrations including a self-portrait by Pushkin and the portrait of a Russian commander by Aivazovsky.

Manuel Sarkisyanz

A Modern History of Transcaucasian Armenia

A *Modern History of Transcaucasian Armenia* is an erudite, sometimes witty, occasionally brilliant, and always readable introduction to our history and culture. The book is divided into many sections and subsections—over a hundred, to be exact. Although mainly derivative, the section devoted to literature is fairly detailed and competently done. Separate chapters are devoted to such important literary figures as Khachatur Abovian, Raffi, Rafael Patkanian, Berj Broshiants, Ghazaros Aghayan, Shirvanzadeh, Avedik Issahakian, Hovannes Toumanian, Charents, Bakounts, and several others. Writers of the diaspora, including Constantinople, are not included.

Born in Kharkov in 1923, Manuel Sarkisyanz studied archaeology and history at the University of Teheran, the Asia Institute of New York, and the University of Chicago. After teaching at American and German universities, he established himself in Heidelberg, where, since 1967, he has been director of the political department of the South Asian Institute of the University of Heidelberg. He has authored several scholarly works (in German) on South Asia and Russia. As far as I know, the work under review is his first venture into Armenology.

In his preface, Professor Sarkisyanz writes that he decided to write a modern history of Armenia "in order to contribute to a wider acquaintance with frequently forgotten facts of a tragic but rich history of the oldest among the nations constituting the Eurasian empire of Russia." His interests lie mainly in the nineteenth-century Czarist period of Armenian history, generally regarded "as a mere prelude to the Armenian Soviet Republic." Though this section is well done, the Soviet period is, in my view, even better. The treatment of complex issues is authoritative,

Privately printed, Leiden, 1975.

201

penetrating, and lively. Even when he speaks of such grim epi-
sodes as the Stalinist purges of the 1930s, the author reveals a
sense of irony that, like the smile of the Cheshire cat, appears and
disappears with hardly a word of warning. Speaking of the first
wave of purges in the years 1929–36, during which old Bolsheviks,
second-generation Armenian Communists, and Party Secretary
Khanchian were liquidated, Sarkisyanz writes: "[Aramais] Yer-
nekian was . . . removed from the Party's Central Committee for
his 'nationalism.' Another of its old Bolshevik members, Kostia
Aivazian, became intoxicated and in this state publicly condemned Beria's narrative. He too was expelled from the Central
Committee—for alcoholism as well as nationalism." Sarkisyanz
further explains: "In theory, when the Transcaucasian Federal
Soviet Republic was dissolved in 1936, Armenia became a 'sov-
ereign' Soviet Republic, 'voluntarily' united with—and constitu-
tionally guaranteed the right to secede from—the Soviet Union.
Yet, in practice, an entire generation of Armenian Communists
was exterminated for allegedly desiring to secede from Soviet
Russia." Sarkisyanz sums up his masterful exposition of the
purges thus: "the purgers themselves were purged between Janu-
ary 1938 and February 1939. Then, in June 1939, Soviet Armenia's
political police passed from the Russified Armenian Khvorostov to
the Russian Alexei Korotkov"—two names that to the English
reader   may   sound   dangerously   like   Tweedledee   and
Tweedledum.

There are many such unexpected and ironic touches in Sarkisyanz's text. At one point, for instance, he writes that World War II
not only accelerated the emancipation of women in Armenia (they
were needed in industry and transportation), but it also "caused
an improvement in the position of the Armenian Church in the
Soviet Union. The Communist regime needed the Church to
endorse its war efforts." What was opium to Marx became, nearly
a century later, a useful Machiavellian tool to Stalin.

   On the debit side, I noted a number of inaccuracies and an
astonishing number of misprints, only a fraction of which are
mentioned in the long list of errata. On pages 290–92, for instance, I noted the following inaccuracies: "Nairo [sic] Zorian" is
confused with Stepan Zorian; Charents's birthplace is given as
Magu, Iran—instead of Kars, on the Russo-Turkish border; "Dan-
teagan Arasbel" (Dantesque Legend), one of Charents's better-
known poems, is translated as "Legend of Dante"; Gourgen Ma-
hari is said to have been "liquidated" in 1936—he died in 1969.

Sylva Gaboudikian

Mosaic of My Soul with the Colors of the Map

"But tell me: dost thou know my lady Silvia?"
"Is she not hard-favoured, sir?"
"Not so fair, boy, as well-favoured."
SHAKESPEARE, *Two Gentlemen of Verona*

IN 1964, FOLLOWING A TRIP to the Middle East, Sylva Gaboudikian published her impressions in a big book (531 pp.) entitled *Caravans Are Still on the Way.* Translated into Russian and published in Moscow in 1969, *Caravans* received a favorable review in *Soviet Literature* (November 1970), which among other things said: "The book is well composed with the main idea—that Soviet Armenia is the real home of all the toiling Armenian people wherever they may be living—passing through the entire narrative."

In *Mosaic of My Soul,* Sylva Gaboudikian writes of her travel impressions of Canada and the United States, where she spent four months in 1973–74. But as the title suggests, *Mosaic* is much more than a travel diary. In addition to being a panorama of the Armenian communities in Canada and the United States (their leaders, their composition, degree of assimilation, character, activities) it is a self-portrait with many divagations on literature, politics, history, and autobiography. From these pages, Sylva Gaboudikian, undoubtedly one of the most widely admired Armenian poets of our time, emerges as a woman of untiring energy and insatiable curiosity about her fellow Armenians—be they establishment types, eccentric rebels, successful businessmen, obscure poets, musicians, painters, singers, professors, editors,

Sovetakan Grogh, Yerevan, 1976.

millionaires, paupers in tenements, hippies. "There is something melancholy about him, something 'helpless.' I wonder why that is," she writes of an Armenian hippie by the name of Kasbar to whom she is introduced by a fellow Armenian in Montreal.

His views are well-founded, mature, lofty. And yet notwithstanding his tall stature and solid build, he looks like a baby to me, a big baby.

"Tell us, Kasbar, how do you feel about yourself? Do you feel like an Armenian?"

"I suppose I do, yes; but . . . one's nationality is not important. It is much more important to be a man and to love one's fellow men. It is through love that we shall reach God."

"What about Naregatsi? Have you heard of him?"

"No, I haven't. Who is he?"

"He is a poet who lived in the 10th century. He too wanted to reach God."

"Is he an Armenian?"

"He is. If you read him, you'll love him. He was a great poet, one of the greatest, like Dante and Shakespeare. Odars who have read him in French and Russian translation have expressed enormous admiration for his work."

There are engaging portraits of such well-known personalities as surgeon and scholar Dr. Hampar Kelikian, director Nishan Parlakian, poet and political activist Shahan Natali, authors Levon Surmelian, Antranig Antreassian, Vahe Haig, Puzant Granian, and many, many others.

Here is another poignant encounter:

Once, in Fresno, when during a visit I felt tired and a little weak, I begged my hostess to allow me a few moments to myself so that I could rest. I had barely had a chance to place my head on the pillow when the door opened and in came one of the guests, a thin, withered old man.

"Please, forgive me," he began, "I am from Kharpert, Napoleon Ayadjayan, I have orchards here . . . I went to Armenia, I saw Yerevan" his face was all wet with tears now. "I don't have a wife and children; I don't have a country of my own . . . I would like to come and live in Armenia for a while—not as a tourist—for at least two, three months . . . I would like to get up every morning, go to the kindergarten, stand by and watch the children . . . I don't need anything else. I just want to stand there and watch . . . I have no children of my own, but they are all my children . . . I am not

very rich, but whatever I have I want to leave to Armenia, to Armenian schools."

His tears were coming down in torrents now. I was silent. I didn't know what to say. It was as though I were participating in a sacred ritual, a confession, an oath, which should not be interrupted at any cost.

As this passage and the one quoted above suggest, Sylva Gaboudikian is at her best when dealing with individuals who are more or less passive, "helpless," and therefore in need of her understanding and compassion. But like all people of strong political convictions, she can be as tough as a commissar against critics of the regime. Even skeptics do not escape her wrath. When a wealthy Armenian widow expresses concern over her compatriots in Soviet Armenia, Gaboudikian allays her fears by saying: "The people? . . . They are fine, they're living." "Are they satisfied?" the widow asks next. "They are satisfied." "Are they happy too?" "They're happy too. . . ." "How's the regime, did you get used to it?" "We got used to it." "You have to get used to it, I suppose, what else can you do?" At which point, Gaboudikian makes the following comment:

I would like to tell her to concern herself with the affairs of her own spiritual salvation. Is it any of her business to inquire after the regime and whether or not we got used to it? . . . It's none of our business whether she is a millionaire who owns oilwells in Iraq and factories in the United States . . . I would like to ask her: Who are you? What have you contributed to the world? to mankind? to your country? to your people? If you have contributed nothing, then we would like to forget all about you. We would like to forget you even if you could buy the whole world with your money.

Coming from an "ambassador of good will," this animus is rather shocking. Wealth may be suspect; but so is power—the power to fill the Gulag with millions of prisoners.

On another occasion she interrupts a long diatribe to ask: "Am I preaching?" Of course she is, and she knows it. Rhetorical questions and partisan polemics are accepted, even encouraged modes of expression in the Soviet Union. She simply conforms. But one cannot help wondering how much more effective and relevant her work would be without these encumbrances and inconsistencies. Inconsistencies: While in California, she rebukes Levon *(I Ask You, Ladies and Gentlemen)* Surmelian for no longer writing in Armenian; but when an Armenian writer in

Toronto asks her what the chances are of having one of his works published in Armenia, she dismisses him ("I cut him short," in her own words) by saying: "We don't publish works written in Western Armenian, especially when the author happens to be affiliated with the *Hamazkain*." In view of the fact that she recounts this episode as if it were a victory against the enemies of the people, one is justified in suspecting that she is not simply voicing the policy of the Soviet literary establishment but her own convictions. And here, may I be allowed a digression? If we agree that Armenia and Armenian culture are precious to all Armenians wherever they may be, we shall also have to agree that the Armenian diaspora is a reality whose survival is dependent on the survival of its culture. Not to promote this culture is therefore to condemn it to gradual extinction. As an intellectual, Sylva Gaboudikian is no doubt aware of all this. She must also be aware of the fact that Western Armenian, as a language, is easily accessible to Eastern Armenians, and that it was in Western Armenian that some of our greatest 19th and 20th-century authors wrote. But even assuming for the sake of argument that Western Armenian were, like Chinese, incomprehensible to Eastern Armenians, that would not necessarily mean that books written in Western Armenian ought to be unavailable to the Soviet-Armenian reading public. Many Canadian and American libraries catalogue and circulate books in Chinese and Japanese, in Polish and Russian, sometimes even in Eastern Armenian—languages that are incomprehensible to the overwhelming majority of the population.

Mosaic suffers from a number of other deficiencies. It is at times too verbose, gossipy, and repetitive. Irrelevant encounters and chitchat abound. There is an old Armenian prayer:

> *O Lord, give me inner tranquility in order that*
> *I may accept*
> *That which is unacceptable.*
>
> *O Lord, give me courage in order that*
> *I may not accept*
> *That which is unacceptable*
>
> *O Lord, give me wisdom in order that*
> *I may differentiate*
> *Between the first and the second.*

Sylva Gaboudikian is familiar with this prayer, because she quotes it in its entirety on page 500. She should have placed it at the head of page one.

Grant Matevossian

The Orange Herd

O NE OF THE MOST promising Soviet-Armenian writers, Grant
Matevossian was born in 1935 in a small village called Akhnitsor, not far from Yerevan. In 1961 he published a sketch of village
life entitled "Akhnitsor," which became the center of considerable
controversy. Satirical and comic in tone, this short piece depicted
village life with unprecedented, and by Soviet standards, unusual
honesty. Eventually the editors of *Soviedagan Kraganutiun,* the
literary journal where the story appeared, were removed, and
Matevossian himself was severely reprimanded by the Party leadership.

In *The Orange Herd,* the first English-language publication of
the author's work, Akhnitsor has become Tsmakut, and Tsmakut
may soon become as familiar a place to Armenian readers as
Gabriel Garcia Marquez's Macondo and Gabriel Chevallier's
Clochemerle have become to American readers.

The inhabitants of Tsmakut, a small Armenian village where
time has stood still, are, in the words of the author, "buried away
in the woods and don't even know what's going on in the world.
And, what's more, they don't give a damn. They mow the grass,
stack the sheaves, milk the cows, tend the flocks, churn butter,
make cheese and raise cattle. If at least they'd be closer to the
railroad, but no, they *have* to live miles from no place."

Matevossian shares with Marquez and Chevallier a fondness for
describing a series of people, events, and conversations that are
exaggerated and at times bizarre. His prose teems with detail and
his plots are veritable labyrinths of subplots where even animals
and plants are as lovingly observed as human characters. "The
sunflowers were silently following the sun," we read at one point,

(Translated by F. Glagoleva)
Progress Publishers, Moscow, 1976.

"the earth under the tomato rows was absorbing water, a pear dropped from the pear tree, the deep buzz of a bumble bee broke in on the monotonous hum of the bee-garden, the school principal's wife appeared on the path." And here is Alkho, a horse, daydreaming:

He would wander about in his valley, drinking water from the spring, swishing away a fly or two, thinking of whatever he wanted to as he wandered leisurely about. Then he would lie down in the sun and stretch out, and a fox passing by would think the horse was dead. The fiery-red fox would sit down nearby, gaze at him doubtfully and lick its chops, and then Alkho would suddenly snort. He would snort so loudly the fox would be gone in a flash. Ah, then Alkho would bound up in the best of spirits. He would spot a mare at the far end of the valley. She would have a broad rump, her coat would be chestnut and she would be standing in the green meadow.

Like Leacock's famous horseman, Matevossian's prose seems to be riding madly off in all directions in a whirlwind of dust. And in the eye of this whirlwind stands the narrator: sensitive, vulnerable, often confused and exasperated by the obtuse villagers, but above all, ambitious and drunk with the wine of future glory.

Alexandre Dumas wallowed in fame and was surrounded by adoring women, and that was me; Fieldmarshal Kutuzov slept through a decisive battle, and that was me; our king Artavast walked proudly to the executioner's block, past that slut Cleopatra, and that was me too. There was my Nobel Prize, a cozy supper in the Latin Quarter. . . . And that kitten Brigitte Bardot. And various snatches of conversation: "I despise you," "The Emperor has asked you to come," "Tell his majesty that I shall be detained for an hour."

Though at times verbose and distracting, *The Orange Herd* is an amusing and sometimes brilliant work that should not be ignored.

S. H. Varjabedian

The Armenians:
From Prehistoric Times
to the Present

"THE ARMENIAN MASSACRES became proverbial," said Antonio Gramsci in an essay written in 1916, "but they were words that sounded hollow and failed to conjure up images of men with flesh and blood." Things are not much different today. Despite the wide popularity of William Saroyan's short stories *(My Name is Aram)* and autobiographical books *(Here Comes/There Goes/You Know Who* and many others) and more recently of Michael J. Arlen's *Passage to Ararat* (which is a successful amalgam of historiography, autobiography and travelogue), and notwithstanding the existence of such scholarly works as Sirarpie Der Nersessian's *The Armenians* (1969) and David Marshall Lang's *Armenia: Cradle of Civilization* (1970), Armenians have repeatedly failed to make their history and culture known to the English-speaking world— Saroyan and Arlen, for instance, have little or nothing to say about Armenian music, literature, art and architecture.

In his efforts to cover Armenian history and culture from remotest times to the present in less than 200 pages, Varjabedian is inevitably too sketchy and often unenlightening. His exaggerated fondness for such vague and ultimately impure words as *famous, interesting* and *talented* may indicate haste or a superficial approach or perhaps an inability to distinguish between what is significant and what is ephemeral. The absence of an index and an adequate table of contents doesn't improve matters. As a result *The Armenians* is a flawed even if at times informative and useful work for nonspecialists who know Armenians only as a people that have given a million victims to the Holocaust of 1915.

Privately printed, Chicago, 1977.

209

Edward Topchian

The Concept of Renaissance

THIS POSTHUMOUS COLLECTION of book reviews, essays, and miscellaneous pieces is divided into three sections: the first and the most extensive (427 pages) is devoted to Armenian literature; section two contains essays on Russian writers; section three (about a dozen pages altogether) contains public addresses on official themes like "The Ideal of Brotherhood" and "Soviet Multinational Literature" (whose combined message is: Soviet literature has always been on the side of progress, brotherhood, peace, and everything that promotes love and happiness).

Topchian, a widely read scholar, is as much at home in Armenian literature of all periods as in Russian, English, French, and German literatures. From the Introduction (which is written by his son Stepan Topchian, himself the author of two scholarly works on Raffi and Shirvanzadeh) we learn that he studied literature under some of the greatest names in Soviet (Armenian as well as Russian) scholarship—including Manoug Abeghian. In order to produce a short essay he often read as many as ten books.

Of particular interest in the present collection are Topchian's masterful essays devoted to Levon Shant (nearly 50 pages long) and to Armenian literature of the Diaspora, where the works of Shahan Shahnour, Vahe Haig, Vahan Tekeyan, Antranig Antreassian, Zareh Vorpouni, Vahe Vahian, Garabed Sidal, Vahram Dadrian, Levon Mesrob, Peniamin Noorigian, Levon Surmelian, William Saroyan, and a number of others, are examined and assessed. Unfortunately, since this essay was written in 1946 and never updated, several important figures of the diaspora are not discussed.

Whenever Topchian chooses to write about writers as unique phenomena (instead of social beings with preconceived Marxist labels) he reveals a sensitive mind and a perceptive intelligence.

Sovetakan Grogh, Yerevan, 1977.

But whenever he approaches his subject with Pravda-inspired clichés, the results, I regret to say, are fit only for home consumption. Though in some ways *The Concept of Renaissance* may be regarded as an important contribution, it is, as a result, also a deeply flawed one.

Topchian's "dichotomy" is not hard to explain. He was first and foremost an establishment figure. He occupied several important administrative posts and from that point of vantage attacked, in addition to Dudintsev's *Not By Bread Alone*, some of our most widely admired writers—Sero Khanzatian and Zarzant Darian, among others—for "crude distortions of Soviet life . . . . which drive the reader into an atmosphere of degenerate, easy-living glory"—whatever that may mean. Though in the present volume Topchian manages to avoid such "crude" journalistic formulas, he nevertheless tends to resort to black-and-white extremes of judgment. For instance, in describing Shahan Shahnour's fictional characters, Topchian tells us that they are a miserable, confused lot because they failed to join the French proletarian movement. We read also that in his fiction, Antranig Antreassian criticizes "bourgeois culture and the inhumanity of the capitalist system"—the implication being that the Soviet system is all heart. The essay on Charents emphasizes his revolutionary writings—*Soma, The Demented Crowds, All-Poem*—at the expense of his latter, anti-Soviet verse—for which Charents was eventually arrested and either murdered or forced to commit suicide in a Yerevan jail (about which, predictably enough of course, Topchian says nothing). Ignored are also the Stalinist purges (during which at least 20 million men, women, and children were done to death, not to say some of our greatest writers)—which makes one wonder how it is possible to say anything relevant about Soviet life and literature while ignoring these facts. As Solzhenitsyn points out in his recently published third and final volume of *The Gulag Archipelago:* "If words are not about real things . . . what is the good of them? Are they anything more than the barking of village dogs at night?"

Yervant Odian

Comrade Panchoonie

ONE OF OUR most prolific and literate satirists, Yervant Odian (1869–1926) was born in Constantinople into a wealthy family of diplomats and intellectuals. He began to write early. "First thing I did after I learned how to read and write was to publish a hand-written newspaper," he tells us in one of his autobiographical essays. "In it I recorded the fights between the maid and the cook, the day's menu, the people who came to see my father, and miscellaneous other occurrences." He goes on to say that the paper had only three readers: his father, his mother, and an aunt who happened to be staying with them at the time.

A lifelong bachelor and a gargantuan consumer of hard liquor, Odian was also an indefatigable traveler who at one time or another lived and worked in virtually all the major population centers between London and Bombay.

Reserved in emotion, a stoic, Odian was a pleasant, mild-mannered man who had a Chekovian distaste for all ideas and ideologies and by extension political parties, committees, and organizations. But I think it would be more accurate to say that what Odian detested most was the individual who by joining a group, any group, behaved according to its tenets and in the process shed part of his humanity. In *Comrade Panchoonie* he excoriates "revolutionaries," but elsewhere (notably in *The Councillor's Wife* and *Family, Honor, Morality*) it is the hypocrisies of the bourgeoisie that he exposes with devastating results—which, by the way, may explain why his works, though written in Western Armenian, have been published and widely circulated in Soviet Armenia.

Odian's prose—beautifully captured by Jack Antreassian in this

(Translated by Jack Antreassian)
St. Vartan Press, New York, 1977.

expertly done translation—is unadorned, direct, accessible. It is said that Jonathan Swift would summon his servants and have his proofs read aloud to them, and then alter his writing until the servants fully understood it. Odian may not have adopted this method, but judging by the results, he might as well have done so. *Comrade Panchoonie* may even be viewed as a savage attack on the misuse of language and political rhetoric. "With all his passion for talking," Odian writes in the short biographical sketch of Panchoonie which introduces this epistolary novel,

little Panchoonie misused words repeatedly, often corrupting their meaning altogether. One day he picked up a valuable vase from the table and slammed it to the floor, shattering it into a hundred pieces.

Scolded by his father, Panchoonie justifies his act of vandalism by saying, "I fixed it."

"What do you mean you fixed it? You broke it, you little devil."
"No, father, I fixed it," the boy insisted.

From a foolish meddler, Panchoonie develops into a dangerous zealot convinced that his cause will change the course of human affairs for the better and that he himself is absolutely vital to the success of that cause. It must by now be clear to the reader that Panchoonie (literally "Has-nothing") is a character *sui generis*. He bears no resemblance to Don Quixote or Sancho Panza—he lacks Panza's horse sense and the Don's noble innocence (confronted with a windmill he would probably "fix it" as an instrument of bourgeois exploitation even if that meant starving the neighboring villages). In Saroukhan's drawings—some of which are veritable Breughelian canvases teeming with anecdote and village life— he appears as a slightly undernourished and maniacal Trotsky in a perpetual state of agitation, eyes forever popped out and veins on the point of rupture. When a whisper will do, he screams at the top of his voice, reminding us of Nietzsche's dictum that "Anyone with a very loud voice is almost incapable of thinking subtleties." Panchoonie has no use for subtleties. He lives on a strict diet of black-and-white extremes and contradictions. In one of his seething letters to the Central Committee (which invariably end with the by now legendary words *Mi kich pogh oughargetzek*— Send a little money) he writes:

"We are all Armenians, we are brothers. Why can't we live together? Why must we fight?" that filthy bourgeois kept repeating,

not being able to comprehend that conflict is the basic condition of life, that class conflict is essential to socialist victory, and that it is impossible to do any good at all without at least a little blood-shed. . . .

In vain did I repeat that violent class conflict must be waged between us, that they had to use against us every evil means at their command—betrayal, false accusation, force; without these it would not be possible to have a dirty bourgeois class, the exis-tence of which was essential if we were to wage our noble revolu-tionary struggle against it.

Panchoonie is a funny book, but like all genuinely funny books it is also deadly serious. As one reads it one is haunted by the question "To what extent is our social existence still in the hands of Panchoonies?" It is *this* that lends Odian's book tragic dimen-sion and relevance, that is to say, *universality*.

J. Karnusian

Return to the Ararat Plateau

THROUGHOUT ITS MILLENNIAL HISTORY Armenia has been repeatedly invaded, divided and subdivided between powerful neighboring empires. The situation hasn't changed to this day. Most of historic Armenia is now under Turkish control—the native Armenian population having been exterminated or driven out during World War I. An estimated four million Armenians now live in Soviet Armenia and the neighboring republics of Georgia and Azerbaijan; another two million are scattered all over the globe, with large concentrations in the Middle East and the United States.

As an ethnic group and a political force, Armenians in their diaspora remain hopelessly fragmented and divided. There are two main political organizations: those who are resigned to the Soviet presence in Armenia (or rather what remains of Armenia), and the nationalists, who are unwilling to give up their dream of a free and independent homeland. There are in addition two fairly large contingents, one of which may be described as "nonpartisan" and the other as "assimilationist."

In his short pamphlet Karnusian attempts to reconcile these four disparate groups of the diaspora into a single political force. As he himself is willing to concede at the outset, his approach lacks originality. It is, in point of fact, utilitarian in scope and, like all such attempts, lacks both depth and vision. His style moreover—analysis of the present malaise, followed by a constructive program—is constantly vitiated by an unfortunate either/or approach that simplifies past complexities and distorts present realities. Some of these distortions may be dismissed as more or less academic, but others will inevitably generate further controversy and polarization. Consequently *Return to the Ararat Plateau* at times becomes a symptom of the malaise it tries to cure.

(Translated by Aris Sevag)
A. R. Press, New York, 1979.

Chaké Der Melkonian-Minassian

Politiques Littéraires en U.R.S.S. depuis Les Débuts à Nos Jours

IN 1957 KHRUSCHEV SAID, "The highest social destiny of art and literature is to mobilize the people to the struggle for new advances in the building of Communism." Half a century before—in 1905, to be exact—Lenin put it more bluntly: "Literature," he said, "must become an integral part of the Party."

Since every aspect of Soviet life is controlled by the Party, it would be absurd to expect that literature would be accorded exceptional treatment. The question that immediately arises of course is whether literature can exist without freedom; and more specifically: when civil servants (who, by definition, have no interest in ideas, only in power) are authorized to dictate to writers what to write and how to write it, whether the resulting product can be called *literature* by any stretch of the imagination.

Freedom, Kant thought, was the principal issue philosophy must address. In our own days, Sartre has stated that the function of literature is to reveal our own freedom to ourselves. Sartre has even gone so far as to maintain that there has never been any good book "whose purpose was to serve oppression." One does not write for slaves: "writing is a certain way of wanting freedom."

All this talk of freedom, Soviet Marxists would have us believe, is a petty-bourgeois camouflage that seeks to maintain only one type of freedom at the expense of all others: that of the rich to exploit the poor.[1] Without justice, we are informed, freedom is bound to degenerate into economic slavery. That may indeed be true, but what these same Marxists have so far failed to explain is whether justice (or for that matter any ideal) can be defined, let alone conceived, without freedom. What happens to justice in a

---

Les Presses De L'Université du Quebec, Montreal, 1979.

land where bad men are free to commit unspeakable crimes and good men are not even allowed to call them criminals? Under Stalin, and in the name of an ideal (was it justice, order, equality, territorial integrity? Did anyone bother to explain? did anyone dare to ask?) millions of innocent people disappeared in the Gulag—among them some of the greatest names in Soviet literature—and when men of good will tried to expose these crimes, they were labeled "enemies of the people" and "tools of imperialism" and thrown out of the country—this of course only if they were internationally recognized and respected names; the fate of less well known figures has been harsher.

When the talented young poet Iosif Brodsky was accused of parasitism and put on trial, he tried to explain to his Soviet judge that poetry comes from God. When asked by the judge "Who put you on the list of poets?" Brodsky—instead of asking the judge who had put *him* on the list of judges—retorted: "Who put me on the list of human beings?" If anything, this short dialogue—or rather two monologues that never cross—demonstrates that the Soviet system recognizes neither God nor human beings, only the Party and those who are willing to serve it. In Stalin's words: "The base produces the superstructure so that it can serve the base."[2]

Sooner or later a Soviet writer, in order to continue to function—that is to say, write, publish, survive—must declare himself either *for* or *against* the Party. There can be no dialogue, dissent, criticism, refutation.

These thoughts are prompted by a new book by Dr. Chaké Der Melkonian-Minassian which tells a familiar and in many ways predictable story—not however without its short-term complexities and surprises—which may explain why highly sophisticated and intelligent writers like Louis Aragon, Ilya Ehrenburg, and our own Zabel Yessayan, Axel Bakounts, and Yeghishe Charents were, for a while at least, enthusiastic supporters of the regime. It is a story that has been told before[3] but never with as much thoroughness and documentation. Dr. Der Melkonian-Minassian does not simply summarize the outline of the plot, but includes long passages (translated here for the first time) from Soviet editorials published in *Pravda, Izvestia,* and other official organs. The reasoning here has a simple-minded yet frightening inevitability. It is easy to understand how an ordinary citizen could be led into believing that to silence intellectuals is a form of social hygiene instead of a typical fascist ploy.[4]

When, in a recent interview, I asked the author to speak of the genesis and development of this study, she replied: "It began with an interest in Soviet-Armenian literature. But I soon came to realize that our literature could not be understood without taking into consideration the literary politics of the Kremlin—which meant a close study of editorials in official publications like *Pravda, Literaturnaia Gazeta, Novy Mir, Voprosy Literaturi;* also resolutions of Conventions of the Central Committee, writings by political leaders, declarations, manifestos, etc." This may explain why, for a change, developments in Armenia are not ignored but discussed at length. There are, in addition, verbatim translations from the Armenian of several important documents, one of which is the notorious "Declaration of the Three"—the three being Charents, Azat Veshtouni (1894–1958), and Gevorg Abov (1897–1965)—published on June 14, 1922.

Born in Beirut and educated at the American University there and at the Sorbonne in Paris, Dr. Chaké Der Melkonian-Minassian has edited a number of Armenian and French publications in the Middle East and France. In addition she has authored two previous books: *Contes et legendes armeniens* (1964) and the most thorough and competent study of our national epic titled *L'Epopée populaire armenienne David de Sassoun* (1972). She is now a professor of literature at the University of Quebec, in Montreal, a post she has held since 1969.

Les Politiques littéraires en U.R.S.S. fully deserves a wider audience, and it is to be hoped that soon an enterprising publisher will issue an English translation of it.

NOTES

1. In a recent speech, delivered before the Supreme Soviet in Moscow, Leonid Brezhnev stated: "What real rights and freedoms are guaranteed to the masses in present-day imperialist society? The 'right' of tens of millions to unemployment? . . . Or the 'right' to live in perpetual fear of the omnipotent underworld of organized crime?"

2. In *Marxism and Linguistic Questions.*

3. The number of books on this particular topic are many. For the interested reader, I have selected below only those in the English language:

Political Control of Literature in the USSR: 1946–1959 by Harold Swayze (Harvard University Press, 1962)

Literature and Revolution in Soviet Russia: 1917–1962—A Symposium, edited by Max Hayward and Leopold Labedz (Oxford University Press, 1963)

On Socialist Realism, by Abram Tertz (Pantheon Books, 1960).

The Cult of Optimism: Political and Ideological Problems of Recent Soviet Literature, by Walter N. Vickery (Indiana University Press, 1963).

4. "The primary aim of fascism," Roland Barthes has said, "is always and everywhere to liquidate the intellectual class."

Interviews

Jean-Marie Carzou

J ournalist, author, educator, film director and producer, Jean-
Marie Carzou was born in Paris in 1938 and educated at the
prestigious Ecole Normale Superieure. His articles have appeared
in such respected journals as *Le Monde, Combat,* and *Quotidien
de Paris.* His books include *Cinquante Vietnam* (1969), *Armenie
1915—un genocide exemplaire (1975),* and *Caida (1977).*

He has written and directed several television documentaries
on subjects that have ranged from Nietzsche, Vermeer, and Mal-
raux to Oliver Messiaen, Madame de Sevigné, George Sand, and
Boulez. His father, Jean Carzou (Carnig Zouloumian) is a re-
nowned painter and stage designer; his mother, Nane Carzou, is
the author of a highly informative and literate travel diary titled
Voyage en Armenie (1974).

AB: In an article published last year in the *New York Times* (April
9, 1977), C. L. Sulzberger traces the present militant mood of
the Armenians to a speech made by you in Marseilles, in
which you are said to have called for coordinated acts against
Turkey. What are the facts behind this allegation?

JC: It is true that when I made that speech on October 1973,
terrorism had not yet been contemplated in Armenian circles. If my speech provoked this form of action, that may be
due to the fact that I was asked to speak on the Armenian
Question, and perhaps because since 1915, all efforts
through official channels to have the Armenian genocide
recognized as a crime against humanity had been totally
ineffective. As a result, one could no longer ignore terrorism
as a means in the defense of our cause.

AB: What exactly did you say in that speech?

JC: Well, I said that in the world we live in, whenever the political
and military avenues are blocked, terrorism seems to be the
only viable alternative for people whose very existence is
being threatened. But let me quote: "If in recent years terrorism has become a viable and acceptable alternative, that is

223

because it offers to the destitute and to those who are without any means of survival, the possibility, desperate yet effective, to attract world attention. We are by now familiar with
the excesses and errors of terrorism—the Palestinians and
Tupamaros furnish numerous instances. And I believe that, if
the Armenians of Europe decide to undertake terrorist actions against the Turks, I have no doubt in my mind that they
will make headlines and they will thus bring back the un-
solved problems of the Armenian question. But please note,"
I added: "terrorism may soon degenerate into vulgar bandit-
ry if it is not coordinated with a whole program of other
actions which must express the will of a community whose
very existence is in peril. It is not enough to throw three or
four bombs and to organize ten meetings. There must be an
uninterrupted series of actions in the name of a cause which
must itself be actual and deeply felt."

AB: How did your audience react to these words?

JC: The older people and the officials were angry, the youth
enthusiastic. Since then, events have proven me right. Until
then, Turkish pressure to restrain the publicity of my book
(Armenie 1915–un genocide exemplaire) had been more or
less successful. But this same pressure was totally ineffective
whenever, following terrorist acts, the media reminded the
world of the 1915 genocide. In a world in which might is right
and force more valued than reason, violence remains the
only alternative for victims of injustice. But let me reiterate
that this violence cannot have any practical results without
the presence of a community near the occupied territories.

AB: About your book Armenie 1915: could you tell us what it was
exactly that made you decide to write it?

JC: Simply because until 1974 there wasn't a single French work
available on this subject. My intention was to produce a work
that could be easily located in a library by anyone who was
interested in reading about the Armenian genocide. In addition I thought that such a work could be extremely useful in
our daily task of acquainting our French compatriots with
certain historic events now long forgotten.

AB: Was your book widely reviewed in France?

JC: I already mentioned Turkish pressure, often quite effective,
on the state-controlled radio and television. It is a well-
known fact that in a cynical world, the representatives of a
State with which one has important ties—political, military,

and economic ties—have more influence than scattered victims without representation. Notwithstanding this, however, my book received favorable reviews in *Le Monde* and *France Soir*. I was myself invited to discuss the book on French, Belgian, and Swiss radio. So far 14,000 copies have been sold, and it is now available in paperback.

AB: Tell us more on Turkish reaction to your book.

JC: The Turks, as a rule, limit themselves in putting pressure through official channels and maintain an outward silence. Even so, after each broadcast, they wrote letters of protest and sometimes sent diplomats to participate in debates on radio and television programs.

AB: Is the book being translated into any other languages?

JC: So far it has been translated only into Greek (Athens: Kedros Editions). There are other translations in progress. But I would particularly like to see it translated into English and distributed in the United States.

AB: What are you working on now?

JC: I am at the moment working on a number of projects as a writer as well as a TV producer and director. Concerning my Armenian-interest work, however, I have the following plans: (1) to publish translations of Armenian literary works and documents on the genocide; (2) to produce a documentary film that, like my book, will acquaint the French public with the Armenian genocide; and (3) to publish another work on the Armenian Question since 1915, in which I will analyze our failures to have the genocide recognized; what we can do about it now; on the existence of Armenian political parties and factions in the diaspora; the role of Soviet Armenia, etc.

AB: Tell us something of your work on French televison.

JC: From 1968 to 1974, as an executive on French television, I was able to make decisions on the conception and implementation of a number of educational programs, choice of authors and topics, etc. Since then, I have dedicated my efforts as a writer to the preparation of programs devoted to such figures as Nietzsche, Vermeer, Jung, et alii. During all of 1976 I devoted a great deal of time and work on the presence of immigrant workers in France.

AB: Of the recent French translations of Armenian-interest works, which one impressed you most?

JC: I'm now reading with enormous interest Michael J. Arlen's *Passage to Ararat* which appeared recently here in French translation. My reading, as a rule, is limited to the testimony of survivors of the massacres.

AB: Do you follow artistic and intellectual developments in Soviet Armenia?

JC: Only from afar, unfortunately, and mainly through contacts with Armenian artists who visit us in Paris.

AB: Do you plan to visit the United States soon?

JC: Certainly. I am very eager to meet with members of the Armenian-American community, which gives one the impression of being active, well organized and efficient.

AB: What about Soviet Armenia?

JC: I hope to be able to go there later this year.

AB: Your mother is an accomplished writer: did she have any influence on your decision to become a man of letters?

JC: I don't think so, no; though, without any doubt, the artistic and intellectual climate of my family must have had something to do with my decision to choose literature as my profession, which dates back to when I was seven or eight years old.

AB: In your book *Armenie 1915,* you refer to the fact that Armenians are fascinated to the point of obsession with their famous men—Khachaturian, Mikoyan, Saroyan, Aznavour. Could we indulge for a moment or two this national weakness of ours and assess the importance and significance of the work of some famous French-Armenians? Let us begin with the late absurdist playwright Arthur Adamov. What is your opinion of him?

JC: I have no doubt in my mind that he is a great playwright and that his work will retain its power and relevance for a long time to come. I regret very much not having made his personal acquaintance while he was alive.

AB: The novelist Vahe Katcha?

JC: He is a writer of great charm, talent, and inventive ability. *L'Homme qui troubla la fête* (The Man who Spoiled the Fun) happens to be a favorite of mine; also *Le huitieme jour du Seigneur* (The Eighth Day of the Lord), which I hope to adapt someday for television.

AB: Film director Henri Verneuil?

JC: He is a good friend of mine and a man who has thoroughly mastered his profession.

AB: Who are, in your view, the Armenians presently living in France who are destined for greatness?

JC: The youth, this third generation following the genocide, that has manifested that it has the initiative and passion to act and move things.

Hampar Kelikian

An emeritus professor of orthopedic surgery at Northwestern University in Chicago, Dr. Hampar Kelikian was born in Hadjen, Cilicia (formerly Armenia Minor) and came to the United States shortly after World War I. The author of several monumental medical texts (in English)—*Hallus Valgus: Allied Deformities of the Forefoot* (1965), *Congenital Deformities of the Hand and Forearm* (1974), and others—and a collection of essays (in Armenian and English) titled *A Doctor and Modern Literature* (1964), he has also published many stories, poems, and essays in such literary periodicals as *Ararat* (New York), and *Nairi* (Beirut).

William Saroyan has said of him: "He is an enormity, both as a brilliantly creative surgeon and as a human being. His kindness, understanding, intelligence, and humor are instant, constant, and inexhaustible, whether he is with a child in a hospital or with a poet at a dinner table . . . He is a genius, and therefore immediately understood, but also impossible to fully understand. There is always more to be noticed, recognized, and understood."

AB: Dr. Kelikian, do you have a favorite saying or maxim—the kind that guided you throughout your life?

HK: No. I believe in hard work.

AB: You have said that literature was your first love. Do you sometimes regret your decision to become a surgeon?

HK: No. I love both surgery and literature.

AB: If you were to name the person who influenced you the most, who would it be?

HK: My father.

AB: Have you written anything about him?

HK: Hamasdegh once insisted that I write a biography of my father, whose name was Yeghishe, Yeghishe Gakvonts—the Turks called us Kekloghlou, and in official papers we were called Keklikian; some bureaucrat here dropped a 'k' and I am now called Kelikian. In any case, Yeghishe Gakvonts, my

228

father, was a colorful character—if you read Kazantzakis's *Zorba the Greek* you'll get an inkling of the kind of man my father was . . . When Hamasdegh insisted that I write a book about my father, I sat down and produced some fragments—anecdotes, reminiscences.

AB: Were they published?

HK: Yes, but in a sterilized form, which made me give up the whole thing in disgust.

AB: Who was the guilty party?

HK: Someone with the mentality of a dehumidified deacon. He's no longer with us, so I won't mention his name. Like most of our editors he couldn't understand that there are no such things as immoral words. Words are innocent. They don't have to bear the seal of approval of a teacher or preacher before they are printed. There is only one type of immoral speech—that which fakes. The trouble with most of our writers is that they are squeamish, clerical-minded, castrated—mentally and morally. And they use the dictionary much too much. They practically bury their characters under avalanches of lifeless verbiage. That editor who deleted certain colorful expressions of my father's didn't live long enough to read some recent American novels—things like Philip Roth's *Portnoy's Complaint*, which many critics regard as a masterpiece.

AB: Tell us more about your father.

HK: He was close to nature, down to earth. He had mountain air in his blood. People who live on mountains use basic words. My father had no schooling. He let go whatever leaped on his tongue. No restraint. He couldn't and didn't turn and twist what he had to say to suit this or that occasion. He had no patience with preachers. Once, in Beirut, when a *vartabed* made a long-winded speech about me, my father hollered: "Tell me how much money you want from my son and I'll give it to you myself, but for chrissake stop this damn nonsense!" On another occasion, when the Catholicos asked him why he never went to church, my father replied: "For 95 years your god has forgotten me. If I go to church now he may remember me and take away my soul."

AB: Your father sounds like a man ahead of his time.

HK: He was at least fifty years ahead of *me*. Let me tell you another story about my father. Once when he was very sick, a devout Christian visited him and kept urging him to pray and repent. "Whatever for?" my father demanded to know. "So that the good Lord will open the gate for you." "Gate? What gate?" "That of heaven, of course." "Will you be going there too?" my father wanted to know, and the other said: "I certainly hope so." "In that case," my father said, "please ask your good Lord to send me to the other place—that's where all my friends are, you see. I'm sure I'll feel much more comfortable there." By the way, my father didn't do a thing for me—never helped me financially. He told me so himself once. "But you gave me things money can't buy," I told him, and he said: "Money is money: without it you can't live. You're saying that because like all intellectuals you under-stand nothing about money." My father wasn't a rich man, but he knew how to live, how to love, how to laugh. Never in my life have I met anyone who could laugh like my father—mountain-resounding laughter.

AB: Hamasdegh was right. You *should* write a book about him.

HK: He was my hero, my father was. On a horse he looked like Kevork Chavoush, Antranig, Vartan himself. He may not have been a brave man, but he was a compassionate one. He made me godfather to two beggars so that I'll provide for them.

AB: Why do you say he may not have been a brave man?

HK: He loved life too much. People who love life can't be brave. I remember when I was a boy there was some gossip about him and the attractive wife of a Turk. My father and I had no secrets. We spoke openly about everything between heaven and earth. So I asked him if there was any truth in these rumors, and he said: *"Che, yavrous!"* (None, my boy!)
"She was attractive, was she not?" I asked.
"Very."
"Were you not tempted?"
"Am I not a man?"
"How could you resist then?"
"She was someone else's property. I don't like hurting peo-ple, especially weaklings, and her husband was a weakling."
He died at the age of 98—my father did. I was on my way to see him for the last time when I heard of his death. I must have smiled because I remember my son saying: "Dad, you're smiling instead of crying." "I'm thinking of your grandfather," I told him. "It is impossible to think of him without smiling." My father didn't like tears. He surrounded himself with laughter wherever he went.

AB: I read somewhere that when Saroyan read your first novel, he said: "We have been friends for a long time, let's not spoil it." Are you still friends?

HK: We are closer than ever.

AB: What happened to the novel?

HK: Gathering dust.

AB: You say somewhere that we (Armenians) have never coveted our neighbor's land, never subjugated other people, nor exploited them. We have only tried to surpass others by erecting monuments of beauty inside and around us. To what extent do you think Armenians in America have lived up to this ethos?

HK: We have had some shopkeepers who thought of money first.

AB: Dr. Kelikian, who are some of your favorite Armenian writers?

HK: Zohrab, Zarian, Zabel Yessayan, Shahnour, Varoujan, Toto-vents, Charents, Bakounts, Derian, Issahakian, and some others . . . Maro Markarian, Grant Matevossian, Sylva Gaboudikian . . .

AB: Did you read Sylva Gaboudikian's last book, *Mosaic of My Soul?*

HK: Not all of it, no.

AB: What did you think of her characterization of you?

HK: She's right: I *am* crazy in the loving way she describes.

AB: One of your last essays is devoted to Zabel Yessayan. Could you tell us what it is about her that makes her a particular favorite of yours?

HK: She was one of our ablest writers—no doubt about that. She has produced some cheap propaganda—like *Prometheus Unchained,* which she wrote to please the commissars, who expressed their gratitude by sending her to Siberia where she died—but she has also written some excellent fiction, things like *The Waiting Room*: you should translate that into English. I would like to do it myself but I don't have the time. It is not long—about 60 pages. She wrote it in French when she was twenty-five, after which she translated it into Armenian. Her French was excellent. Many of our writers lived in Paris for a while, even attended classes at the Sorbonne, but she was the only one who came out of there with a degree.

AB: Is *The Waiting Room* autobiographical?

HK: All her things are—every word of hers is based on lived experience. And she had an insatiable lust for life. It hasn't

come out in book form, by the way. And the periodical in
which it appeared is now extinct. She wrote it shortly after
the Dreyfus affair. The heroine of the novella is a Jewess by
the name of Eva. She is married to a weakling and falls in love
with a stronger character, a doctor—a man with "the eyes of a
lion." Zabel's husband was also a weakling and she too fell in
love with a stronger character—a Turkish officer. Everything
she wrote is autobiographical—*The Gardens of Silihdar, Shirt
of Fire, Barba Khachik*. She idolized her uncle Khachik who
married a Greek prostitute. *Barba Khachik* is based on his life.
It could have been the great Armenian novel, but before she
had a chance to revise it, she was purged. That's the problem
with Armenian literature: our greatest writers were either
murdered by some despotic regime or died of tuberculosis in
their twenties, or were forced to become shoemakers or
party functionaries. Whenever a writer joins one of our political parties, that's the end of him as a creative artist.

AB: Charents is another poet about whom you have written a
great deal. Would you assess his work for us?

HK: Charents was short and ugly. He had an enormous pro-
boscis—a Jimmy Durante schnozzle on a small, compressed
face. He was sick—a morphinist. Also a heavy drinker. Without discipline—both in life and in his writings. Unlike Varoujan and Derian, he had no university education. Without
restraint, arrogant, passionate, garrulous, ill-tempered, spontaneous—a real revolutionary, a born genius. He was our
François Villon. But then all great writers or artists have been
abnormal—they all suffered from some sort of sickness—
amorality . . . Dostoevsky was an epileptic and he raped an
eleven-year-old girl—Nabokov's *Lolita* is based on a suppressed chapter from *The Possessed*. Verlaine, Oscar Wilde,
André Gide, Proust, E. M. Forster, Auden, Genet, Cocteau
were all homosexuals. I dare you to mention a single great
writer who was a law-abiding, decent, normal citizen.

AB: Chekhov.

HK: He was a sick man—died of tuberculosis at 40. And did you
know that he fell in love with an Armenian girl? He even
wrote a story about her—it's called "The Beauties." I could
tell you things about Issahakian and Charents, and certain
other major poets of ours, but I don't wish to offend the
sensibilities of your readers. What is strange about Charents

is that he decided to write—and poetry at that: and *what poetry!*

AB: Did you ever meet him?

HK: When I went to Armenia in 1937, Charents was in jail. I asked Avedik Issahakian to take me to him but Issahakian said: "He's a wreck, a walking skeleton. He curses and screams whenever they are late with the morphine." If the Stalinists had not killed him, Charents would have killed himself.

AB: 1937—isn't that the year in which Bakounts died?

HK: And many others. 1937 is the year of the second major blood-letting of Armenian intellectuals, 1915 being the first. It was a gloomy atmosphere . . . Bakounts and Charents were good friends, by the way, but they were entirely different characters. Bakounts remained a loyal nationalist to the end. Charents wavered and was at times taken in by the propaganda of the commissars.

AB: What are your own political convictions?

HK: Politics don't interest me and I have never belonged to a political party. You no doubt are familiar with the story of the three Armenians who went to heaven—one a Tashnag, the other a Ramgavar, and the third a Chezok (non-partisan). The angel who was assigned to look after their needs—keep them happy—asked the Tashnag if he had any particular wish, and the Tashnag said: "I would like to see all Ramgavars in hell." Next the angel turned to the Ramgavar and asked him the same question. "I would like to see all Tashnags in hell," the Ramgavar said. The angel then turned to the Chezok, who said: "I am a simple man with no particular wishes of my own; but I *would* like to see my friends happy. Please, go right ahead and grant their wishes."

AB: Dr. Kelikian, a final question: What are you working on now?

HK: A medical text on the human ankle, also essays on Daniel Varoujan and Vahan Totovents.

AB: What about the biography of your father—do you plan to finish that?

HK: I might.

AB: I think you should. I, for one, shall look forward to it.

(1978)

Puzant Granian

Born in Cilicia (formerly Armenia Minor) shortly before World War I, Puzant Granian was educated in Alexandria (Egypt) and New York. He is now a resident of Los Angeles. A leading poet, critic, playwright, and educator of the diaspora, he has published several collections of verse, travel impressions, essays, and the novel *The Armenian Comedy* (Beirut, 1965). One of his books, titled *My Land, My People* (Los Angeles, 1978), is available in English.

AB: There are a number of characters in your novel, *The Armenian Comedy*, who have the odor of reality. Pasha, the mysterious, chain-smoking ex-fedayee for instance—

PG: That's Rouben.

AB: And Adamian, the famous poet and teacher—

PG: Aghbalian, Nikol Aghbalian.

AB: Hamo, the political activist—

PG: Ohandjanian.

AB: Who were they in real life?

PG: Rouben Der Minassian, better known as Rouben of Sassoun, or simply Rouben, was of course one of our greatest guerrilla fighters and the author of a monumental autobiographical work titled *The Reminiscences of an Armenian Revolutionary,* which is regarded as a classic in its field. Aghbalian was an eminent statesman, scholar, and educator. Ohandjanian was likewise a statesman—president of the Free and Independent Republic of Armenia from 1918 to 1920 and, after its downfall, a highly influential community leader in the diaspora; also with Levon Shant and Aghbalian, one of the founders of the Hamazkain and its lifetime president.

AB: Tell me more about them.

PG: First let me say that I met all three when I was a boy—that's when I believed in men and gods. They are all dead now but to me they are more alive than many so-called "live" people I know. I think of them constantly—they continue to live in me, through me, around me. These men live in me as spiritual forces—how can they be dead? They are at the roots of my being. Where do they end and where do I begin? Hamo Ohandjanian was an impressive sight, a splendid man, a powerful personality, yet humane, extremely sensitive and compassionate, totally incapable of hurting anyone. He could and did dominate without thirsting for power and issuing commands. An undeniable moral force. His authority seemed to flow naturally from his being—was, in fact, an extension of his personality. Manipulating others, cheating, wheeling and dealing—these things were beyond him. He was credulous to the point of being naive—couldn't imagine anyone lying to him, for instance. During World War II, I remember, in the middle of an argument, I once overheard him say: "Churchill does not lie!" He made you think of the Old Testament line that says God created man in His own image. Another one of his pet beliefs was that one should repay evil with hard work. Get busy, he would say, and you'll forget the evil done to you. And that's what he did himself despite his advanced age. Hard work was the most effective antidote to difficulties, problems and conflicts of all kind. "Old age is a mode of perception and I've never felt old," he would say. He was an optimist with an indestructible faith in our Cause. No one, nothing, could shatter this faith. He had seen his people suffer and he had himself suffered a great deal—including exile in Siberia, where his health had been permanently damaged.

AB: What did he do for a living?

PG: He was a doctor and a very good one, too—a near infallible diagnostician, it was said. Once, I remember, I went to see him with a minor complaint. I didn't feel well. Probably nerves. Couldn't sleep. I knew there was nothing wrong with me physically, but I felt sick all the same—it was like an obsession. After hearing me out, he said: "Don't worry, everything will be all right and you'll feel better soon." Gave me some pills, asked me to return next morning for an injection, talked to me at length on the present political situation. Refused payment. That's the kind of man he was. Sometimes, after examining his destitute patients, he would even slip some money under their pillow. On another occasion, I remember, one of us—may have been me—made a speech in his honor (it was his birthday, which he always liked to celebrate with great pomp), saying things like, "We trust and admire you because you are one of those rare beings who live by what they preach." "You could all be like me, if you wanted to," he said. "I have no particular aptitude or gift."

AB: That's exactly what J.S. Bach once said—"If anyone were to work as hard as me, he would achieve as much, perhaps even more."

PG: He probably meant it, too. I know Hamo did. And there is some truth in that—at least as far as Hamo was concerned. He had no particular talent or gift. He was not a brilliant orator, a profound intellectual, or a political thinker. But he was an *idealist*. When he walked into a room, he radiated authority and inspired respect. Men like that don't exist any more.

AB: What about Rouben of Sassoun?

PG: He was another fascinating character—a formidable presence, strong, enigmatic, withdrawn, with an inward stare. A chain-smoker. Medium height, but a man of immense power—spiritual as well as physical. White hair, blue eyes—penetrating, feline. A perpetual smile on his lips. There was something unfathomable about that smile—its origins seemed to be not individual but ancestral, symbolic, archetypal. Seen at close range, his eyes contained sparks, something unpredictable, wild—like those of a tiger about to spring on its victim. One of our giants. Unlike anyone else I've ever known, yet quintessentially Armenian.

AB: In what way did his "Armenianness" express itself?

PG: In his speech, for one—sparse, lean, yet flexible, colorful, agile: he made frequent use of popular sayings and turns of phrase. He knew Armenia thoroughly—its valleys, mountains, roads, villages, towns—he knew it as a geographer, as a military leader, and as an economist; also as a historian and a student of its spiritual heritage. He had this tremendous kinship with the Armenian soil—something that I can't recall anyone else having had to the same degree. He seemed to carry this soil everywhere with him. He also had a profound knowledge of the Armenian people—its traditions, dialects, ethos—likewise of Kurds, Turks, and all the other minorities who lived on our lands. He was a man of the people. A powerful intellect. What else can I say about him? A hard man to capture with words. A simple exterior that concealed a very complex internal life. There is a type of simplicity, someone has said, that is the resolution of many complex and contradictory forces. That was Rouben. Even after you met him you couldn't fully grasp him. His inner world was of the stuff of the incommensurable. You had to sense his special quality—establish a mode of communication that transcended the verbal and the visual. Rouben was a world, an entire people, a great representative of the Armenian spirit—of the Armenian nation and its soil—the very soil that had absorbed the blood and light of innumerable heroes and saints. Tenacious, unassuming, introspective, but deep, with an enormously rich, diversified internal life—crowded with voices and spirits. Generations will pass but he'll live. He was more than an individual self, a temporary being. Though a man of his time, he seemed to live in the past. A splendidly noble life throbbed in his soul. Austere, tough, wild, bloody, but splendidly noble. Giants walked within him, they fought and fell, like the sun behind the mountains. His eyes looked at you but he didn't see you, didn't hear you, he lived in a different realm. Probably haunted by the memory of comrades-in-arms, killed long ago. He may have felt he ought to have died with them. He had no business leading a normal, day-by-day existence. He may even have felt guilty.

AB: You mentioned his *Reminiscences*.

PG: A literary masterpiece of epic cast. The style is lean, almost ascetic, but it has immediacy and an ability to communicate complex images and events in a few words.

AB: Tell me about Nikol Aghbalian.

PG: Aghbalian was my teacher. An incomparable orator—white hair, bearded, deep blue eyes that never looked directly into your face but past you at a certain point slightly above the horizon. Though fully aware of his powers there was no trace of arrogance in him. Like Ohandjanian, he elicited respect and admiration without trying. A very sociable, gregarious man who loved banquets, meetings, and in general surrounding himself with people. He drank moderately. Loved to sing songs by Sayat-Nova. He sang with a deep baritone. He was born in Tiflis, in the same neighborhood as Sayat-Nova. A truly cosmopolitan figure—educated in the Kevorkian Jemaran in Etchmiadzin, then in Petrograd, where he had studied linguistics under the celebrated Nikolai Marr; in Moscow he had studied Russian literature; at the Sorbonne, in Paris, philosophy under Bergson. A restless man, seldom satisfied with himself and his surroundings, always searching, traveling—Iran, the Balkans, most of Europe, Russia, Egypt, the Middle East. Minister of Education in the Republic of Armenia, he established the first university in Armenia, and the first man to perceive Charents's genius, which he encouraged and helped. Also co-founder of the Hamazkain and the Beirut Jemaran—a great educational institution. An able scholar whose works include important essays on Armenian philology, a *History of Armenian Literature*, monographs on Sayat-Nova and Movses Khorenatsi, many essays, political reflections, reminiscences, insightful analyses of the works of his contemporaries. A writer of undeniable genius who scattered and dissipated his energies in a thousand extraliterary activities. Sometimes I'm asked if there was any particular field in which he excelled. Somewhere Aghbalian himself says: "Some people think of me as a critic. Others, as a scholar. Still others have a different view. As far as I can tell, I am many things and I am nothing." He was a man torn between his duties as a public servant and an intellectual in love with ideas. To specialize in a particular field, one must work in isolation. As a community leader, Aghbalian couldn't afford doing that. He was a man of his time. With Auguste Comte he believed that a man is first and foremost a social being, and sociology was for him the queen of sciences. But there was also something of the Russian intellectual in him— intense commitment to an ideal. He was first a citizen, then a poet. Art must serve the people—he shared this belief with Tolstoy and Levon Shant among others.

AB: Is it true that he preferred to lecture rather than write?

PG: Yes. On a podium he was an overpowering presence. No one could project as much depth, vigor, and substance as he. A phenomenally gifted public speaker. His knowledge of Armenian literature and culture in general was intimate and deep. The Armenian temperament, the Armenian *voki*, had no secrets from him. He had explored all its facets and manifestations. There was something of the prophet in him, something of the spellbinding power of a visionary and a mystic. Anyone who has come in direct contact with him bears his mark. He was more than his work. Sometimes great artists can be mediocre individuals. Wagner was a giant among composers, but a moral midget. Not Aghbalian. There was something of Socrates in him, who, as you know, didn't write a single line.

AB: In more specific terms, how would you describe his influences on you?

PG: He was my only true teacher. I studied under Levon Shant, too—he taught me the Armenian language. Aghbalian, on the other hand, inspired in me the Armenian *voki*. It was also Aghbalian who reinforced my mystical tendencies.

AB: You said that he was an idealist. In what way did this idealism manifest itself besides words?

PG: When the Communists overthrew the Republic of Armenia in 1921, Aghbalian escaped to Iran, but his wife and children remained behind and were kept as hostages. The Communist regime tried to lure him back by making promises, but he refused to return. When a man like that speaks of sacrificing everything to an ideal, he is bound to make a profound impression on a boy. I remember after meeting him I had this feeling that my life would never be the same again.

AB: Tell me about Gostan Zarian. Did you know him well?

PG: Very well, yes. Both as a writer and as a man.

AB: What's your assessment of him as a writer?

PG: A powerful voice, a brilliant stylist, one of the most daring explorers of the Armenian *voki*—

AB: Like Nigol Aghbalian?

PG: Yes. Aghbalian, by the way, was a great admirer of his. Zarian is a unique phenomenon in our literature. Some Armenian writers, after they discover *odar* cultures, lose interest in their own. It was the other way around with Zarian. He discovered Armenian culture and language after he had familiarized himself with *odar* cultures and became convinced that ours was one of the greatest in the world; and unlike most of his contemporaries, he wasn't simply *influenced* by Western literary trends, but was *part* of these trends—having produced a substantial body of work in French and other languages: works that were highly regarded by his contemporaries and peers. A thoroughly sophisticated mind who felt at home in all the arts— music, painting, sculpture—also history, psychology, philosophy, the natural sciences. A deep thinker. Original. Never impersonal or academic. In some ways he reminds me of Bach. Everything he wrote bears his strong individuality. A fascinating combination of East and West. His Armenian actually is a curiously attractive mixture of the West- and East-Armenian variants: it has the musicality of the East and the refinement of the West. But Zarian combined East and West in even more profound ways. His technical apparatus is Western, but his vision and symbolism are thoroughly Eastern. He saw gods and spirits in everything. He believed that all things, the universe as a whole, is in constant flux. Change was the only reality. In Zarian's world everything moves and flows—mountains, the earth, trees— they all flow toward self-fulfillment. Chaos toward a new order. This movement is the only permanent thing in the world. Zarian's art consists in capturing from transient phenomena that which is permanent and durable.

AB: Some critics have called his style theatrical.

PG: It is, yes, but in a Wagnerian sense—manly, elemental, overpowering. Like Wagner, Zarian had a deep interest in the racial past of his people—its legends, myths, archetypes. One of his last books, as a matter of fact, dealt with Armenian mythology. He called it *The Book of Legends*. I remember that when I paid him a visit in 1961 at his Berkeley home, which, appropriately enough, was on Olympus Street, he talked about it a great deal. "Now that we have been fragmented and scattered all over the world," he said, "we must find a common ground on which to stand. Archetypes like Vahagn, Anahit, Ara the Beautiful, Tigran—nothing much has been written about them so far." I asked him if he planned to include David of Sassoun in his book. "No," he said. "One shouldn't touch David of Sassoun, because Toumanian and Issahakian have already written about him."

AB: How would you assess his poetry?

PG: Let's say I prefer his prose.

AB: Tell me something about Zarian, the man. Is it true that he was a notorious womanizer?

PG: And proud of it, too! Once, in the presence of others, he boasted that he had loved "in lakes and forests, in the grass, by the moonlight." He could be on occasion something of a *fanfarone*—a braggart. But his speech, like his writing, was pure music—it had rhythm, authority, individuality, and it never failed to communicate a striking image or idea.

AB: What else can you tell me about him?

PG: He was shabbily treated by his fellow Armenians. Institutions and individuals promised to finance the publication of his last book, but nobody did anything for a long time. Finally, the Catholicos from Etchmiadzin, during a visit in California, assured him that his book would be published in Yerevan if he agreed to return there; which he did, but again nothing happened. The only books the Soviets published were heavily edited versions of his novel *Ship on the Mountain*, which had already come out in Boston in 1943; and the narrative poem *The Bride of Tetrachoma*, also published in Boston in 1930. All his major works—the autobiographical *Traveler and His Road; Gods and Countries;* the Charents study *Bancoop and the Bones of the Mammoth*, and others—masterpieces all—remain unpublished there to this day.

AB: Somewhere in *The Traveler and His Road*, I think, he says: "It's a terrible thing being a writer and belonging to a small nation. It's even worse being an Armenian writer."

PG: He knew what he was talking about.

(1980)

Views

Cross-Examinations

E ver since he began to publish more or less regularly, Ara Ballozian has been asked many questions by a variety of people. In what follows he brought together some of these questions and his answers.

Q.   What made you decide to become a writer?

A.   I'm not sure. Sometimes I suspect I became a writer because I couldn't be anything else. I didn't have enough capital to go into business, for instance. I could have been a farmer had my father left me a farm . . . I like all kinds of work!

Q.   Do you believe writers are born or made?

A.   Both.

Q.   To which category do you belong?

A.   To the third—I should never have been a writer.

Q.   Why do you say that?

A.   It took me twenty years to break into print and I'm still having serious problems. My books have been rejected so many times by so many different publishers that if I were to collect and bind all the rejection slips I've received so far, I would end up with a volume as thick as *War and Peace* and *The Brothers Karamazov* combined.

Q.   What is for you the most difficult thing about writing?

A.   The English language.

Q.   *That* I would never have guessed.

A.   I am an Armenian, born in Athens (Greece), and educated in Venice (Italy). I adopted the English language rather late in life.

Q.   Like Nabokov.

A.   Not quite. Nabokov was educated in England. Besides, he had an English governess and could speak the language fluently even as a child—much better than Russian, or so he tells us in his autobiography. Even so, when he began to write

245

in English, he was repeatedly criticized—by, among others, Edmund Wilson—for being stilted and un-American.

Q. He happens to be a favorite writer of mine.

A. Mine too.

Q. I'm glad we agree.

A. He fascinates me even when he speaks of subjects I have no interest in.

Q. Such as?

A. Butterflies, chess, Pushkin, incest. Even when he expresses eccentric views—

Q. Such as?

A. His dislike of Thomas Mann, Sartre, and Dostoevsky, for instance—I find him insightful and stimulating.

Q. Perhaps I should confess that I've so far failed to appreciate Mann—he seems so pompous, unfeeling, ponderous. I assume he's another favorite of yours.

A. He was, and to some extent still is, yes. I must have read his *Magic Mountain* at least seven times. At the moment I am rereading with enormous enjoyment another novel of his— *Joseph the Provider,* the last volume of his biblical tetralogy: a work of Wagnerian dimensions. It is one of the most wildly humorous books I've read. Mann is generally respected and admired for his formidable erudition, depth, subtle irony, elegant style, etc. Someday, I suspect, he will be recognized as one of the greatest humorists of our time.

Q. I'm afraid his humor has so far escaped me.

A. Give him another try—begin with *Confessions of Felix Krull,* his last unfinished novel. And try his essay on Chekhov, which he completed shortly before his death.

Q. I will, though I don't have much time for reading any more. What about you? Do you read a great deal?

A. Perhaps more than I should, but not half as much as I used to—that is until two, sometimes three in the morning. In those days I didn't simply love or admire a writer, I was *obsessed* with him—a feeling akin to carnal passion. I would read his entire output several times; I would read everything that was available about him—in books, old magazines, newspapers. I would breathe and live in his atmosphere. In my Simenon phase, for instance, I would dream Simenon dreams, write Simenon novels during my walks, or at night, in bed, before falling asleep—that's where I still do most of my writing by the way. I would in fact perceive reality like a character out of Simenon. Confronted with a problem, I would ask myself, how would a Simenon character solve it? In my Saroyan phase, I would write, or rather force myself to write, a Saroyanesque short story every day. . . . Let me also add that it wasn't just writers that I became obsessed with, but painters, political leaders, film directors, composers. In my Gandhi phase, for instance, I became a vegetarian; in my J. S. Bach phase, I began work on a gigantic organ passa-caglia—

Q. Let me confess another blind spot of mine: the music of Bach. He has always seemed to me so academic and imper-sonal—*"Germanic"* is I suppose the right descriptive term— just like Thomas Mann.

A. That indeed was my initial impression of both Mann and Bach—Germanic, alien, cold, irritatingly methodical, all head and no heart. "A sublime sewing machine," Colette once called Bach. Even knowledgable men like Berlioz, Nietzsche, and Tolstoy seem to have had a natural antipathy for Bach's music. In one of his novels, *The Cossacks,* I think, Tolstoy says that the beauty of Bach's music is a figment of the imagination. In our own days, the eminent American music critic B. H. Haggin has described Bach as one who goes "through the motions of saying something while actually saying nothing." Bach's own son, Johann Christian Bach, himself a distinguished composer, referred to him as an "old fogey."

Q. Can all these people be wrong?

A. And how!

Q. Tell me, what was it exactly that made you change your mind about Bach? Anything particular happened to make you see the light?

A. It was more like lightning, as a matter of fact. It happened while I was listening to Wanda Landowska's recording of the *"Well-Tempered Clavier, Book One"*—which is known in mu-sical circles as the Old Testament of music (Book Two being the New Testament)—and more particularly the D-major Fugue, No. 5, a very short piece, about two pages and less than three minutes long—it sounds more like a gorgeous processional march, a dazzling royal fanfare rather than a fugue; brilliant, yet restrained, a thoroughly honest piece of work, so spontaneous that it might as well be an improvisation. That little fugue was a revelation to me. After listening to it—*experiencing* it, I should say—I felt there was meaning to life after all. I also understood why critics have called Haydn shallow, Beethoven rhetorical and verbose, Grieg schmaltzy, Wagner barbarous, Rachmaninov an emotional exhibitionist, and Mahler and Bruckner longwinded.

Q. Tell me about Bach, the man—what was he like?

A. He was a bundle of contradictions: extremely sensitive but not morbid; a dreamer but also a formidable craftsman; a mystic but also a man of healthy appetites who enjoyed a good meal, a bottle of wine—married twice and fathered about twenty children. Arrogant yet also genuinely modest— he actually admired, copied, and adapted music by composers that were his inferiors. He was an enormously intelligent man. He must have had an approximate awareness of his own greatness, but he was also totally unaware of his posthumous fame—perhaps because he was too busy working (he composed even on his deathbed when he was completely blind) to have any time for such, more or less, academic games as assessing his own reputation in relation to predecessors or contemporaries.

Q. Have you written anything about Bach?

A. Only scattered notes. But it is one of my ambitions to produce a short volume about his method—creative process— with many musical quotations from his works, though this has already been done to some extent by Albert Schweitzer, among others.

Q. Who are the writers that influenced you the most?

A. There are so many of them that I doubt very much if I can come up with a complete list on the spur of the moment. But I'll try. Dostoevsky, Chekhov, Tolstoy, Turgenev, Bernard Shaw, Simenon, Raymond Chandler, Thoreau, Aldous Huxley, Thomas Mann, Gandhi, Kazantzakis. Shall I go on? There must be a hundred more, some of whom (mostly Armenian poets and novelists) may not be easily recognizable names.

Q. I noticed that you included the names of Simenon and Raymond Chandler—

A. In that connection perhaps I should have added the names of Dashiell Hammett, Rex Stout, and Eric Ambler.

Q. Have you written or do you plan to write a mystery novel?

A. No. I prefer to write about things that I have first-hand knowledge of.

Q. Is everything you write autobiographical?

A. More or less, yes.

Q. I've noticed that writers as a rule don't like discussing that particular aspect of their work. You said "more or less." What do you mean exactly?

A. I mean that most of the details in my fiction are auto-biographical, but the arrangement of these details may be, and often is, pure fantasy.

Q. In one of your stories, the narrator says that after reading his first Sherlock Holmes story he decided to become a detective. Is that an autobiographical statement?

A. It is. I think perhaps at one time or another I have wanted to be practically everything you care to mention—including a garbage collector and a politician: forgive the Freudian association.

Q. And yet, you chose writing, why?

A. I'm shy and anti-social by nature. I like solitude—well, not quite, but let's say I get easily bored with small talk, partisan politics, gossip. Writing is a solitary business—

Q. So is composing music.

A. Originally that's what I wanted to be, a composer. And may I add that I've made and continue to make more money as a church organist than as a writer. As a writer, I should have starved by now. As an organist, I manage to survive—pro-vided, of course, I avoid all the charms of the bourgeoisie. More to the point, it is extremely difficult to become a com-poser without many years of formal study in a conservatory, which I couldn't afford. To be more specific: I come from the lower classes—make it depths. When my father died, he left little money—no money, as a matter of fact; just a few debts. I don't mind admitting that. I'm even willing to admit that during the last 20 years my income has never risen above the poverty line. To be more accurate about this, I've no doubt in my mind that an average plumber makes more money in a couple of months than I made during the last 20 years as a writer.

Q. Does that include books?

A. It does, yes.

Q. How many?

A. Four so far—a couple more should be coming out soon.

Q. Tell us more about your books.

A. None of them is an accurate reflection of the type of work I do—most of which is either in manuscript form or scattered in obscure periodicals.

Q. What type of books are the ones that have come out so far?

A. Mostly commissioned works—translations from the Armenian, an anthology, a text on Armenian history and culture.

Q. *Commissioned*—does that mean you were paid for writing them?

A. No, not always. And even when I was paid, the sums involved were so insignificant that they barely covered such basic expenses as coffee and vodka.

Q. Vodka?

A. Vodka, yes.

Q. Is alcohol for you a source of inspiration?

A. O no! More like a means for survival. A well-known Armenian writer by the name of Yervant Odian was asked once why he drank so much and he replied, "To drown my sorrows." Was he successful in drowning them, he was asked. "No," he said, "the rascals are excellent swimmers." And speaking of rascals, plumbers, and related topics: let me tell you another story. A couple of weeks ago I had a minor problem with a dripping faucet and called a plumber from the Yellow Pages. He came. He wasn't alone. He brought with him a little boy—probably his kid—and let him watch what he was doing. He worked for no more than five minutes. The kid didn't do a thing. Shortly thereafter I received an enormous bill, and when I questioned it, I was informed that the kid was a fully qualified plumber and that I had to pay for his labor too. When I said I would do no such thing, I was threatened with legal action.

Q. Moral of the story?

A. Writers are a disorganized lot. They are individualists, and you can't organize individualists. If plumbers—most plumbers at any rate—are better off than most writers, that's because they know something writers don't know: in order to survive in this world, an individual must surrender part of his precious individuality. That is to say, get organized.

Q. Would you be willing to do that?—surrender part of your individuality?

A. As things stand, that's a highly hypothetical question.

Q. Do you know many writers?

A. Until very recently I didn't know any, but ever since I went into the book-reviewing business, I've met many. As a matter of fact, the overwhelming majority of my correspondents are now writers.

Q. That sounds interesting.

A. Not quite. Writers, as a species, are arrogant and self-centered. Demanding. Praise they are willing to accept, but criticism, never! Whenever I've dared to criticize any of them, I've been accused of ignorance, laziness, stupidity, lack of understanding. You want to lose a friend? Try reviewing his book.

Q. I suppose, like the rest of us, writers too have their blind spots.

A. Namely their ego.

Q. Are you aware of your own blind spots?

A. If I were, they would no longer be blind, would they?

Q. What about defects?

A. Defects by the dozen, the hundred. I discover new ones every day. I would enumerate them for you but I'm sure it would be an uninteresting list.

Q. Tell us one or two anyway.

A. If you wish. One, I go to extremes. Two, I take words literally.

Q. I do too. But is that really a defect?

A. It is for me, because it doesn't allow me to function effectively. Generally speaking, people tend to regard excessive love of solitude as a socially undesirable trait in an individual. I don't regard my own love of solitude as a defect because It allows me to concentrate on my work, to be productive.

Q. You said you go to extremes. In what way?

A. I tend to exaggerate the importance of certain details. A nasty word may depress me for days. The memory of an insignificant event may haunt me for years—I mean literally. Things that happened 30, 35 years ago make me writhe and moan with shame and anger to this day.

Q. You said you take words too literally—could you expand on that?

A. I suppose that comes from using words as tools—a writer's disease. When a politician, or anyone else for that matter, promises to do x, y, z, knowledgeable people know that what he is expressing is an equation with many variables—that is to say: I'll do x, y, z, if conditions a, b, c, prevail—which, needless to add, never do. Something always happens to alter circumstances, needs, judgments, perceptions. Life is, after all, a veritable mafia of variables. People who take promises literally—that includes me—don't realize that a promise may indicate an intention, never a postponed fait accompli.

Q. If I understand you correctly, you seem to be advocating cynicism.

A. Skepticism, maybe. A healthy acceptance of the fact that people should be approached with sympathy and understanding rather than tough, rigid standards of judgment.

Q. What about men who make false promises, deceive, lie, cheat?

A. Such men often count on their victims' vanity and greed, and to be taken in by them is a sign of immaturity.

Q. You mentioned the plumber who tried to cheat you and threatened legal action.

A. The legal action was meant to intimidate me. But when I refused to be intimidated, he backed down. Have you ever noticed that bluffing is a swindler's favorite mode of negotiation?

Q. Tell us something about your daily schedule.

A. I read, write, research, read some more, rewrite—very monotonous.

Q. A quiet, sedentary life.

A. I try to make it quiet, but sedentary, no. There is a lot of legwork in writing. Whenever I work on a non-fiction project, I find that I spend more time walking from one shelf to another, going up and down staircases in libraries than actually writing at my desk. Sometimes after spending an entire morning walking around in the library I may end up with a single line, which I may not even include in the final version of the book or the article.

Q. Do you rewrite a great deal?

A. I rewrite more than I write. Writing for me is like mosaic work. Sometimes, in order to write an essay of five pages, I may end up with fifty pages of notes, which I then proceed to edit, select, arrange in such a way that a pattern will emerge.

Q. Did you always work that way?

A. No, no. It evolved gradually. That's why I find most books that set out to teach a novice how to write very depressing, even misleading. Any method that is received from the outside is bound to stifle originality.

Q. Would you say that one of the most important things about writing is that one should never give up? And that one should work hard every day, no matter what?

A. Of course, but one should also enjoy what one does. One should never force oneself to write. Writing is something that one lives with constantly, 24 hours a day. The act of writing itself is only an insignificant detail of the whole process. And one can live constantly only with something one loves—really loves.

Q. What kind of advice would you give to a young man who plans to be a writer?

A. I don't feel qualified to advise anyone. My case is far from typical. I had to spend 20 years trying to overcome the language barrier. And the advice I was given during these years was completely useless. Once, for instance, a writer advised me to attend lectures delivered by other writers, try to talk to them afterwards, ask for their help and advice on how to go about publishing my stuff—in other words, improve my connections. It is much more important that a writer improve himself rather than his connections. The truth of the matter is, if your work is good, even your enemies will want to help you because in the process they'll be helping themselves. But if it's bad, even your best friend can't help you. To paraphrase Thoreau, if you have God on your side, who needs friends?

Q. There are no formulas or professional secrets then.

A. That's the only secret—the fact that there are no secrets.

Q. What about inspiration?

A. The more I write, the more convinced I become that all that talk about inspiration is nothing but uninspired nonsense.

Q. But you do believe in concentrated, hard work.

A. Like most of my fellow men who don't belong to the privileged classes, I have always worked eight hours a day, six, sometimes seven days a week. I have done so for almost 20 years now. For a long time I had no choice. And now that I am financially independent, it is too late. Daily work has become a habit, and habits, as everyone knows, are easier to keep than to give up.

Q. Financially independent? I thought you said your income never rose above the poverty line.

A.   It may seem paradoxical to say it, but it remains nevertheless a fact that I am both destitute and financially independent.

Q.   Could you explain that paradox?

A.   Anyone can do it. All that's required is that one give up all luxuries.

Q.   Luxuries? Such as?

A.   Anything that is not bread and books, of course.

Q.   I see. No, I don't think *anyone* could do it.

A.   Very easy. You know, for 25 years I was tormented by this problem of financial independence. I envied the rich because they had it, and loathed the poor because they were condemned never to have it. I was wrong. Thoreau is beautiful on this topic. Read him.

Q.   Do you think life has treated you unfairly?

A.   Yes, of course,—sometimes. Sometimes I also think I've been damn lucky.

Q.   Lucky in what way?

A.   Lucky because things could have been much worse.

Q.   Do you have any recurring dreams?

A.   Daydreams, yes. I often dream of what life would be like living in a country where writers are needed in the same way that, say, plumbers and garbage collectors are. But perhaps that's too much to ask from our fellow men.

Q.   I find most Europeans are disgusted with our commercialism. How do you cope with that particular aspect of our life here?

A.   I consider it a minor inconvenience in a world filled with major scandals.

Q.   Such as?

A.   Decay, disease, pollution—chemical as well as moral, political, and aesthetic.

Q.   Do you think of death often?

A.   I'm not sure if I *think* about it, but I am reminded of it constantly: daily catastrophes announced on the radio and seen on TV, traffic accidents, the setting sun, pain, indifference, sleep, hospitals, ambulances, funeral homes (there are two of them in my neighborhood), memories—

Q.   What is your attitude toward death?

A.   It varies. There are times when I look forward to it as a form of liberation. At other times, I am horrified by it. At still others, I am totally indifferent.

Q. What about God? Are you a believer?

A. I'm not sure. I may be described as a non-believer with many doubts. I suspect if God exists, he is so different from what men generally think that whether he exists or not, or whether one believes in his existence or not, won't make one bit of difference one way or the other.

Q. I detect traces of mysticism in that reply.

A. Perhaps. I am willing to admit that I was tempted by mysticism once, and very probably, in a major crisis, I shall resort to it again. To me, mysticism is a faculty with which we may introduce meaning and order into chaos. But a meaning that transcends common sense and logic, and is therefore non-verbal and non-transferable. That's why I find most books and schools of mysticism as useless and mercenary as books and courses on creative writing.

Q. Are there any books you like to reread?

A. Rereading is now a luxury I can no longer afford. But there was a time when I never got tired of rereading *Hamlet*, Sartre's memoirs *The Words*, Mann's *Magic Mountain*, Toynbee's *Reconsiderations* (volume 12 of his *Study of History*), certain things by Chekhov—"The Lady with the Pet Dog," "A Boring Story"—sometimes also translated as "A Tedious Tale"—Raymond Chandler's *Farewell My Lovely*, Dashiell Hammett's short story "Dead Yellow Women"–

Q. What is it about Chandler and Hammett you find so attractive?

A. Their use of slang. Slang for me is the purest and most spontaneous form of poetry—like Gregorian chant is the purest and most spontaneous form of music: functional, economical, the real response to a real demand—no posturing or artifice, no technique and machinery.

Q. Have you ever had what's known as writer's block—when your mind went blank and you couldn't write any more?

A. Yes, once or twice—that's when I used to write only fiction. Ever since I began translating and writing nonfiction, however, I haven't had that problem.

Q. Do you have any favorite mottos?

A. Hundreds of them. As a matter of fact, I have a notebook filled with favorite sayings which someday I hope to publish—privately if possible.

Q. Would you care to quote one of these sayings?

A. "For what is a man profited if he shall gain the whole world and lose his own soul? Or what shall a man give in exchange for his soul?"

Q. Amen.

(1979)

Conversations with Ara Baliozian

by John Antikian

On a number of occasions in July and August 1984, John Antikian visited Ara Baliozian in his home in Kitchener, Ontario, and conducted a series of interviews that were later broadcast on CFMU-FM, the multicultural radio program of McMaster University, in Hamilton, Ontario. Though somewhat abridged, the following transcription reflects faithfully the contents of their conversations.

Q. I see from the list of your published books that so far you have translated three volumes by Gostan Zarian—*The Traveller and His Road, Bancoop and the Bones of the Mammoth,* and *The Island and a Man.*

A. I have a fourth as well as a fifth almost ready for publication.

Q. Could you tell us more about them?

A. The first consists of selected passages from *Countries and Gods.*

Q. What is it about?

A. Impressions of Spain and the United States with—as always with Zarian—colorful characters, encounters, and stimulating conversations and meditations on a large variety of topics that have lost none of their relevance.

Q. And the other book?

A. That one is a biographical work, or rather a collection of interviews and reminiscences by noted contemporaries of Zarian. We have biographies of many minor writers and party hacks, but none so far of Zarian. My volume will begin to fill that gap—make it abyss.

Q. Am I right in assuming that Zarian is a favorite writer of yours?

A. Yes, of course. But he also happens to be one of our most important writers. Even his detractors will concede that.

Q. He has detractors?

257

A. Many more than he deserves.

Q. Who are they?

A. Political partisans, commissars, philistines, charlatans, benevolent benefactors, phonies, wheeler-dealers—the kind of
scum he exposed and ridiculed in his books.

Q. Is Zarian's name now better known in the English-speaking
world as a result of your three translations?

A. I doubt that very much, no. Sometimes I get letters from
fellow Armenians informing me that what I am doing is extremely valuable because I am making our literature known
to the world at large. There are also those who insist that I
translate this or that writer because he deserves to be better
known in the English-speaking world. The sad truth is that
neither Armenians nor the world at large gives a damn about
Armenian literature.

Q. Yet you go on translating.

A. I do, yes. I have become a hopeless pessimist who somehow
continues to function as an incurable optimist. I suppose I
must have ink instead of blood in my veins.

Q. How does one go about making the name of an obscure yet
important writer better known?

A. With patience and perseverance—extreme patience and un-
wavering perseverance: the kind that stretches from here to
eternity.

Q. Let me rephrase the question: Tell us what you have done so
far to make Zarian's name better known in America.

A. I like to believe I have translated key passages from his vast
body of work with some degree of accuracy—accuracy of
meaning as well as style (or so some of my Armenian re-
viewers—who are not easy to please—have said); after which
I have tried to persuade publishers to invest their money in
him. On at least two occasions I was successful—though it
wasn't easy; but when I failed to find a publisher for my third
translation, *The Island and a Man,* I decided to use my own
savings. It looks like I'll have to do the same with the fourth
as well as fifth volumes.

Q. What do you do after the book comes out?

A. I send away about 100 copies to miscellaneous weeklies,
literary periodicals, writers, critics, journalists, friends, hoping they will review it. Most of them will ignore it, of course.

Q. Most? Could you be more specific?

A.   A conservative estimate would be 98 percent.

Q.   *That* many?

A.   But even if one of them reviews it you're in luck, because sometimes the review is read by librarians, which means that the book is ordered by a few libraries . . . not Armenian libraries, however; Armenian libraries don't waste any money on books; they expect and usually get free copies and after they receive them they seldom bother acknowledging. They seem to think accepting to catalogue a book should be in itself sufficient recompense.

Q.   But if a few Canadian and American public libraries catalogue a book, in a way they make it available to millions of readers, don't they?

A.   Theoretically, yes. It is only the exceptional reader, however, who will check out a book with whose contents or author's name he is not already familiar. A case in point: our local library serves over a hundred thousand people and has had a copy of Zarian's *Traveller* on its shelves for three years now, yet the book has never been borrowed. And I mean not even once.

Q.   Not even once?

A.   That's right. Not even once. That bears repeating.

Q.   We are back where we started from.

A.   Exactly. A vicious circle. There are no golden rules or magic formulas, and even if there were, I am neither a magician nor do I have enough gold with which to make rules. I must do things the hard way, which takes time. If anything, this business teaches you to be patient. Very patient. There is hour-patience, day-patience, month- and year-patience. I'm talking about decade- and century-patience. I wouldn't be surprised in the least if after waiting for years and decades absolutely nothing happens. I don't believe in the fairy tale that says if a writer is good he will be discovered sooner or later. After all, we Armenians neglected Zarian for fifty years, and we go on neglecting him. We have translated and retranslated relatively minor writers, but we have consistently ignored Zarian. The complete works of derivative scribblers have been issued by the State Publishing House in Yerevan, but so far no more than one heavily censored and bowdlerized volume by Zarian.

Q.   I might as well confess here and now that I too have ne-

glected Zarian. I haven't read any of his works. Would it be
possible for you to explain his appeal in a few words?

A. He was a giant. He had a gigantic appetite for ideas, for
people and places. He loved life. He loved the details of life.
He is not an easy writer to sum up. All my translations contain
detailed introductions and commentaries explaining, analyzing, and assessing his achievement, style, world-view. How
would you sum up the achievement of a Bach or a Mozart?
Supreme creative powers? Forceful original inventiveness
and intellectual control? Infectious exuberance? The ability
to create an irresistible magic circle?

Q. What about his philosophy of life?

A. He has no systematic philosophy like, say, Jean-Paul Sartre. If
anything he promoted a healthy skepticism of philosophic
systems that promise to solve all our problems. Let's say he
had an eye for the variable in life—its psychological depths,
its social implications, its political angularity. Imagine, if you
can, a combination of Dostoevsky, Thomas Mann, and Kazantzakis. He was a penetrating judge of character—of individuals, societies, nations, cultures, civilizations—and
penetrating to the point of being prophetic. Long before
writers like Gide, Silone, Koestler, and Solzhenitsyn, for example, he analyzed and criticized the practice of Marxism-
Leninism in the USSR after spending a number of years there
in the 1920s—not as a tourist but as a teacher and reporter,
which may explain the hostility of commissars toward his
works.

Q. I assume Zarian is better known in the diaspora, then.

A. Well, no, not quite. The few Armenians in the diaspora who
are familiar with his work, know him only as the author of a
novel, *The Ship on the Mountain,* and a short 50-page epic
poem titled *The Bride of Tetrachoma.* Most of his important
works—like *Bancoop, Countries and Gods, The Island and a
Man*—have not yet been published in book form anywhere.

Q. Where do you find copies for your translations?

A. In old issues of the *Hairenik* Monthly of Boston—that's where
Zarian first published his works serially.

Q. Do you have a set of old *Haireniks?*

A. No, I don't. What I do is beg friends in large metropolitan
centers to locate a complete set in some dingy basement or
abandoned bookcase and xerox the relevant pages. Not an
easy task.

Q. Can you explain why they haven't been published in book form yet?

A. Because there are no Armenian publishers in the diaspora. Printers, by the dozen; but publishers, none! What we have instead are so-called cultural foundations that operate like private clubs and mafias. Some of these foundations—like the Gulbenkian Foundation in Lisbon, for instance—are not even interested in Armenian literature, let alone English translations of Armenian literary works. It is interesting to note that the Gulbenkian Foundation promotes the translation of *odar* books into other *odar* languages—there is even a Gulbenkian Prize for the best translation of the year, but for some incomprehensible reason it prefers to stay away from Armenian literature altogether . . . which is odd because some established Armenian authors have been on its staff, and at least one of these authors was very eager to see his works translated into English.

Q. And what happened?

A. He died a disappointed man, alas.

Q. So there is some kind of rough justice in this world after all.

A. One is tempted to reach that fantastic conclusion, yes. As for our benevolent benefactors, who occasionally subsidize the printing of Armenian works: generally speaking these gentlemen have no real interest in ideas. Patriotic mumbo-jumbo they are willing to tolerate, but genuine works of literature, never! It is no surprise that at one point in his *Bancoop* Zarian dismisses Armenian millionaires as "hoodlums."

Q. In the homeland, collaborators and commissars; in the diaspora, hoodlums and mafias. Another vicious circle?

A. Exactly.

Q. Do you see a way out?

A. Whenever I am asked that question, I reply: Yes, of course. I believe in miracles!

Q. Do you really?

A. Do I have a choice? Imagine a drowning man in the middle of a stormy ocean surrounded by hungry sharks. He hears a voice asking, "Do you believe in miracles?" Though he suspects the voice is a figment of his own imagination, and even as he is being devoured by the sharks, he screams, "Yes, I do!!!" And that's our situation now. I have friends—both Armenian and *odar*—who are convinced that Armenians be-

long to the dustbin of history, and that I am wasting my time
promoting Armenian literature. And yet, here we are, two
Armenians discussing Zarian in the middle of nowhere for a
Canadian multicultural radio program. I have no idea how
many people will listen to our words, but let us assume that
at least one of our listeners will be curious enough to get a
copy of Zarian, and after reading it he will recommend it to a
friend . . . and so on as in a chain reaction. This is wishful
thinking on my part, of course, but it is also within the realm
of possibility. Perhaps what I'm trying to say is that to the
discerning eye life may indeed be a series of situations pregnant with unforeseen possibilities that may verge on the
miraculous. On a more mundane level: sooner or later our
philistines in the diaspora and our collaborators in the homeland may come to realize that patriotic mumbo-jumbo and
propaganda are crap and they cannot go on dishing it out as
if it were rose-jam. They cannot fool all the people all the
time. Today it's the Poles, the Afghans, and some isolated
dissidents like Sakharov, Solzhenitsyn, and Paradjanov; yesterday it was the Hungarians and the Czechs; tomorrow,
perhaps the Georgians, the Armenians, and even the Russians. A system that relies too much on propaganda is
doomed to failure. And on the day the system fails, Zarian
will be given a chance to find his rightful place in our literary
pantheon.

Q.   In the meantime, is there anything we can do in the diaspora,
     I mean to improve matters?

A.   The diaspora presents a different and a somewhat grimmer
     situation. Sophisticated readers are already convinced that
     there is no such thing as Armenian literature and culture;
     remember the final pages of Michael Arlen's *Passage to Ararat*
     wherein he informs us that since we Armenians have failed to
     create a new culture we might as well give up and assimilate.
     I've also met Armenian professors who have asserted that
     when it comes to literature, the Turks are ahead of us be-
     cause they have produced more Nobel candidates. In a way,
     by assimilating, the average Armenian of the diaspora is act-
     ing on this assumption, too. He is voting with his feet, as the
     saying goes. I have literate friends who urge me to translate
     well-known writers like Baudelaire and Mallarmé; others
     want me to write critical works on writers like Mann and
     Hemingway. These friends seem to be totally unaware of the

fact that there are hundreds, perhaps even thousands of translators and scholars who are subsidized by their own governments and miscellaneous cultural foundations to produce works on these internationally recognized writers. But Zarian continues to be ignored simply because he wrote in Armenian and because the position of our establishments on both sides of the Iron Curtain is so insecure that they must avoid dissent at all cost.

Q. Speaking of miracles: Isn't the fact that we Armenians survived for millenia despite many adversities—wars, invasions, massacres, a genocide, dispersion, exile—a miracle of sorts?

A. Perhaps at this point we should define our terms. What do we mean by *survived?* After all, a great many of us did *not* survive. And here I'm not only talking about the two million who perished in the Ottoman Empire between 1894 and 1922, and the countless victims of Stalin's Great Terror in the 1930s, but also our communities in Eastern Europe—Bulgaria, Rumania, Poland, Hungary, the Ukraine. They have all vanished without a trace. These were prosperous, well-organized communities with their own press, schools, churches, legal system. I mention this to dispel the notion that God is on our side, that's why we survived until now, and we are destined to survive to the end of time. I have met Armenians who are so convinced of this that they do nothing but drag out a useless and parasitical existence. To me that's not survival. On the contrary, it is worse than death. To live as a creative force—*that* is the only kind of survival worth talking about.

Q. In that case, how would you assess our chances of survival?— assuming of course things will be going as they have been for the last decade or so.

A. The rate of intermarriage and assimilation in the United States and Canada has been alarming. An Armenian-American sociologist has just published a book on the subject with all kinds of charts and statistics. Our prospects are grim. We don't have to consult statisticians and sociologists to realize this, of course. All we have to do is look around us—at our communities, at our friends and relatives, at ourselves. We remain hopelessly fragmented, disoriented, disorganized, scattered. I live in a small town with about a hundred Armenian families. During the last 25 years I've seen only about a dozen of them. I know about the rest only because I see their

names in the telephone book. I once had a telephone conversation with one of these Armenians; it was in connection
with some department store business. I had to give my name
and address to some clerk, at which point I heard him saying,
"So you're an Armenian." "How did you guess?" I wanted to
know. "I'm Armenian, too," he replied. "How come I never
see you around?" I said. "I stay away from ethnic activities"
was the answer. I have since come to realize that this type of
Armenian who avoids his fellow Armenians is the rule rather
than the exception. Even some committed Armenians prefer
to stay away. The other day I received a letter from a highly
cultured Armenian lady saying, "We are Armenians from the
Caucasus area and very proud of our heritage. We don't mix
with the local Armenian colony because most of them are
Turkish-Armenians. Everything is different about them. Mentality, character, cuisine. They use sugar, we use honey; on
the whole we prefer natural products." And here we are, two
Armenians speaking in English because most of our audience
can't understand the language and because we are no longer
as fluent in Armenian.

Q. But isn't it true that we have more Armenian community
centers and schools today in the United States and Canada
than ever before? Wouldn't you consider that a move in the
right direction?

A. I'm afraid I don't share your faith in buildings. We can build
schools and centers but can we make of them centers of
intellectual ferment? The church was at the height of its
power when the faithful met in catacombs. It was the construction of St. Peter's in Rome—as a matter of fact—that split
the Catholic church apart. Just because we can afford building schools and centers it doesn't necessarily follow that we
can also inspire our boys and girls to cherish their traditions
and culture. How can we when our leadership is in disarray
and when our cultural organizations preach culture but practice pilaf and shish-kebab? A fellow Armenian—a retired old
man—once said to me: "How come I never see you at our
community center? Drop in once in a while. We can play a
game of tavlu and have a cup of Turkish coffee." Again, don't
think this type of Armenian is the exception. On the contrary.
Baronian's, Odian's, and Zarian's books are populated by this
type of poltroon for whom Armenian culture is nothing but
Mesrob Mashdots, Vartan Mamigonian, the eternal snows of
Ararat, and of course the Turkish massacres. I have friends

active in miscellaneous Armenian political and cultural organizations who love to deliver fiery speeches in public, but in private and after a couple of drinks they will concede that they are fighting a lost war.

Q. Can't we hope that the next generation of leaders will be more progressive and committed?

A. Whether this hope will be justified remains to be seen, of course. What we need in the meantime is some degree of honesty and integrity in our organizations—the exchange of ideas rather than insults. Dialogue. Divisions and factions can be useful if they engage in dialogue. I don't see that happening, however. Even our most venerable institutions—our churches and monasteries—are now riddled with scandals. Our clerics have now degenerated into a bunch of Levantine wheeler-dealers in pursuit of profit. Do you think these characters mean what they say when they preach unity? Do you think a single one of them would even entertain for a fraction of a second the idea of relinquishing any of his titles and privileges for the sake of unity? When they hold forth on unity, they remind me of boa constrictors preaching unity to an audience of rabbits. Unity is strength, they say, therefore consent to be swallowed up and digested. Boa strength, rabbit death.

Q. I'm sure there must be some kind of psychoanalytical explanation for this type of conduct.

A. Yes, of course. We are, after all, the remnants of the Ottoman nightmare that lasted six centuries. We have not yet shed a "victim" mentality. We want to *survive* at all costs—even if it means the ultimate extinction of the nation. Even if it means selling Oriental rugs in cathedrals. You may not be aware of this, but some of our churches advertise the sale of Oriental rugs in the *New York Times*. I'm told these sales are very profitable because they are tax-deductible and they attract a lot of *odar* money.

Q. But why do Armenian churches find it necessary to engage in such questionable, not to say nefarious, activities?

A. I asked that same question once of an insider and was informed that Armenians are not churchgoers, that as a rule the Sunday collection plate doesn't bring in more than a couple of hundred dollars, and that their total expenses run into millions. Some of these churches employ as many as fifty people: secretaries, accountants, public relations personnel, fund-raisers, financial experts, janitors, editors. They issue a large variety of printed matter and voluminous newsletters wherein their own activities are publicized in great detail. A bishop shakes hands with a politico and he makes the front page, for instance. A senile old couple donates a couple of thousand dollars, and they too make headlines on the front page.

Q.   And Armenian-American communities tolerate this without a word of protest?

A.   To use the word *community* in reference to Armenian-Americans is an overstatement. The vast majority of Armenian-Americans are either assimilated or alienated. As for the very few who consider themselves committed Armenians: they are divided between fellow-travelers who are convinced that the Kremlin is the best thing that happened to us during the last thousand years, and those who clamor for a free and independent homeland. Both groups agree on one thing: the diaspora is only a temporary thing on the verge of collapse, hence not worth bothering about.

Q.   Well, on the other hand, can't they see that the whole concept of an independent homeland is a Utopian daydream?

A.   An independent homeland may indeed be a distant dream; what is far more important and infinitely more accessible, however, is the rediscovery within us of *independence* and *homeland* as states of mind, as attributes of character, as sources of strength and individuality. Before we demand independence we should develop into a nation *worthy* of independence. A man may be politically free and independent yet be the slave of innumerable petty problems, prejudices, and complexes. Before we contemplate unification and independence we should attempt to resolve our contradictions, otherwise we will be working against our own aims and interests: which is what we have been doing, preaching one thing and doing the exact opposite. Our enemies—the Stalinists and before them the Turks—seem to have done much more than murder thousands and millions of our brothers. They seem to have shattered something very deep in our consciousness: our integrity and self-respect, the way we perceive ourselves, our fellow men, and the world. Perhaps that is why we prefer flattery and patriotic mumbo-jumbo to honest and objective assessments of our situation. In a sense we are still in mourning. We are not yet ready to *live*—to face facts, to confront reality. We have not yet emerged from a state of paralyzing shock.

Q. Have you published anything in this vein?

A. Yes, I have, but there is nothing new in what I'm saying. In point of fact I have been doing nothing but paraphrasing Zarian.

Q. What kind of reactions have you been getting?

A. The fanatic and lunatic fringe tends to be more vocal and aggressive. I have discovered that explanations work only with fundamentally decent and reasonable men, who tend to keep to themselves. Even so, I have had a number of positive responses—some of it in the form of letters to the editor.

Q. Tell us about the negative responses.

A. It's been mostly from fellow travelers and what I call "chic Bolsheviks": wealthy Armenian-Americans who pose as patriotic supporters of the homeland. Let me give you an example. One of these characters once telephoned from a distant American city and for nearly two hours tried to convince me that Russians were our big brothers, and that we needed them more than they needed us, and that they are so good to us that even our capitalists in America support the homeland, and that if it weren't for the Russians, the Turks and the Azerbaijanis would tear us to pieces, and so on and so forth. I have noticed that our fellow travelers try to avoid speaking of the regime, or the Kremlin and our puppet government in Yerevan; they prefer to harp instead on the "homeland" and the "Russian people," thus identifying the people with the regime, which of course is a total falsehood; because the ordinary Russian or Armenian living in the USSR has more reason to loathe the regime than any outsider like myself. At an unguarded moment, this fellow Armenian demanded: *"How do you expect to have the support of the homeland if you criticize it?"* At no time have I criticized the *homeland*, of course. Why should I criticize Mount Aragats and Lake Sevan? Or for that matter, my brothers and sisters who are the real victims of this drama. What I have criticized is the Kremlin and its collaborators; I don't consider *them* homeland. On the contrary: they are our real enemies and oppressors. But let us, for the moment, ignore that aspect of the argument. What horrifies me about this type of Armenian who promotes passive acceptance of the regime is that he expects writers, *all* writers, including those who live and work in the Free World, to function as hirelings of the Soviet propaganda machine. This is worse than fascism. Instead of trying to oppose fascism, our chic Bolsheviks (and there are a surprising number of them) want to export it to the Free World. We may live in democracies, but in reality, in the depths of our hearts, we continue to be subjects of the Sultan. Some of these Armenian-Americans are even more Turkish than the Sultan and more Bolshevik than Stalin. They view the Kremlin's totalitarianism as a form of benevolent paternalism because in the Ottoman Empire both the intellectuals and the people were slaughtered, whereas in the USSR the intellectuals are only castrated and the people allowed to vegetate. That's progress for you. I have discovered that just because an Armenian lives under a democratic form of government it doesn't mean that he understands the fundamental principles of democracy: things like human rights, freedom of speech, freedom of the press, freedom of movement, accountability, to govern is to serve, one is innocent until proven guilty, the right to dissent, to criticize, to debate. Or, if they recognize the validity of these rights, they reject their universality, which is even worse—the attitude that we, Armenian-Americans, deserve these rights and privileges but our brothers in the homeland do not—because they don't know any better. This attitude is a byproduct of the American tourist mentality. Armenia is a nice place to visit. (By Armenia they mean Yerevan, of course.) They go to Yerevan as tourists, walk through a couple of boulevards, talk with members of the priviligentsia, and they come back home with superlatives. Everything is magnificent! Everything is great! Sakharov and Solzhenitsyn are misguided nuts, Paradjanov, a syphilitic black marketeer. Our dancers, our artists, our poets—they are the best in the world. The average tourist, of course, is not exactly a reliable authority. Anyone who knows anything about literature and the performing arts will tell you that everything is hopelessly mediocre and amateurish. I have never been there myself, but I get a large variety of printed matter, some of which seems to have been written by half-wits for an audience of morons. An Armenian lady, a former concert pianist who contributes regularly to the Armenian-American press, once told me, "Whenever I attend an Armenian recital, I always write a glowing review, not because I don't know any better—as some of my readers may suspect—but because I always try to be positive and encouraging." That is to say, patronizing and paternalistic. When I started reviewing books for the Armenian press about ten years ago, I had a similar attitude until I met some of the writers I had reviewed: they struck me as arrogant, ruthless, mean-spirited charlatans, the kind of scum that should be buried rather than praised. It never pays to spread pleasant lies in order to avoid harsh realities.

Q.   What are you working on now?

A.   More translations and critical essays.

Q.   Do you plan to publish these essays in book form?

A.   I might, yes.

Q.   Have you decided on a title?

A.   I have several tentative titles, one of which is *Common Fallacies*.

Q.   Could you name a couple of these fallacies?

A.   That we Armenians will never amount to anything because we are too few, too weak, and politically too inexperienced; that we have produced only one major writer, William Saroyan.

Q.   I'm familiar with these lines.

A.   Armenians who voice these fallacies cannot be aware of the fact that the Greeks of Athens who initiated a new culture 2500 years ago didn't even number half a million: a nation may be militarily weak but morally strong. Revolutions are started by a couple of individuals in a dingy basement.

Q.   What about our lack of political experience and leadership?

A.   I don't consider that a fallacy as much as an expression of our inferiority complex. The inaccuracy of a statement is sometimes less important and revealing than the reason why the statement is made. All children are incompetent, but every parent knows that to harp on its incompetence will inevitably hamper the child's development. I might be willing to agree that we, Armenians, are a politically misguided and naive bunch, but I refuse to conclude that *that* is an incurable disease or a permanent state. We lack political experience because we haven't had our own political environment for almost ten centuries. Even so, I am personally acquainted— and I'm sure you are too—with fellow Armenians who, given the chance, could be as effective leaders as Reagan, Mrs. Thatcher, the Ayatollah, or any other contemporary leader you care to mention. We may be ignorant, but we can learn. Armenians, as a matter of fact, have produced many important political leaders in alien environments. Some of the greatest imperial dynasties of the Byzantine commonwealth were founded by Armenians. In our own century we have produced men like Krikor Zohrab, Anastas Mikoyan, Governor Deukmejian—all of whom reached the heights of political power in totally alien, not to say hostile, environments. Zohrab was a charismatic leader, a spellbinding orator, a man of integrity and courage, in addition to being an internationally respected jurist and a master of the short story. He could have been a far more progressive and enlightened leader than Talaat, Enver, Jemal, and Ataturk put together—and Turkey would have been better off today.

Q.   What about Saroyan being our only major writer?

A.   Armenians who say that, I suspect, confuse greatness with fame and popularity, both of which are impure concepts. Zohrab and Zarian are totally unknown in the English-speaking world; *that* does not make them *minor* writers. At this particular time someone like Michael Jackson is probably far more popular than Sibelius and Bartok; *that* doesn't make him greater than Sibelius and Bartok. Armenians who downgrade their own literature and culture forget that during the last century alone we, as a people, lived under two of the most brutal regimes in the history of mankind—regimes that ruthlessly and systematically exterminated all our intellectual and political leaders. In 1915 alone the Turks murdered fifty of our ablest intellectuals, among them Zohrab. The same thing happened two decades later in Soviet Armenia—Charents, Bakounts, Zabel Yessayan—our greatest poet, short story writer, novelist respectively; all victims of Stalin's Terror. Inevitably these martyred leaders were replaced by spineless opportunists with a highly developed instinct of self-preservation: the very same people who now preach collaboration in the homeland and promote fragmentation in the diaspora, after which they maintain with some degree of self-satisfaction that we will never amount to anything. Let us imagine, for the sake of argument, the following scenario: The Indians of the New World outnumber the white settlers, and at one point they decide to get rid of them. They proceed to massacre as many as they can and they deport the rest back to Europe, which, in the meantime, has reverted to a

primitive form of warlike totalitarianism wherein every ves-
tige of creative freedom is ruthlessly and systematically strangled. Now then, my question is: How many of the American
writers and statesmen we know and respect today would be
mentioned in contemporary reference works and texts?
Would there be such a thing as 20th-century American literature or culture or for that matter history? Because, if you
think about it, this is what happened to us. To say therefore
that we will never amount to anything is to accept the role
assigned to us by the bloodthirsty predators of this world.
That is why I maintain that an Armenian may be the
shrewdest man on earth when it comes to selling rugs and
making money, even amassing fortunes, but he remains
hopelessly naive in the world of ideas—so much so that he
will recycle enemy propaganda believing it to be the truth,
the whole truth and nothing but the truth. My quarrel isn't
with these fools and dupes, however, but with those hirelings
who are fully aware of what they are doing and why they are
doing it.

Q.   You mean members of our establishment in the homeland.

A.   Exactly!

Q.   But suppose they promote dissent: How far would they go?

A.   They wouldn't go anywhere, of course. They would be certified as lunatics and immediately replaced by more cooper-
ative junior members. This has happened already. And it
keeps happening all the time, as a matter of fact. Anyone who
exhibits any sign of courage, integrity, and character, is by-
passed, demoted, eliminated . . . which is what I am saying:
we are at the mercy of a ruthless master and his hirelings who
pretend to have our interests at heart.

Q.   In other words, we have no choice but to collaborate passively with the regime.

A.   If you like. What I refuse to accept passively, however, is the
aggressive, intolerant, and even arrogant attitude of our Soviet-Armenian quislings. I have seen some of these commissars in action. They visit the diaspora and assume a
morally superior stance toward us renegades. They deliver
homilies on patriotism, dedication, and other noble ideals.
They try to convince us that they never had it so good and
that we have no business living in the diaspora. They insult
those who dare to disagree with them. They make empty

promises to those who vacillate. Let me be more specific. Since every Armenian writer of the diaspora dreams to be published in the homeland, they assure these writers that a volume of their selected works is in the works. Years pass. Nothing happens. In the meantime, this poor jerk in the diaspora proves he is a good boy by writing favorable articles about the regime. That's how they managed to lure Zarian back to Yerevan. They promised to publish his complete works. Only the first volume came out, however, and that with so many censored passages and alterations that it turned into a major scandal. The whole project had to be abandoned because it revealed the total moral bankruptcy of the Soviet-Armenian literary establishment. Zarian was given a desk job in some library, allowed to vegetate, then buried—literally as well as figuratively. He is only a faint memory now. Once in a while he makes short appearances in memoirs by contemporaries, none of whom seems to have read his works (or is willing to confess that he has read them).

Q. What I fail to understand is why Zarian allowed himself to be taken in? Surely he must have known what would happen.

A. No doubt he suspected. His decision to go back was prompted not so much by the attractiveness of the Soviet offer as by the degeneration of the Armenian diaspora. To understand the degree of this degeneration, you must be a full-time writer. As a matter of fact, there are no full-time Armenian writers. Very probably I am the only one, and I don't even qualify as an Armenian writer because I write in English. If you want to know what it means to be dependent on the charity of swine, dedicate your life to Armenian literature.

Q. Am I right in assuming that you wouldn't encourage a young man to adopt writing as a career?

A. I certainly wouldn't. I'm not a sadist. Encouraging a young man to become a writer would be like thrusting martyrdom on him—destitution, solitary confinement, asceticism, and an endless series of humiliations.

Q. I would like to end this talk on a more positive note, if I may.

A. Whatever for? So that we will not spoil the appetites of our bourgeois audience?